Page deliberately left blank

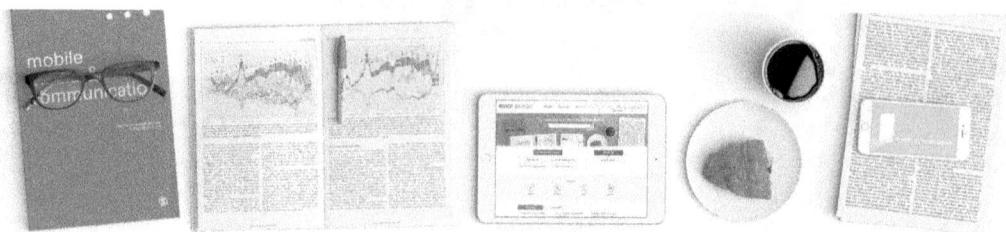

THE
ANNALS

of the American Academy of Political and Social Science

VOLUME 689 | MAY 2020

Do Networks Help People to Manage Poverty? Perspectives from the Field

SPECIAL EDITORS:

Miranda J. Lubbers
Autonomous University of Barcelona

Hugo Valenzuela García
Autonomous University of Barcelona

Mario Luis Small
Harvard University

⑤SAGE

Los Angeles | London | New Delhi
Singapore | Washington DC | Melbourne

The American Academy of Political and Social Science

202 S. 36th Street, Annenberg School for Communication, University of Pennsylvania,
Philadelphia, PA 19104-3806; (215) 746-6500; (215) 573-2667 (fax); www.aapss.org

Origin and Purpose. The Academy was organized December 14, 1889, to promote the progress of political and social science, especially through publications and meetings. The Academy does not take sides in controverted questions, but seeks to gather and present reliable information to assist the public in forming an intelligent and accurate judgment.

Meetings. The Academy occasionally holds a meeting in the spring extending over two days.

Publications. THE ANNALS of The American Academy of Political and Social Science is the bimonthly publication of the Academy. Each issue contains articles on some prominent social or political problem, written at the invitation of the editors. These volumes constitute important reference works on the topics with which they deal, and they are extensively cited by authorities throughout the United States and abroad.

Subscriptions. THE ANNALS of The American Academy of Political and Social Science (ISSN 0002-7162) (J295) is published bimonthly—in January, March, May, July, September, and November—by SAGE Publishing, 2455 Teller Road, Thousand Oaks, CA 91320. Periodicals postage paid at Thousand Oaks, California, and at additional mailing offices. POSTMASTER: Send address changes to The Annals of The American Academy of Political and Social Science, c/o SAGE Publishing, 2455 Teller Road, Thousand Oaks, CA 91320. Institutions may subscribe to THE ANNALS at the annual rate: $1257 (clothbound, $1419). Individuals may subscribe to the ANNALS at the annual rate: $134 (clothbound, $197). Single issues of THE ANNALS may be obtained by individuals for $41 each (clothbound, $58). Single issues of THE ANNALS have proven to be excellent supplementary texts for classroom use. Direct inquiries regarding adoptions to THE ANNALS c/o SAGE Publishing (address below).

All correspondence concerning membership in the Academy, dues renewals, inquiries about membership status, and/or purchase of single issues of THE ANNALS should be sent to THE ANNALS c/o SAGE Publishing, 2455 Teller Road, Thousand Oaks, CA 91320. Telephone: (800) 818-SAGE (7243) and (805) 499-0721; Fax/Order line: (805) 375-1700; e-mail: journals@sagepub.com. *Please note that orders under $30 must be prepaid.* For all customers outside the Americas, please visit http://www.sagepub.co.uk/customerCare.nav for information.

THE ANNALS

© 2020 by The American Academy of Political and Social Science

Editorial Office: 202 S. 36th Street, Philadelphia, PA 19104-3806
For information about individual and institutional subscriptions address:
SAGE Publishing
2455 Teller Road
Thousand Oaks, CA 91320

For SAGE Publishing: Peter Geraghty (Production)

From India and South Asia, write to:
SAGE PUBLICATIONS INDIA Pvt Ltd
B-42 Panchsheel Enclave, P.O. Box 4109
New Delhi 110 017
INDIA

From Europe, the Middle East, and Africa, write to:
SAGE PUBLICATIONS LTD
1 Oliver's Yard, 55 City Road
London EC1Y 1SP
UNITED KINGDOM

International Standard Serial Number ISSN 0002-7162
ISBN 978-1-0718-2375-0 (Vol. 689, 2020) paper
ISBN 978-1-0718-2376-7 (Vol. 689, 2020) cloth
First printing, May 2020

Information about membership rates, institutional subscriptions, and back issue prices may be found on the facing page.

Advertising. Current rates and specifications may be obtained by writing to The Annals Advertising and Promotion Manager at the Thousand Oaks office (address above). Acceptance of advertising in this journal in no way implies endorsement of the advertised product or service by SAGE or the journal's affiliated society(ies) or the journal editor(s). No endorsement is intended or implied. SAGE reserves the right to reject any advertising it deems as inappropriate for this journal.

Claims. Claims for undelivered copies must be made no later than six months following month of publication. The publisher will supply replacement issues when losses have been sustained in transit and when the reserve stock will permit.

Change of Address. Six weeks' advance notice must be given when notifying of change of address. Please send the old address label along with the new address to the SAGE office address above to ensure proper identification. Please specify the name of the journal.

THE
ANNALS
of the American Academy of Political and Social Science

VOLUME 689 | MAY 2020

IN THIS ISSUE:

Do Networks Help People to Manage Poverty? Perspectives from the Field

Special Editors: MIRANDA J. LUBBERS, HUGO VALENZUELA GARCÍA, and MARIO LUIS SMALL

FORTHCOMING

Refugee and Immigrant Integration: The Promise of Local Action
Special Editors: KATHERINE M. DONATO and ELIZABETH FERRIS

The Reassertion of the Regulatory Welfare State
Special Editors: DAVID LEVI-FAUR and AVISHAI BENISH

Keywords: poverty; social exclusion; social networks; social support; relational mechanisms; coping strategies; network poverty

Do Networks Help People To Manage Poverty? Perspectives from the Field

By
MIRANDA J. LUBBERS,
MARIO LUIS SMALL,
and
HUGO VALENZUELA
GARCÍA

In 2018, a staggering 38 million Americans, about one in every nine, faced income poverty. Seventeen million of them experienced deep or extreme poverty, defined as a household income below 50 percent of the household's poverty threshold (Semega et al. 2019). Extreme poverty has almost doubled between 1995 and 2016 (Brady and Parolin 2019). Given the magnitude of the problem both in the United States and worldwide, it is hardly surprising that poverty has had a steady place on the agenda of the social sciences. Nonetheless, not all of its features have received equal attention. A recent literature review of the causes of poverty (Brady 2019) distinguished between three dominant explanations for poverty: individual behaviors and risk factors (e.g., unemployment, single motherhood,

Miranda J. Lubbers is an associate professor in the Department of Social and Cultural Anthropology and director of the Research Group GRAFO at the Autonomous University of Barcelona in Spain. She investigates personal networks, migration, poverty, social exclusion, and social cohesion. Her recent work appears in, among others, Social Networks, Human Nature, *and the* International Migration Review. *She is coauthor of the book* Conducting Personal Network Research: A Practical Guide *(Guilford Press 2019).*

Mario Luis Small is Grafstein Family Professor of Sociology at Harvard University. His research interests include urban poverty, inequality, culture, networks, and case study methods. He is the author of Villa Victoria: The Transformation of Social Capital in a Boston Barrio *(University of Chicago Press 2004),* Unanticipated Gains: Origins of Network Inequality in Everyday Life *(Oxford University Press 2009), and* Someone to Talk to *(Oxford University Press 2017).*

Correspondence: mirandajessica.lubbers@uab.es

DOI: 10.1177/0002716220923959

cultural schemas, and repertoires guiding behaviors), structural factors (e.g., the economic and demographic context), and power and institutions that create policies affecting poverty rates (e.g., by redistributing resources, investing in capabilities, or "disciplining the poor"). Both structural and institutional explanations have included meso-level factors, such as neighborhoods and organizations. These meso-level conditions have also received attention in other reviews (Desmond and Western 2018; Small and Newman 2001) and special issues (e.g., Allard and Small 2013; Friedrichs, Galster, and Musterd 2003; Lee et al. 2015).

In contrast, a meso-level concept that has received far less attention in such reviews for its role in poverty is that of social networks. This limited attention is surprising, since poverty is profoundly relational (Desmond and Western 2018; Hall 2019; Walker 2014) in the sense that it is lived, managed, negotiated, and reproduced in relationships with others. Research into social networks and poverty has made it clear how important it is to pay attention to the role of networks in how people experience, cope with, and seek to escape poverty. Nonetheless, researchers have drawn widely diverging conclusions. Some authors have emphasized how networks are an essential survival mechanism, whereas others find that they exacerbate the risk of social exclusion, and still others present alternative perspectives. It is unclear how these contrasting findings can be consolidated.

This volume aims to push our understanding of the role of social networks in the day-to-day subsistence of families and individuals suffering economic hardship further. We have two objectives: (1) we seek to update the literature with new, fieldwork-based evidence on how networks affect how people cope with poverty; and (2) we aim to refine and expand on the theoretical processes through which networks are mobilized in times of need. The multiple causal pathways between network conditions and poverty remain only partly mapped out. While many social relationships emerge in organizations in which people routinely participate (Small 2009), little is known about the conditions under which these organizations contribute to the creation of social capital among their clients or participants. The studies and results reported in this volume intend to inform theory, substance, and practice by expanding on the many ways networks are related to poverty.

Hugo Valenzuela García is an associate professor in social and cultural anthropology at the Autonomous University of Barcelona. His main research interest is economic anthropology (poverty, precarious work, peasantry, entrepreneurship, work, consumption) and he has conducted fieldwork in Malaysia, Mexico, and Spain. He is associate editor of the Journal of Organizational Ethnography.

NOTE: We thank the RecerCaixa program for their research support to Miranda Lubbers and Hugo Valenzuela (RecerCaixa, 2015ACUP 00145), which also helped us to organize the workshop "Who cares? Relational mechanisms involved in the day-to-day subsistence of families and individuals struggling with poverty" in Barcelona on February 7–8, 2019, at which the articles in this volume were originally presented. We thank Harvard University and its Project on Race, Class and Cumulative Adversity, funded by the Ford Foundation and the Hutchins Family Foundation, for research support to Mario L. Small. The articles in this volume benefited from the generous feedback of the other participants of the workshop, as well as of the anonymous reviewers. We thank Thomas Kecskemethy and Emily Babson for their support and advice at all stages of this project.

In this introductory article, we first provide a brief overview of the different types of effects that networks can have on well-being. Then, we review the interdisciplinary literature on the role of social networks in coping with poverty to help the reader to situate the contributions of this special issue. We discuss three contrasting perspectives on networks among the poor that have dominated the literature: pervasive solidarity, pervasive isolation, and selective solidarity (Raudenbush 2016). The perspectives are partly analogous to traditional perspectives on the organization of personal networks in modern society, where community is "saved" (or "found"; Drouhot 2017), "lost," or "liberated" (Wellman 1979). Then, we outline the contributions of the articles presented in the current volume. The collection of articles provides new evidence and theory of how networks are mobilized in poverty, showing the wide empirical variation in network access and returns among the poor and analyzing the roles of organizational brokerage and evolving networking practices that may help to explain contrasting outcomes. We conclude with a brief discussion of pathways for future research.

Network Effects and Well-Being

In their daily lives, people interact with partners, relatives, friends, bosses, workmates, and other acquaintances in similar and different economic conditions. These relationships can give access to valuable resources, including money and goods, information, time and skills, counsel and consolation (e.g., Taylor 2011); and obtaining access to them may be an important ingredient of coping strategies (e.g., Adler de Lomnitz 1975; Desmond and Gershenson 2016; Edin and Lein 1997; González de la Rocha 1994; Newman 1999; Stack 1974) as well as an aid for social mobility (Domínguez and Watkins 2003; Granovetter 1973). The vast literature on *social capital* and *social support* has uncovered how resources are exchanged in networks (Lin 2001; Cohen, Underwood, and Gottlieb 2000). Research has shown that intimate relationships, such as kin and close friends, give the most emotional support, care, and tangible assistance, but acquaintances can complement those relationships in many ways (Fingerman 2009; Small 2017). Networked individuals can also coordinate their actions and share resources to achieve *collective efficacy* (Sampson 2004) and to *pool risks* (Fafchamps and Gubert 2007). For example, villagers in the Global South often protect themselves against health and income shocks by sharing crops with relatives, neighbors, and friends; providing mutual labor services; or starting a common fund for costly, unforeseeable events such as funerals (e.g., Fafchamps and Gubert 2007).

Still, the impact of networks is not one-dimensional. Networks can just as well drain resources, as implied by the concept of *negative social capital* (Portes 1998), i.e., "the pressure on an individual actor to incur costs by virtue of membership in social networks or other social structures" (O'Brien 2012, 378). Social relationships serve as conduits for not only social support but also values, norms, social pressure, and control. Through social learning and normative pressure, people may adopt either beneficial or harmful coping strategies. Furthermore, *structural violence* (Farmer 2004; Galtung 1969), i.e., "the methodical and often subtle processes through which social structures disadvantage and harm certain groups of people" (Hodgetts et al. 2014, 3), is reproduced and normalized in everyday interactions, "essentially cementing the disadvantage initiated by larger macro- and meso-level forces" (Smith 2010, 4). In this regard, interpersonal relations also play a role in *shaming, stigma,* and *exploitation* (e.g., Del Real 2019; Levine 2013). For example, family and friends can be judgmental about a person's welfare reliance rather than supportive, thereby replicating and normalizing state and public discourse about the causes of poverty. In sum, networks can have intricate effects on individual well-being.

Social Networks and Poverty

Pervasive solidarity

Contemporary research on the role of social networks in the day-to-day subsistence of the poor in cities can be traced back to two pioneering books, one published closely after the other. Both give ethnographic accounts of poor families that are in sharp contrast with Lewis's theory of the "culture of poverty" (1959, 1998), which posits that negative features such as personal and family disorganization cause persistent poverty. Although the theory has been criticized for various reasons (see, e.g., Bourgois 2001; Lamont and Small 2008; Ryan 1971; Streib et al. 2016), its basic assumptions continue to be visible in behavioral theories of the causes of poverty (Brady 2019) and in punitive welfare policies.

The first of the two books is *All Our Kin*, written by anthropologist Carol Stack (1974), now a classic in the field of urban poverty and social networks. Stack performed three years of ethnographic fieldwork in an income-poor, African American neighborhood in a Midwestern city in the United States, starting in 1968. She observed that the people in this neighborhood managed to survive economic hardship by building upon extensive domestic networks of exchange that were local and mainly kin-based. Within these networks, "food stamps, rent money, a TV, hats, dice, a car, a nickel here, a cigarette there, food, milk, grits, and children" (1974, 32) were exchanged. Figure 1 illustrates one such domestic network from the point of view of a married couple, Magnolia and Calvin Waters, as narrated and visualized in different ways by Stack. The figure shows that at least forty adults were reported to participate in the system of exchanges. Most of them were divided over eight local households with fluid boundaries (often extended families), tied to the couple by real and *fictive kinship* ties, close friendships, and children. The exchanges were seemingly voluntary, but participation in these networks required reciprocation. "Sometimes I don't have a damn dime in my pocket, not a crying penny to get a box of paper diapers, milk, a loaf of bread," explained Magnolia's daughter, a young single mother with three children. "But you have to have help from everybody and anybody," she continued, "so don't turn no one down when they come round for help" (Stack 1974, 32).

FIGURE 1
Illustration of the Domestic Network of Magnolia and Calvin Waters, as
Explained by Stack (1974)

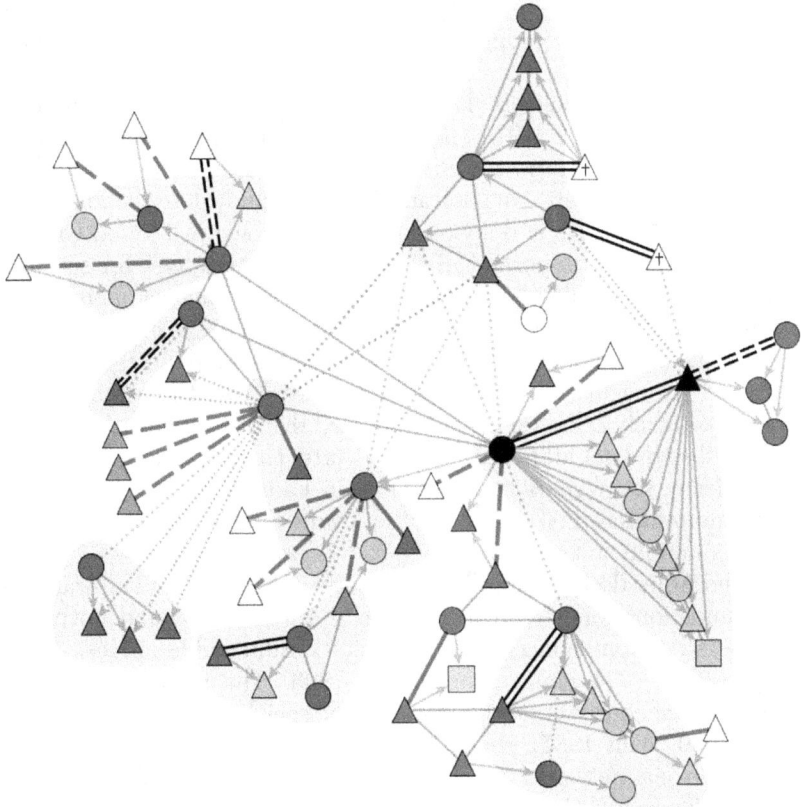

Legend

Node color

■ Member of focal couple
■ Adult participant
■ Child (< 18 years of age)
□ Adult non-participant
  (ex-partners or deceased)

Shaded Area

  Domestic unit (household), April 1969

Node shape

△ Male
○ Female
□ Gender
  unknown
† Deceased

Edge color and shape

A══════ B   A and B are married
A ══ ══ B   A and B are divorced
A▬▬▬▬▬ B   A and B have consensual
            relationship
A ▬▬ ▬▬ B   Past consensual relationship
A──────— B   A and B are siblings
A───────▸ B   A is parent of B
A·············▸ B   A and B are friends
A ············▸ B   A is a caregiver to B

NOTE: Own elaboration based on Stack's (1974) description on pages 94–100 and her charts
C and D. There are small deviations between Stack's text and her graphs, such that the presented graph is approximate.

The system of generalized reciprocity underlying the extensive networks reported by Stack revealed a high level of family organization, contrasting the culture of poverty theory. Mutual sharing was enforced by social control and community sanctions. Even though these systems formed an important survival strategy, Stack (1974) warned that the obligations they created toward kith and kin made it impossible for people to create surpluses, thus making escape from poverty difficult.

Concurrently, anthropologist Larissa Adler de Lomnitz published *Cómo Sobreviven los Marginados* (1975), later translated into English as *Networks and Marginality: Life in a Mexican Shantytown* (1977). Based on surveys and ethnographic fieldwork done between 1969 and 1971, the study described how internal migrants residing in Cerrada del Cóndor, a shanty town in Mexico City, coped with poverty. The most important of three observed strategies for survival was reciprocity, the sharing of favors and scarce resources with local family members and neighbors in similar situations, a strategy for which it was imperative to form dense, local social networks of trust. Fictive kinship (*compadrazgo*, i.e. godparenthood) and strong male bonds (*cuatismo*) were created to strengthen these networks. Like Stack, Adler de Lomnitz showed that these networks guaranteed survival, but they did not lift people out of poverty. The book started a large tradition of studies in social support and poverty in Latin America (see for an early review Enríquez-Rosas [2001]) that is often overlooked by the English-speaking academic community investigating the networks-poverty nexus.

Stack's and Adler de Lomnitz's studies, conducted in distinct cultural settings, laid the foundations for later research into social networks and poverty (e.g., Bazán Levy 1998; Domínguez and Watkins 2003; Edin and Lein 1997; González de la Rocha 1986, 1994; Paugam and Zoyem 1998). This research has benefited from the simultaneously emerging theories of social support (e.g., Kahn and Antonucci 1980; Wills 1985), social capital (e.g., Lin and Dumin 1986; Portes 1998), and personal networks (e.g., Fischer 1982; Wellman 1979). Much of the empirical work confirmed the relevance of informal support for people experiencing poverty. For example, Newman (1999) observed that the working poor, both native-born and immigrants, relied on extended family networks of the type described by Stack. "None of them would have been able to manage these responsibilities [of earning a living and raising children] were it not for the fact that each in turn has made the extended family the core of her life," Newman noticed (1999, 196). She also acknowledged the role of typically older, welfare-recipient neighbors in the collective efficacy of dealing with poverty in some neighborhoods, by "keep[ing] watch over children and property, while the working poor are on the job" (Newman 1999, 223). Others reaffirmed that low-income mothers in poverty draw upon extensive networks, including relatives, close friends, boyfriends, and children's fathers for their survival (Domínguez and Watkins 2003; Edin and Lein 1997; Henly, Danziger, and Offer 2005; Nelson 2005), while these networks simultaneously impede social mobility (Domínguez and Watkins 2003; Henly, Danziger, and Offer 2005). Edin and Lein (1997) estimated the financial contribution of these networks to household budgets. Using interviews and detailed budgetary analyses of nearly 400 low-income mothers, they found that a substantial portion of the total budget of welfare-reliant mothers (17 percent) and low-income wage-reliant mothers (21 percent) came from unreported gifts from network members. More recently, Raudenbush (2020) showed that low-income African Americans who were cut off from formal healthcare also used their social networks to access medicines, medical equipment, and insurance cards. This access could improve their health, but moving beyond formal healthcare could also seriously harm it. Research in former Soviet states documents similar extensive support systems, named *blat*, i.e., the "use of personal networks for obtaining goods and services in short supply and for circumventing formal procedures" (Ledeneva 2009, 257; cf. Caldwell 2004; Ledeneva 1998).

Together, this body of research shows that people in poverty consistently use extensive networks of kin (often matrifocal) and other close relationships, mostly with people in similar economic conditions, to compensate for a lack of resources, adopting systems of generalized reciprocity. A parallel can be drawn with Wellman's concept of "community saved" or "found" (Drouhot 2017; Wellman 1979), in which typically densely knit, local networks give ample social support on the basis of communal solidarity. The blending of the social and economic spheres reported in this literature may be surprising, but researchers have long established that economic activity is an integral part of intimate relationships in all societal strata (Zelizer 2005).

Pervasive isolation

Nevertheless, various scholars have challenged the assumption that the poor can rely on family networks for their survival (e.g., González de la Rocha 2007; Roschelle 1997). Some have called for more attention to the "disastrous consequences" (Roschelle 1997, vii) that policies based on such an "untrue, but also perilous" (González de la Rocha 2007, 48) assumption could have for the many people who do not have such networks. This work suggests that support networks have eroded in contemporary societies, and that people in poverty are mostly on their own. Indeed, some large-scale surveys have shown that the poor, who most need informal support, are the least likely to have it (e.g., Böhnke 2008; Harknett and Hartnett 2011).

The network disadvantage reported in this body of research is a result of both lower *network access*, that is, the poor may have a lower number of resources embedded in their networks (also called *network poverty*; O'Brien 2012; van Eijk 2010) and lower *network returns*, whereby the poor may have similar access but obtain fewer benefits from their networks (Pedulla and Pager 2019). The first—network access—depends on the size and composition of support networks. Empirical evidence shows that support networks shrink after entry into poverty (Böhnke and Link 2017; Mood and Jonsson 2016), and that the poor have smaller networks than the more affluent (Marques 2012; van Eijk 2010). Furthermore, processes of *homophily* (i.e., the tendency to form social ties with people with similar characteristics; McPherson, Smith-Lovin, and Cook 2001), intergenerational transmission of poverty, and geographical segregation mean that the networks of low-income individuals typically comprise equally resource-poor individuals (e.g., Tigges, Browne, and Green 1998), limiting network access. This was vividly illustrated by Mahler (1995), who showed that poor Central and South American immigrants in the United States did not have the financial resources to give support to one another, and lost the systems of reciprocity they had had in their countries of origin as a result. However, they believed that their compatriots were unwilling rather than unable to help them (i.e., they believed they had network access, but not returns), creating environments of distrust. Similarly, Menjívar (2000) demonstrated that income-insecure Salvadoran immigrants in the United States could not provide the support to recent immigrants they are normatively expected to give, due to economic scarcity; she labeled such relationships "fragmented ties." The network poverty had negative repercussions in the creation of social capital in the community of co-nationals.

A second potential source of network disadvantage, network returns, implies that individuals in poverty are not able to benefit from the resources that are embedded in their networks (Pedulla and Pager 2019). Newman (1988), for example, found that downwardly mobile individuals had relationships with middle-class people who had sufficient resources, but it was difficult for these individuals to keep up with their friends' costly lifestyles. While friends invited them at first without expecting much in return, "eventually the unspoken rules of reciprocity put an end to that" (Newman 1988, 3). More generally, Offer (2012) argued that the expectation and obligation to reciprocate hinder the participation of the poorer sections of society in informal exchange networks. In her study, poor women in Israel were either excluded from support networks to avoid resource drain, or they withdrew themselves from networks to avoid exhausting other people's resources or being stigmatized. Wherry, Seefeldt, and Alvarez (2018) showed how potential help providers often refused to give help that might not be reciprocated or otherwise limited it to avoid resource drain.

Other motivations also explain limited network returns. Smith (2005, 2010) showed that unemployed African Americans tended to know employed peers who held relevant job information that could help them get ahead, but they were often let down when they asked them for job referrals (cf. Marin 2012; Newman 1999). Potential job referrers tended to be worried about their own reputations with their bosses, and only helped people they believed were trustworthy, with whom they had strong ties, or when the two were embedded in densely connected networks (among other explanatory factors). Consequently, to avoid rejection, job seekers obtained an attitude of "defensive individualism" (Smith 2010), choosing not to reach out to people who might be able to help them.

Poverty spells can also widen the income or power gap in dyadic relationships, which makes them less sustainable, as people run out of things to share (Newman 1988). But these gaps also create other difficulties. First, the difference in resources between two people may lead the lower-income person to feel shame. Many scholars have noted the association between poverty and shame (Baumberg 2016; Walker 2014; Lister 2016). Lavee and Offer (2012) show that low-income women in Israel only see themselves as deserving of informal support if they are or have been economically productive, with which they reproduce the common discourse regarding welfare recipients' deservingness of formal support. Out of shame, benefit recipients in the UK often decide not to disclose their recipient status to their loved ones to avoid being stigmatized (Garthwaite 2015). As a result, many are wary about activating their networks for support.

Second, differentials in power or income can create "dangerous dependencies" (Scott, London, and Myers 2002) in personal relationships. Lavee (2016) found that isolation led (mostly single) low-income mothers in Israel to depend materially on men with more resources, in exchange for sex. Whether these relationships were disguised as partnerships or not, the women, according to Lavee, commodified their bodies to obtain help for their families. Lavee explicitly rejects conceptualizing such exchanges as social support and calls this survival strategy "the slippery slope of dependency."

Third, these differences can generate distrust. For example, Levine (2013) observed that low-income mothers in the United States distrusted bosses, case workers, child care providers, boyfriends, and even family members, as these relationships were either characterized by a power differential, which could expose them to mistreatment, or by unaligned interests. This impeded the women's use of childcare, them getting married, or getting a job, and thus limited their chances of upward mobility. Similarly, a New Zealand study observed that the poor perceived case workers as abusive, disrespectful, disinterested, and judgmental, scrutinizing every aspect of a person's life in exchange for social support (Hodgetts et al. 2014). Finally, Del Real (2019) reported how low-income undocumented immigrants in Southern California had what she called "toxic ties" with documented partners, relatives, and friends, i.e., relationships that are intentionally or unintentionally exploitative, demeaning, or abusive as a result of the power differential in these relationships (see also Offer and Fischer [2018] for research on difficult ties). They could be reported by them, robbed without the legal means to press charges, or otherwise exploited. In this sense, these relationships reproduce what researchers have called the legal violence that the state's immigration laws inflict on them (Menjívar and Abrego 2012).

In sum, the work described in this section suggests that the poor cannot rely on their networks for support in the same way that the more affluent can due to restricted network access and returns. Support can exacerbate vulnerabilities and create shame and distrust, encouraging people to cope with adversity mostly individually. This body of research suggests that the relationship between poverty and networks may contribute to cumulative disadvantage (DiMaggio and Garip 2011). We can draw a parallel with Wellman's "community lost" perspective (Wellman 1979; Drouhot 2017), where social solidarity has eroded in impersonal, unstable communities.

Selective solidarity

Why do empirical studies find such divergent models for social support in poverty? Has pervasive solidarity become a thing of the past (Hogan, Eggebeen, and Clogg 1993), when networks were mostly dense and local (Wellman 1979), family structures more extensive, and employment opportunities more widespread (e.g.,

González de la Rocha 2007)? Do some people in poverty encounter solidarity while others in similar circumstances face isolation (Klärner and Knabe 2019; Marques 2012), and if so, what explains this difference? Or can solidarity and individualism coexist in the same individuals or communities?

Raudenbush (2016) argued that solidarity and distrust are two frames for thinking that can be adopted by the same individuals toward different people. To capture this compatibility, the author introduced a third perspective, which she called "selective solidarity," based on fieldwork among African Americans in a public housing development in a large U.S. city. In contrast to Stack's informants, most individuals interviewed by Raudenbush talked about "staying to them-selves" more than they did in the past due to neighborhood violence and instabil-ity, although they still selectively mobilized ties with friends or neighbors for much needed social support.

Other studies also found aspects of both solidarity and distrust in the same communities, even though in different forms than observed by Raudenbush (2016). For example, Bourgois and Schonberg (2009) conducted ethnographic fieldwork in a community of homeless injection drug users living around "Edgewater Boulevard" (fictive street name) in San Francisco—a case of extreme poverty and vulnerability. The homeless members of this community had varying relationships with their families: Some had parents who always welcomed them in their homes, others had conflict-ridden relationships with family or were abused by them in the past, and still others were completely estranged from them. Among themselves, however, they had constructed a community, where reciprocity and moral economy coincided with deep distrust for the *same* net-work members (in contrast to Raudenbush [2016]). As the authors explained, "Begging, working, scavenging, and stealing, the Edgewater homeless balance on a tightrope of mutual solidarity and betrayal as they scramble for their next shot of heroin, their next meal, their next place to sleep, and their sense of dignity—all the while keeping a wary eye out for the police" (Bourgois and Schonberg 2009, 9–10). Since most heroin injectors were unable to survive on their own, they relied on others. However, "gifts often go hand in hand with rip-offs" (Bourgois and Schonberg 2009, 9–10).

Another variant of the selective solidarity perspective was given by Desmond (2012), who studied evicted tenants living in a trailer park in Milwaukee. They too faced chronic poverty and destitution. Their cases showed neither pervasive solidarity nor complete isolation. Evicted tenants tended to have financially het-erogeneous families, with some relatives experiencing similar and others better conditions. "Every tenant I met relied on kinfolk for some kind of assistance," Desmond wrote, "Yet to meet their most pressing needs (e.g., food, shelter, child care), tenants often relied more extensively on disposable ties than on relatives" (2012, 1305). He used the term "disposable ties" to label a type of tie that has features of both strong (intimate) and weak (superficial) ties. It refers to newly created relationships that are rapidly thickened to increase the exchange of sup-port, reaching high levels of closeness, contact frequency, and aid, but these ties also rapidly burn out due to excessive demands. While they contributed to day-to-day survival, they also increased the instability in individuals' lives.

Together, these studies parallel some aspects of Wellman's "liberated community" (Wellman 1979) in the sense that they evoke loosely knit and transient social networks, with narrow, mostly specialized support exchanged in one-on-one relationships. Such networks are difficult to maintain without sufficient resources (Drouhot 2017), such as in poverty. Therefore, the picture that the studies in this section paint diverts from Wellman's description of liberated communities.

In sum, the literature provides contrasting but also partially complementary perspectives on the importance of social support networks in the daily survival of the poor. The observed differences may be explained by the characteristics of the populations under study (e.g., single mothers, evicted tenants, the working poor, recent immigrants, homeless drug users, the downwardly mobile, each with varying degrees of economic needs), by the macro-level conditions under which they were studied (e.g., different welfare structures, family structures, and levels of geographical mobility), or perhaps even by the various research methods (Raudenbush 2016). For example, by using ethnographic fieldwork, forming part of concrete households, and conducting participant observation, Stack may have observed higher levels of support than others. More research is needed to understand under which conditions social support networks can be sustainable in poverty and how this sustainability can be improved.

About This Volume

Researchers have investigated the role of social networks in poverty over the past 50 years, and together these studies have shown that, depending on local conditions, (1) networks can both aid the survival of poverty and hinder upward social mobility; (2) networks can fail to be a source of effective support among the poor, leading to isolation, vulnerability, or relational dependencies; and (3) solidarity can co-exist with isolation and distrust, even within the same relationships. This volume aims to improve the theoretical and evidence base of these findings. The volume is distinct from previous research in two ways.

First, it adopts an international perspective, presenting studies from the United States, Mexico, the United Kingdom, Spain, Turkey, and Germany. This viewpoint can shed light on the particularity or universalism of the association between social networks and poverty, as social networks function in part as a reaction to macro-level conditions (e.g., Ledeneva 2009). Moreover, an international perspective can help poverty researchers to examine the limits of adopting national policy-based assumptions, categories, and classifications and presuming these to be universal (Wacquant 2002). This kind of reflexivity has benefitted migration scholars, who have questioned, among other things, the naturalization of differences between migrants and citizens and of national borders (Dahinden 2016; Nowicka and Cieslik 2013; Wimmer and Glick Schiller 2002; Lubbers, Verdery, and Molina 2020). An international perspective should be equally important to poverty researchers.

Second, the work presented here is multidisciplinary; contributors include sociologists, anthropologists, economists, social geographers, and criminologists. Though all papers are either based on or directly informed by fieldwork, the research methods used range from ethnographic observation and qualitative interviews to structured network measurement, surveys, and financial diaries. Qualitative and quantitative methods complement one another in important ways in poverty research (see Small 2011). In this context, qualitative methods bring to light the complexity of the lived experiences of people in poverty (Newman and Massengill 2006), the meaning people attach to their circumstances, and the complex mechanisms through which they use or fail to use their networks. Such methods also often give voice to populations who do not commonly participate in policy-making nor in academic discourse. Quantitative methods allow for breadth, for comparison across cases and over time, and for the contextualization of cases in larger social patterns.

The volume is organized around three themes: (1) the nature of exchange relations in the networks of the poor, (2) the role of organizations in the networks of the poor, and (3) the relation between poverty and other disadvantages in the networks of the poor.

The nature of exchange relations in the networks of the poor

The first section examines the nature of exchange relations in personal networks among the poor. Mercedes González de la Rocha begins with a conceptual article informed by decades of fieldwork that she conducted in Mexico. She shows that, as a result of increases in poverty, social support has become increasingly commodified, where people expect that support must be remunerated. She discusses how this tendency exacerbates social exclusion.

The second article again touches on the connection between economic and social relations (Zelizer 2005). While research has shown that social support matters, there is little evidence on the daily and weekly volume of financial exchanges among people in poverty (but see Edin and Lein 1997). Olga Biosca, Neil McHugh, Fatma Ibrahim, Rachel Baker, Tim Laxton, and Cam Donaldson use unique data based on financial diaries over a six-month period to understand the extent to which financial support contributes to the day-to-day subsistence of forty-five income-insecure individuals in the UK. Consistent with the selective solidarity perspective, they find that the diarists use the social capital embedded in their networks of family members and friends both pervasively and strategically. Over six months, diarists exchanged an average of £870 (approximately 1,143 USD[1]) with one or a small number of family members and friends, who usually experienced similar economic conditions and lived nearby.

In the third article, Miranda Lubbers, Hugo Valenzuela García, Paula Escribano Castaño, José Luis Molina, Antònia Casellas, and Jorge Grau Rebollo examine why some individuals manage to get support and others do not. The authors present findings from a mixed-methods research among sixty-one households in Spain, a country with a Mediterranean welfare system that is based on the assumption that the family is the main provider of welfare. The authors find that network access and returns vary greatly between households. Many networks are, however, less densely connected and more transient and individualistic than those described by Stack and Adler de Lomnitz. In these conditions, support provision transforms the network by violating its norms, such that prolonged a-reciprocal support often leads to conflicts and rejection.

The role of organizations in the networks of the poor

The second group of articles examines the brokerage roles that organizations may have in the creation of social capital for low-income individuals. Social capital results not only from individual agency but also from the opportunities for interaction that people obtain within the context of routine organizations, such as schools, work places, associations, food banks, child care centers, and libraries (Small 2006, 2009; Klinenberg 2018). While past ethnographic research within charity organizations has shown that support obtained within institutions often goes substantially beyond what is formally intended (Caldwell 2004; Glasser 1988; Grau Rebollo et al. 2019), less attention has been paid to the factors that determine the level of non-intended, informal support, and particularly factors that allow such support to flow. Scholarly attention to the institutional practices of local and community organizations can help us to understand networks as they manifest themselves in practice.

In the first article of this section, Mario Luis Small and Leah Gose propose a model of the role of routine organizations in the creation of social capital. Building on brokerage theory and based on an extensive review of published field studies, the authors seek to identify the conditions under which routine organizations can significantly contribute to social capital formation among low-income populations. They argue that successful brokerage depends, in part, on the extent to which institutional norms render social interaction among members frequent, long-lasting, focused on others, and centered on joint tasks. The ensuing ties may stimulate generalized reciprocity, a sense of belonging, and access to other organizations.

Joan Maya Mazelis examines a specific case where social capital is successfully created within an organization for people who hardly obtain support from their personal relationships. Based on long-term ethnographic work and qualitative interviews (Mazelis 2017), the author observes that a grassroots organization for people experiencing poverty, the Kensington Welfare Rights Union (KWRU) in Philadelphia, helps to build a sustainable support network among its members. The organization does not have external funds and can thus only succeed if members collaborate—in turn, collective action is successful and creates supportive bilateral ties among members of the KWRU. This article is consistent with Small and Gose's model: the organization demands frequent presence at the office and at rallies, even if there is not always a lot to do; the adherence to the organization tends to be long-lasting; and the organization gives its members joint tasks of activism and encourages mutual help. Mazelis also finds that the sustainability of these ties is further enhanced by fictive kinship processes and organizational conflict mediation.

Finally, Paul Stretesky, Margaret Anne Defeyter, Michael Long, Zeibeda Satter, and Eilish Crilley focus on British "holiday clubs," community-based institutions that attenuate the hunger experienced by children during the summer holidays when they lack access to school lunches. These organizations provide food, but also, as the authors argue, a broad range of activities and other services that are beneficial for resource-scarce households. Based on mixed-methods research in seventeen holiday clubs in North East England, the authors show that holiday clubs broker access to important community networks to help residents living in disadvantaged areas. Their capacity to broker these resources depends to some extent on the personal networks of volunteers and staff.

The relation between poverty and other disadvantages in the networks of the poor

The last set of articles explores the social support networks of populations facing particular challenges in addition to poverty.

Ezgi Güler presents an ethnographic study of social support among a group of transgender female sex workers who compete for clients in a major city in Turkey. The women endure physical and structural violence in their work and lives, and many are estranged from their families. Güler examines whether the women manage to develop supportive relations given the competitive nature of their interactions. She finds high levels of cooperation around safety and even economic resources, but the support was often selective, and relationships as sources of support tended to be precarious and rife with conflict.

Social support is often affected by national regulations, which can remain invisible in studies of a single nation state. Başak Bilecen examines social support transnationally among Turkish immigrants in Germany and the family and friends of these migrants "left behind" in Turkey. She finds that while German social welfare schemes give Turkish immigrants a more secure income, increasing their ability to send remittances, residency-based social policies also limit their ability to provide care to family members in their country of origin. The welfare schemes of Germany alter the power balance in transnational personal relations, giving migrants the "upper hand" in family decisions.

The volume concludes with a thoughtful commentary by Katherine Newman, whose numerous books on downward mobility (Newman 1988), the working poor (Newman 1999), and retirement insecurity (Newman 2019) touch on many of the issues discussed here. Newman expertly locates the articles of this special issue in the larger social and social scientific context and raises a number of thought-provoking questions for future research.

Thinking Ahead

The articles in this volume show that the nexus between social networks and poverty is highly complex. Social support networks can and do provide much needed emotional, material, and financial help and services to those in poverty, but sustained poverty and a-reciprocal material and financial support can also erode networks, augmenting isolation and the social exclusion that poor people already experience in other sectors of their lives. Family relationships are particularly vulnerable in this aspect. In this sense, mobilizing networks is like walking on thin ice: People may go a long way with what networks can provide, but the network can also easily fall apart.

Given the many people in poverty and the continuing rise in inequality (Grusky and MacLean 2016; Lamont and Pierson 2019), policies can be developed that strengthen, on one hand, the social support networks of vulnerable populations to reduce isolation and exclusion, and on the other, the welfare systems on which the poor depend. The work in this volume suggests that routine organizations can help to provide the "infrastructure" for creating and strengthening social networks (Klinenberg 2018). The work also suggests that welfare policies could be better aligned with the precarity, instability, and income volatility in the lives of the poor. Future research could help to further policy developments by studying the association between social networks and poverty in particular interventions or around important changes in welfare schemes. For example, various European countries have been experimenting with a universal basic income. The works in this volume make clear that such interventions will almost certainly have consequences for the networks of the poor, shaping not only household budgets but also broader communities of exchange relations. Broader attention to such interactions will help us to understand the vulnerabilities to which people in poverty are exposed.

Note

1. Calculated with the conversion rate of 1. 3133 that was current as of September 1, 2016, the midpoint of the data collection period.

References

Adler de Lomnitz, Larissa. 1975. *Cómo sobreviven los marginados*. Mexico DF: Siglo XXI Editores.

Adler de Lomnitz, Larissa. 1977. *Networks and marginality: Life in a Mexican shantytown*. New York, NY: Academic Press Inc.

Allard, Scott W., and Mario L. Small. 2013. Reconsidering the urban disadvantaged: The role of systems, institutions, and organizations. *The ANNALS of the American Academy of Political and Social Science* 647:6–20.

Baumberg, Ben. 2016. The stigma of claiming benefits: A quantitative study. *Journal of Social Policy* 45 (2): 181–99.

Bazán Levy, Lucía. 1998. *El último recurso: Las relaciones familiares como alternativas frente a la crisis*. Mexico DF: CIESAS, UNAM.

Böhnke, Petra. 2008. Are the poor socially integrated? The link between poverty and social support in different welfare regimes. *Journal of European Social Policy* 18 (2): 133–50.

Böhnke, Petra, and Sebastian Link. 2017. Poverty and the dynamics of social networks: An analysis of German panel data. *European Sociological Review* 33 (4): 615–32.

Bourgois, Philippe. 2001. Culture of poverty. In *International encyclopedia of the social & behavioral sciences*, eds. Neil J. Smelser and Paul B. Baltes, 11904–7. Oxford: Pergamon.

Bourgois, Philippe I., and Jeff Schonberg. 2009. *Righteous dopefiend*. Berekely, CA: University of California Press.

Brady, David. 2019. Theories of the causes of poverty. *Annual Review of Sociology* 45 (1): 1–21.

Brady, David, and Zachary Parolin. 2019. The levels and trends in deep and extreme Poverty in the U.S., 1993–2016. *Demography*. DOI: 10.31235/osf.io/73myr.

Caldwell, Melissa L. 2004. *Not by bread alone: Social support in the new Russia*. Berkeley, CA: University of California Press.

Cohen, Sheldon, Lynn G. Underwood, and Benjamin H. Gottlieb, eds. 2000. *Social support measurement and intervention. A Guide for Health and Social Scientists*. New York, NY: Oxford University Press.

Dahinden, Janine. 2016. A plea for the "de-migranticization" of research on migration and integration. *Ethnic and Racial Studies* 39 (13): 2207–25.

Del Real, Deisy. 2019. Toxic ties: The reproduction of legal violence within mixed-status intimate partners, relatives, and friends. *International Migration Review* 53 (2): 548–70.

Desmond, Matthew. 2012. Disposable ties and the urban poor. *American Journal of Sociology* 117 (5): 1295–1335.

Desmond, Matthew, and Carl Gershenson. 2016. Who gets evicted? Assessing individual, neighborhood, and network factors. *Social Science Research* 62 (February): 362–77.

Desmond, Matthew, and Bruce Western. 2018. Poverty in America: New directions and debates. *Annual Review of Sociology* 44 (1): 305–18.

DiMaggio, Paul, and Filiz Garip. 2011. How network externalities can exacerbate intergroup inequality. *American Journal of Sociology* 116 (6): 1887–1933.

Domínguez, Silvia, and Celeste Watkins. 2003. Creating networks for survival and mobility: Social capital among African-American and Latin-American low-income mothers. *Social Problems* 50 (1): 111–35.

Drouhot, Lucas G. 2017. Reconsidering "community liberated": How class and the national context shape personal support networks. *Social Networks* 48: 57–77.

Edin, Kathryn, and Laura Lein. 1997. *Making ends meet: How single mothers survive welfare and low-wage work*. New York, NY: Russell Sage Foundation.

Enríquez-Rosas, Rocío. 2001. Social networks and urban poverty. *Development and Society* 30 (2): 79–108.

Fafchamps, Marcel, and Flore Gubert. 2007. The formation of risk sharing networks. *Journal of Development Economics* 83 (2): 326–50.

Farmer, Paul. 2004. An anthropology of structural violence. *Current Anthropology* 45 (3): 305–25.

Fingerman, Karen L. 2009. Consequential strangers and peripheral ties: The importance of unimportant relationships. *Journal of Family Theory and Review* 1:69–86.

Fischer, Claude S. 1982. *To dwell among friends: Personal networks in town and city*. Chicago, IL: University of Chicago Press.

Friedrichs, Jürgen, George Galster, and Sako Musterd. 2003. Neighbourhood effects on social opportunities: The European and American research and policy context. *Housing Studies* 18 (6): 797–806.

Galtung, Johan. 1969. Violence, peace, and peace research. *Journal of Peace Research* 6 (3): 167–91.

Garthwaite, Kayleigh. 2015. "Keeping meself to meself" - How social networks can influence narratives of stigma and identity for long-term sickness benefits recipients. *Social Policy & Administration* 49 (2): 199–212.

Glasser, Irene. 1988. *More than bread: Ethnography of a soup kitchen*. London: The University of Alabama Press.

González de la Rocha, Mercedes. 1986. *Los recursos de la pobreza. Familias de bajos ingresos de Guadalajara*. Guadalajara: El Colegio de Jalisco/CIESAS.

González de la Rocha, Mercedes. 1994. *The resources of poverty. Women and survival in a Mexican city*. Oxford: Basil Blackwell.

González de la Rocha, Mercedes. 2007. The construction of the myth of survival. *Development and Change* 38 (1): 45–66.

Granovetter, Mark S. 1973. The strength of weak ties. *American Journal of Sociology* 78 (6): 1360–80.

Grau Rebollo, Jorge, Paula Escribano Castaño, Hugo Valenzuela-García, and Miranda J. Lubbers. 2019. Charities as symbolic families: Ethnographic evidence from Spain. *Journal of Organizational Ethnography* 8 (1): 25–41.

Grusky, David B., and Alair MacLean. 2016. The social fallout of a high inequality regime. The ANNALS *of the American Academy of Political and Social Science* 663 (1): 33–52.

Hall, Sarah Marie. 2019. *Everyday life in austerity: Family, friends and intimate relations*. Cham, Switzerland: Palgrave Macmillan.

Harknett, Kristen S., and Carolina Sten Hartnett. 2011. Who lacks support and why? An examination of mothers' personal safety nets. *Journal of Marriage and Family* 73 (4): 861–75.

Henly, Julia R., Sandra K. Danziger, and Shira Offer. 2005. The contribution of social support to the material well-being of low-income families. *Journal of Marriage and Family* 67 (1): 122–40.

Hodgetts, Darrin, Kerry Chamberlain, Shiloh Groot, and Yardena Tankel. 2014. Urban poverty, structural violence and welfare provision for 100 families in Auckland. *Urban Studies* 51 (10): 2036–51.

Hogan, Dennis P., David J. Eggebeen, and Clifford C. Clogg. 1993. The structure of intergenerational exchanges in American families. *American Journal of Sociology* 98 (6): 1428–58.

Kahn, Robert L., and Toni C. Antonucci. 1980. Convoys over the life course: Attachment, roles, and social support. *Life-Span Development and Behavior* 3:253–86.

Klärner, Andreas, and André Knabe. 2019. Social networks and coping with poverty in rural areas. *Sociologia Ruralis* 59 (3): 447–73.

Klinenberg, Eric. 2018. *Palaces for the people: How social infrastructure can help fight inequality, polarization and the decline of civic life*. New York, NY: Penguin Random House.

Lamont, Michèle, and Paul Pierson. 2019. Inequality generation and persistence as multidimensional processes: An interdisciplinary agenda. *Daedalus* 148 (3): 5–18.

Lamont, Michèle, and Mario Luis Small. 2008. How culture matters: Enriching our understanding of poverty. In *The colors of poverty: Why racial and ethnic Disparities Persist*, eds. Ann Chih Lin and David R. Harris, 76–102. New York, NY: Russell Sage Foundation.

Lavee, Einat. 2016. Exchanging sex for material resources: Reinforcement of gender and oppressive survival strategy. *Women's Studies International Forum* 56:83–91.

Lavee, Einat, and Shira Offer. 2012. "If you sit and cry no one will help you": Understanding perceptions of worthiness and social support relations among low-income women under a neoliberal discourse. *The Sociological Quarterly* 53 (3): 374–93.

Ledeneva, Alena. 1998. *Russia's economy of favours: Blat, networking and informal exchange*. Cambridge: Cambridge University Press.

Ledeneva, Alena. 2009. From Russia with blat: Can informal networks help modernize Russia? *Social Research* 76 (1): 257–88.

Lee, Barrett A., Stephen A. Matthews, John Iceland, and Glenn Firebaugh. 2015. Introduction: Residential inequality: Orientation and overview. *The ANNALS of the American Academy of Political and Social Science* 660:7–16.

Levine, Judith. 2013. *Ain't no trust: How bosses, boyfriends, and bureaucrats fail low income mothers and why it matters*. Berkeley, CA: University of California Press.

Lewis, Oscar. 1959. *Five families: Mexican case studies in the culture of poverty*. New York, NY: Basic Books.

Lewis, Oscar. 1998. The culture of poverty. *Society* 35 (2): 7–9.

Lin, Nan. 2001. *Social capital: A theory of social structure and action*. Cambridge: Cambridge University Press.

Lin, Nan, and Mary Dumin. 1986. Access to occupations through social ties. *Social Networks* 8 (4): 365–85.

Lister, Ruth. 2016. "To count for nothing": Poverty beyond the statistics. *Journal of the British Academy* 3:139–66.

Lubbers, Miranda J., Ashton M. Verdery, and José Luis Molina. 2020. Social networks and transnational social fields: A review of quantitative and mixed-methods approaches. *International Migration Review* 54 (1): 177–204.

Mahler, Sarah J. 1995. *American dreaming: Immigrant life on the margins*. Princeton, NJ: Princeton University Press.

Marin, Alexandra. 2012. Don't mention it: Why people don't share job information, when they do, and why it matters. *Social Networks* 34 (2): 181–92.

Marques, Eduardo Cesar. 2012. *Opportunities and deprivation in the urban south: Poverty, segregation and social networks in São Paulo*. Farnham: Ashgate Publishing.

Mazelis, Joan M. 2017. *Surviving poverty: Creating sustainable ties among the poor*. New York, NY: NYU Press.

McPherson, Miller, Lynn Smith-Lovin, and James M. Cook. 2001. Birds of a feather: Homophily in social networks. *Annual Review of Sociology* 27:415–44.

Menjívar, Cecilia. 2000. *Fragmented ties: Salvadoran immigrant networks in America*. Berekely, CA: University of California Press.

Menjívar, Cecilia, and Leisy J. Abrego. 2012. Legal violence: Immigration law and the lives of Central American immigrants. *American Journal of Sociology* 117:1380–1421.

Mood, Carina, and Jan O. Jonsson. 2016. The social consequences of poverty: An empirical test on longitudinal data. *Social Indicators Research* 127 (2): 633–52.

Nelson, Margaret K. 2005. *The social economy of single motherhood: Raising children in rural America*. New York, NY: Routledge.

Newman, Katherine S. 1988. *Falling from grace. Downward mobility in the age of affluence*. Berkeley, CA: University of California Press.

Newman, Katherine S. 1999. *No shame in my game: The working poor in the inner city*. New York, NY: Vintage Books: Russell Sage Foundation Edition.

Newman, Katherine S. 2019. *Downhill from here: Retirement insecurity in the age of inequality*. New York, NY: Metropolitan Books.

Newman, Katherine S., and Rebekah Peeples Massengill. 2006. The texture of hardship: Qualitative sociology of poverty, 1995–2005. *Annual Review of Sociology* 32 (1): 423–46.

Nowicka, Magdalena, and Anna Cieslik. 2013. Beyond methodological nationalism in insider research with migrants. *Migration Studies* 2 (1): 1–15.

O'Brien, Rourke L. 2012. Depleting capital? Race, wealth and informal financial assistance. *Social Forces* 91 (2): 375–96.

Offer, Shira. 2012. The burden of reciprocity: Processes of exclusion and withdrawal from personal networks among low-income families. *Current Sociology* 60 (6): 788–805.

Offer, Shira, and Claude S. Fischer. 2018. Difficult people: Who is perceived to be demanding in personal networks and why are they there? *American Sociological Review* 83 (1): 111–142.

Paugam, Serge, and Jean-Paul Zoyem. 1998. Le soutien financier de la famille: Une forme essentielle de la solidarité. *Economie et Statistique* 308 (1): 187–210.

Pedulla, David, and Devah Pager. 2019. Race and networks in the job search process. *American Sociological Review*, 1–48.

Portes, Alejandro. 1998. Social capital: Its origins and applications in modern sociology. *Annual Review of Sociology* 24 (1): 1–24.

Raudenbush, Danielle. 2016. "I stay by myself": Social support, distrust, and selective solidarity among the urban poor. *Sociological Forum* 31 (4): 1018–39.

Raudenbush, Danielle T. 2020. *Health care off the books: Poverty, illness, and strategies for survival in urban America*. Oakland, CA: University of California Press.

Roschelle, Anne R. 1997. *No more kin: Exploring race, class, and gender in family networks*. Thousand Oaks, CA: SAGE Publications.

Ryan, William. 1971. *Blaming the victim*. New York, NY: Random House.

Sampson, Robert J. 2004. Neighborhood and community: Collective efficacy and community safety. *New Economy* 11:106–13.

Scott, Ellen K., Andrew S. London, and Nancy A. Myers. 2002. Dangerous dependencies: The intersection of welfare reform and domestic violence. *Gender and Society* 16 (6): 878–97.

Semega, Jessica, Melissa Kollar, John Creamer, Abinash Mohanty, and Current Population Reports U.S. Census Bureau. 2019. *Income and poverty in the United States: 2018*. Current population reports. Washington DC: U.S. Census Bureau.

Small, Mario Luis. 2006. Neighborhood institutions as resource brokers: Childcare centers, interorganizational ties, and resource access among the poor. *Social Problems* 53 (2): 274–92.

Small, Mario Luis. 2009. *Unanticipated gains: Origins of network inequality in everyday life*. Oxford: Oxford University Press.

Small, Mario Luis. 2011. How to conduct a mixed methods study: Recent trends in a rapidly growing literature. *Annual Review of Sociology* 37 (1): 57–86.

Small, Mario Luis. 2017. *Someone to talk to*. New York, NY: Oxford University Press.

Small, Mario Luis, and Katherine Newman. 2001. Urban poverty after The Truly Disadvantaged: The rediscovery of the family, the neighborhood, and culture. *Annual Review of Sociology* 27:23–45.

Smith, Sandra Susan. 2005. "Don't put my name on it": Social capital activation and job-finding assistance among the black urban poor. *American Journal of Sociology* 111 (1): 1–57.

Smith, Sandra Susan. 2010. *Lone pursuit: Distrust and defensive individualism among the black poor*. New York, NY: Russell Sage Foundation.

Stack, Carole B. 1974. *All our kin: Strategies for survival in a black community*. New York, NY: Harper & Row.

Streib, Jessi, SaunJuhi Verma, Whitney Welsh, and Linda M. Burton. 2016. Life, death and resurrections: The culture of poverty perspective. In *The Oxford handbook of the social science of poverty*, eds. David Brady and Linda M. Burton, 247–69. New York, NY: Oxford University Press.

Taylor, Shelley E. 2011. Social support: A review. In *The handbook of health psychology*, ed. M. S. Friedman, 189–214. New York, NY: Oxford University Press.

Tigges, Leann M., Irene Browne, and Gary P. Green. 1998. Social isolation of the urban poor: Race, class, and neighborhood effects on social resources. *The Sociological Quarterly* 39 (1): 53–77.

van Eijk, Gwen. 2010. Does living in a poor neighbourhood result in network poverty? A study on local networks, locality-based relationships and neighbourhood settings. *Journal of Housing and the Built Environment* 25 (4): 467–80.

Wacquant, Loic. 2002. Scrutinizing the street: Poverty, morality, and the pitfalls of urban ethnography. *American Journal of Sociology* 107 (6): 1468–1532.

Walker, Robert. 2014. *The shame of poverty*. Oxford: Oxford University Press.

Wellman, Barry. 1979. The community question: The intimate networks of East Yorkers. *American Journal of Sociology* 84 (5): 1201–31.

Wherry, Frederick F., Kristin S. Seefeldt, and Anthony S. Alvarez. 2018. To lend or not to lend to friends and kin: Awkwardness, obfuscation, and negative reciprocity. *Social Forces*, 1–23.

Wills, Thomas A. 1985. Supportive functions of interpersonal relationships. In *Social support and health*, eds. Sheldon Cohen and S. Leonard Syme, 61–82. Orlando, FL: Academic Press.

Wimmer, Andreas, and Nina Glick Schiller. 2002. Methodological nationalism and beyond: Nation-State building, migration and the social sciences. *Global Networks* 2 (4): 301–34.

Zelizer, Viviana A. 2005. *The purchase of intimacy*. Princeton, NJ: Princeton University Press.

Of Morals and Markets: Social Exchange and Poverty in Contemporary Urban Mexico

By
MERCEDES GONZÁLEZ
DE LA ROCHA

Based on longitudinal ethnographic research in Guadalajara, Mexico, from the 1980s to present, I argue that there has been a significant change in the availability of mutual help or support networks for the economically disadvantaged. As time and income have become increasingly scarce, people who used to find support in reciprocal social relationships now find that support-givers are in no position to provide assistance for free. Now, people experiencing scarcity find that they must pay for help formerly available through social relations. In other words, care within the family, in contexts of urban poverty, is becoming a commodity. A paradox arises for those who have fewer resources: they are excluded by the market economy, and by resorting to mercantilist values to survive, they are violating moral principles and norms that exclude them even more from social exchange.

Keywords: social networks; poverty; provision of care; monetization of favors

The reach of markets, and market-oriented thinking, into aspects of life traditionally governed by non-market norms is one of the most significant developments of our time. (Sandel 2012)

This article builds on the premise that social exchange is crucial for the survival of all, but particularly the survival of the poorest families. Since Larissa Lomnitz's now classic

Mercedes González de la Rocha is a Mexican social anthropologist at El Centro de Investigación y Estudios Superiores en Antropología Social (CIESAS). She is the author of The Resources of Poverty: Women and Survival in a Mexican City *(Blackwell 1994) and (with Gonzalo Saraví),* Pobreza y Vulnerabilidad: Debates y Estudios Contemporáneos en México [Poverty and Vulnerability: Contemporary Debates and Studies in Mexico] *(CIESAS 2018).*

NOTE: The completion of this article benefited from the comments and suggestions of two anonymous reviewers and the invaluable support of Inés Escobar González. Her help is an example of household cooperation and generosity.

Correspondence: mgdelarocha@gmail.com

DOI: 10.1177/0002716220916700

ANNALS, AAPSS, 689, May 2020

monograph, *Networks and Marginality* (1977), scholarship has widely documented the effectiveness and importance of mutual aid, social norms, reciprocity,
and trust in the lives of the poor. Through mutual aid, individuals and households
lend each other money when in need, and relatives and neighbors cooperate in
taking care of children and the sick, sharing resources, and collectively contributing to the solutions to routine and extraordinary problems (González de la Rocha
1986; Estrada 1995; Bazán 1998; González de la Rocha 1994; Rivera González
2005). In addition to an expansive literature that focuses on social ties and reciprocity in urban contexts, the importance of mutual aid has also been observed
in the Mexican countryside (Velázquez Galindo 2013) and shown to be a highly
valuable mechanism in systems of reciprocity and exchange among transnational
migrant families in contexts of intense migration (Ariza 2017).

Social exchange is the term used here for the transfer of information, goods,
and services (favors) among friends, relatives, and neighbors. Lomnitz (1977)
insisted that social exchange takes place between people who maintain mutual
ties and are united by social relations characterized by trust, as can be the case in
friendship, kinship, or co-parenthood *(compadrazgo)*. Moreover, favors in social
exchange are neither bought nor sold, and they are typically understood by individuals to be separate from markets. While favors frequently co-mingle with
money, they are exchanged in networks of social relations according to the
acknowledged principle of social reciprocity, not market exchange. As the strikingly Maussian popular saying goes, "today for me, tomorrow for you" *(hoy por
mí, mañana por ti)* (Mauss 2000).

Recognizing the paradigmatic importance of social exchange in the survival of
the poor (and the greater prosperity of the nonpoor and privileged; see Lomnitz
and Pérez Lizaur 1993) does not mean rendering it static. Neither is this recognition an obstacle to observing that, in certain contexts and situations, social exchange
can transform and, indeed, deteriorate. Analysis of the factors and contexts that
hinder the capacity to reciprocate has led scholars to suggest that job insecurity,
poverty, and aging are associated with the weakening of social ties and reciprocal
exchange (González de la Rocha 1999; González de la Rocha and Villagómez 2006;
Rivera González 2006; Rabell 2009; Rabell and D'Aubeterre 2009; González de la
Rocha, Moreno, and Escobar 2016). Montes de Oca (2004) argues that informal
systems of care, within and between families, have come under threat for a number
of reasons, among them demographic change, as a smaller number of children
limits the possibilities for care of aging parents. The result is an arguable crisis in
care once based on systems of delayed intergenerational reciprocity. The household and social networks, once cushions in times of economic and personal crises,
now face severe obstacles to softening the challenging effects of economic and
demographic change. The erosion of ties is one of the final consequences in the
deterioration of people's living conditions, one that people try to avoid and manage
by implementing a set of diverse work practices and adaptations to scarcity
(González de la Rocha 1999, 2000, 2001). Within the so-called ocean of resources/
assets (Narayan et al. 2000), two are key to the maintenance of social exchange:
time and money. Money is crucial because, as a good in itself, it flows through
networks in the form of monetary loans, but also as currency mediating the

acquisition of other goods circulating in those networks. Time is fundamental to the act of care: caring for a neighbor's children when there is a medical emergency or for one's elderly parents takes time (Folbre 2001). But social exchange, I have argued, is sensitive to the changes that take place in individuals' material lives. In times of economic hardship, monetary resources and time become too scarce to maintain the social fabric through which flow the goods and services that make up social exchange (Bazán 1999; Estrada 1995; González de la Rocha 1999; González de la Rocha, Moreno, and Escobar 2016). It is under these conditions that social isolation develops, with dire consequences for people's welfare.

From theory grounded on systematic research on the limits of support systems and mutual aid, I focus in this conceptual article on growing evidence of a newly significant phenomenon in Mexico: the monetization of favors.[1] Based on three examples from different countries in contrasting periods, I argue that social isolation can be deadly: people need social relations for survival, but social relations depend on time and money. I then construct a case study from my ethnographic work to demonstrate the opposite situation: the regularity of income and stable, protected employment, enables the construction and maintenance of social ties through which the exchange of favors and mutual aid can flow. This established, I then present key ethnographic and survey findings that explain, for the case of Mexico, the factors and conditions that lead to the observed deterioration of social exchange. I use recently collected data from low-income neighborhoods in Guadalajara to reflect on the monetization of assistance and the buying and selling of favors, once exchanged outside the market following the principle of social reciprocity. This article questions whether we face a crisis in the economy of care, and the extent to which the monetization of favors is—on one hand—evidence of market expansion and—on the other hand—a symptom of increasingly precarious material conditions. To what point is the buying and selling of favors a result of the erosion of social ties and the flow of mutual aid? I thus conclude with a reflection on the intimate relationship of social life and economic activities (Zelizer 2005), on the economy of family values (Folbre 2001), and on the moral limits of markets (Sandel 2012). The title of this article is inspired by 1980s contributions to feminist literature such as the volume *Of Marriage and the Market: Women's Subordination Internationally and Its Lessons*, edited by Kate Young, Carol Wolkowitz, and Roslyn McCullagh and published in 1981/1984. Particularly inspiring was their explicit aim ". . .to develop analytical and conceptual tools to encompass not only economic relations but also what have been called the relations of everyday life" (Pearson, Whitehead, and Young 1981/1984, x); or, in Zelizer's words, the mingling of economic activities and social and moral dimensions of life (Zelizer 2005).

Social Isolation Kills: Three Examples across Time and Space

For Stephen Devereux (1999), informal safety nets—mutual aid—form part of the strategies that people put into practice when they face episodes of food insecurity. Informal safety networks, he argues, can be conceptually defined as a manifestation of social capital, or the "moral economy." Social networks—constituted by extended family, friends, and neighbors—offer protection in periods of need and implement a variety of forms of aid. They encompass transactions that do not take place in the market, including anything from food to cash, from sharing soup to interest-free loans (Devereux 1999).

In his studies of food insecurity in Malawi, Devereux found evidence of a gradual erosion of the moral economy resulting from a combination of factors. He wrote, "The economic explanation has to do with deepening poverty—people complain that everyone looks out for themselves these days because there is no food or cash income to spare to help others" (Devereux 1999, 64). Devereux emphasizes this process and identifies its distinct stages. On one hand, social exchanges tend to increase when there are moderate economic stress factors or idiosyncratic shocks, like the loss of employment or an individual's illness. However, in times of generalized economic crisis, when the economic providers in every household have been severely affected, there are few possibilities for responding to the growing demands for help from the poorest relatives. The literature on famines, Devereux notes, exhibits a clear process by which informal safety nets expand at the beginning of a food crisis and contract when the crisis becomes acute. He refers to this situation as the gradual erosion of the moral economy:

> Informal safety nets are contracting and losing their capacity to buffer the poor against temporary or permanent declines in their income or food production. Survey data collected following the August 1998 devaluation of the Malawi kwacha confirm that informal safety nets are neither substantial nor robust enough to provide adequate support for the poor, and this trend in itself further undermines the resilience of their already fragile livelihood systems. (Devereux 1999, 65)

Several other authors have demonstrated that a lack or loss of income can lead to the erosion of social neighborhood relations (Bähre 2007) and that solidarity networks shrink in contexts of resources (Lauhlin 1974, quoted in Bähre 2007). Others, like Dennis Rodgers (2007), have questioned the flawed epistemology that has analytically endowed the household with a certain intrinsic altruism and naturalized these units as inherently cooperative. While households may indeed be cooperative, the particular characteristics of a given social, political, and economic context can condition households into being highly segmented and noncooperative as well (Rodgers 2007).

The second example I present comes from Catharina Lis's study of social change in Antwerp from 1770 to 1860 (Lis 1986). Her work was inspired by Michael Anderson who demonstrated the centrality of family and kin as sources of assistance to the majority of nineteenth-century English workers in times of illness, unemployment, death of a loved one, or old age (Anderson 1971, 1980). Lis asked whether the less privileged classes in port cities like Antwerp had constructed social networks similar to those of the English textile workers, as Anderson had described, or whether families broke up in contexts where casual labor was the main source of earnings. Are family strategies and reciprocal support the most appropriate or rational responses to growing material insecurity? Change in the occupational structure of this Belgian city produced unemployment and increased poverty, crowding, malnutrition, and high mortality rates, all of which, Lis notes, meant an uncertain future that limited the possibilities for long-term reciprocity (Lis 1986). The cases she reconstructs from historical archives are revealing, three of which I briefly restate here:

1) "In January 1804, a man whose wife . . . had been in prison for five weeks declared that their four children had been taken in by neighbours; since these people were every bit as needy as himself, they could not long continue their charitable action."

2) "In November 1828, a certain Louis Verbrucken asked the poor relief authorities to provide support to a widow who had a small grocer's shop; he and his parents had long helped her, but now their financial means were exhausted."

3) "In June 1846, the neighbours of a very elderly widow wrote to the poor relief authorities that her allowance must be raised: after subtracting rent, she was left with only half a franc a week, wholly inadequate to feed herself; the neighbours often came to her rescue, but that was no longer possible since they themselves now had difficulty making ends meet." (Lis 1986, 158)

According to Lis, mutual aid among the poor lost its effectiveness beyond a certain threshold of poverty. Poor families and individuals who themselves had difficulty surviving could not provide help to others in need. One of the factors in this situation, she notes, is age. In these contexts of scarcity, aging meant that workers lost physical strength and saw the decline or disappearance of their income, which made making ends meet extremely difficult. In these conditions, they could not help others, and they received no assistance because their children were also in need. Lis's findings leave little doubt that the number of married children able to offer a room to their parents had declined, mainly because unemployment left working-class families with a drastic reduction in income:

> The poor relief authorities were alarmed by the gradual disruption of the family life of the lower classes. In 1860 they reported "That one finds but few young couples who are prepared to take in their elders even if the latter receive public support because of their age or an infirmity . . . more and more children desert their aged parents . . . they are obliged to rid themselves of their elders." (Lis 1986, 154)

As a last example, Eric Klinenberg (2002) argues that social contacts and active participation in social support networks with neighbors, friends, and relatives are crucial to survival. His account leaves little doubt about the tragedy of those who lack such support. During the Chicago heat wave of July 14–20, 1995, there were at least 739 more deaths than there would have been at the normal mortality rate or in the absence of above-average temperatures. These deaths, however, were not evenly distributed. The determining conditions of increased vulnerability behind these deaths, Klinenberg relates, were living alone and in conditions of poverty, not going out daily, having no access to transportation, being sick or bedridden, and having few or no active social relations. The victims were mainly men: poor, elderly men who lived alone, did not leave their apartments, and did not have visitors or even receive phone calls. These men lived in social isolation. Moreover, the majority of the victims were African American, while the comparably poor Latino population reported few deaths.

Why did more men die than women? Why did Latinos, at least as poor as African Americans, not suffer the same effects of the heat? Klinenberg suggests that women, more than men, tend to maintain social contacts through daily visits, telephone calls, and social outings. They exchange advice about what to do in case of emergency and keep track of each other's needs, which was crucial during the heat wave. Concomitantly, Klinenberg found that Latinos in Chicago do not live alone; they share their homes with relatives and others, and their daily lives are rarely solitary. In short, social ties reduce vulnerability and provide physical protection against death.

Employment, Social Security, and Social Ties: The Case of Ciria[2]

To contrast these three examples that show that poverty leads to an erosion of social ties and social exchange, I now construct a case study from my ethnographic fieldwork (González de la Rocha, Moreno, and Escobar 2016) to demonstrate that the regularity of income and stable employment enable the construction and maintenance of supportive social relations.

Ciria emigrated from a rural town in the south of Mexico to Mexicali, on the border with the United States, when she was 21 years old. One of her uncles, who had migrated to Mexicali before Ciria and was a pastor in an evangelical church, provided her with shelter, food, and aid to find employment. A few years later, Ciria established a relationship with Julián, a migrant from Western Mexico. Ciria and Julián became a focal contact for many migrants, forging chains of migration involving siblings, relatives, friends, and acquaintances from southern Mexico to the North. Together, Ciria and Julián helped migrants to obtain food and lodging until they found employment and could manage on their own—the same kind of assistance Ciria received when she arrived in the city.

Ciria's employment history is long and diverse. She participated in the family production of subsistence crops, helped her grandfather selling clothes, and assisted her aunt serving food and coffee in an informal cafeteria. Ciria also had paid employment experience in her hometown, mainly as a domestic worker. Her uncle had told Ciria about the employment opportunities in Mexicali, encouraging Ciria to visit and, ultimately, stay in the border city. She found a full-time job in a water heater factory, a business that in the mid-2000s employed 1,500 workers in Mexicali, most of whom were women. When I met Ciria, she was 36 years old and had been working in this factory for the previous 15 years.

At first, Ciria worked the morning shift, but when she gave birth to her daughter, she requested the afternoon shift because she had no one to care for her baby in the mornings. This way, she could go to work in the afternoon while her partner took care of the child. These domestic and labor arrangements enabled the young working mother to carry on earning, avoiding the fate of the many for whom the birth of a child means labor market withdrawal.

Although Ciria's employment at the factory has been stable and comes with social security and health care, she has also worked other jobs simultaneously. Ciria has found these jobs with the help of many of her contacts, taking advantage of her mornings since her daughter started school. She was first a domestic worker in various homes in the city, even if only to sweep the patio or run some errands. Through them and her factory job, she was able to save enough money to buy the lot where she, her partner, and their daughter now live.

She currently carries out two economic activities: a job at the factory and a micro-business of Avon and Fuller products that she sells from home. She sells to neighbors, friends, and the people at the evangelical church where she spends most of her weekends. The profits can amount to 30 pesos for every 100 pesos in sales. While it takes a long time for her customers to pay, she does not worry: she trusts them and considers it money "put away," not lost. She pays for the products from her own pocket and her customers gradually pay her back. Her earnings do not amount to much, but she is content in having extra money to modestly expand her daily consumption. Ciria's micro-entrepreneurship depends on her regular formal employment: she buys the products from her factory wage and sells on credit because she does not depend on sales for her basic subsistence.

Ciria's household economy consists of her wages in the factory (700 pesos a week),[3] her partner's wages (805 pesos a week), her additional—if unpredictable—income from selling Avon and Fuller products, and a weekly grocery voucher from her employer (200 pesos). Although her factory wages are 700 pesos a week, her paycheck is approximately 400 pesos after withholding for social security, healthcare, and employer-enforced savings. While access to social security and health care comes at a cost, Ciria values her factory job for this access above all. She explains that she has stayed on the job to maintain her benefits with the Mexican Social Security Institute (IMSS), the government's pension and the health care system.[4] Ciria does not know how much she makes from the sale of Avon and Fuller products, for the inputs and outputs are hard to quantify; she stocks a variety of deodorants, lotions, and toothbrushes in her home to meet the erratic demand of her customers. She sells from this stock, but also uses it to extend occasional gifts to her acquaintances: "That is why I don't see the profits."

Ciria is a successful network weaver. She has strong ties with other migrants who have gradually arrived in Mexicali. She is part of support systems where material resources, monetary loans, information, housing, and emotional support circulate. It is with this constellation of friends, relatives, and coworkers that Ciria and her partner celebrate anniversaries and special occasions. She is an active member of a group in her church, where she has friends and participates in games, Bible readings, and lunches. They meet every Sunday for general meetings and hold Saturday meetings for younger members. Ciria finds in this religious group a great sense of solidarity, one she values highly. Church members visit and help one another. Although her church includes professionals, such as doctors and lawyers, she believes, "we are all equals . . . we are like a family, you feel each other's pain."

Despite Ciria's clear economic disadvantages, she is relatively privileged. In fact, given the massive number of precarious workers in the country, she is a minority. On one hand, she has a permanent job with access to health care and a wage that is low but contributes to her household economy in a stable way. On the other, she trusts her neighbors, is involved in strong social networks, and actively participates in social and communal life. These qualities are increasingly rare among low-income households in contemporary Mexico (González de la Rocha, Moreno, and Escobar 2016).

Ciria's work life heavily depends on kinship and social networks, and her social networks are robust and strong because she invests significant amounts of time and material resources in them. Ciria is both a formal and informal worker; an employee and self-employed. She has a job that pays stable if low wages, and another that depends on the first and fosters her ability to build and maintain social ties. She has to work a fixed schedule in the factory, but outside those hours she controls her own time and sells Avon and Fuller products on her own.

She receives help from relatives and provides support to others in chains of deferred reciprocity. She is religious and invests an important part of her free time in commitments to her church and the maintenance of its social networks. She likes to socialize and to exchange favors, which her economic situation enables her to do. She has income that arrives predictably every week, and some profits which, while difficult to quantify, allow her to expand consumption and participate in social life. The regularity of her income from stable, formal employment gives her the freedom to buy the products she sells and assume the risks of doing so on her own.

Above all, Ciria's small-scale business thrives with her social relationships. While her case demonstrates the entanglement of economic and social life (a relation that González de la Rocha, Moreno, and Escobar [2016] have analyzed in detail)—or the "mingling" of intimate life and economic activity (Zelizer 2005)—it cannot be glossed as an example of the monetization of favors. Ciria does not sell nor buy favors, but rather expends her resources and builds her business among friends and relatives. In so doing, she manages the delicate balance between social and market exchange. As I explain, however, this balance is far from given and proves highly sensitive to changes in people's material conditions.

The Erosion of Social Exchange

The lives of the great majority of workers in Mexico are very different from Ciria's. In 2006, 60.8 percent of men and 56.9 percent of women had no employment benefits, and more than 70 percent of them had no permanent jobs (García

Guzmán 2009). Ten years later, the National Institute of Statistics and Geography (Instituto Nacional de Estadística y Geografía, INEGI 2016)[5] reported an informal employment rate of 52.4 percent for the nonagricultural employed population and 57.2 percent for the employed population, a rate always higher for women: 56.4 percent of the nonagricultural employed and 57.7 percent of the employed.[6] Mexican workers cannot afford the luxury of unemployment because they do not have access to unemployment benefits. Since protected employment is scarce and limited in entry, and unemployment is an unaffordable luxury, most workers inhabit a world of underemployment and precarity.

With information from the Socioeconomic Conditions Module of the National Survey of Household Income and Expenditures (Módulo de Condiciones Socioeconómicas de la Encuesta Nacional de Ingresos y Gastos de los Hogares, ENIGH) for 2008 and 2010, a descriptive statistics analysis arrived at a result that would be later confirmed by more precise methods: the perception of available social support increases with income.[7] That is, people with higher incomes believe that harnessing social networks is easier. The poorest, on the other hand, say such support is less easy to come by. This positive relationship between income and access to networks is a pattern found across different types of social support: monetary loans, care while sick, help getting a job, being taken to the doctor, getting contributions to make improvements to one's neighborhood, and assistance in childcare (González de la Rocha, Moreno, and Escobar 2012).

There are differences in access to networks by the type of need for which help is sought. Finding someone to take you to the doctor, someone to take care of you when you are sick, and someone to help with childcare are the most accessible types of support, as well as those that people believe are easiest to find. It is more difficult to borrow a month's worth of household earnings or collect money to improve one's neighborhood. Other surveys (Encuesta de Familia y Vulnerabilidad en México, 2006, or Family and Vulnerability Survey)[8] show similar results: urban and rural men and women declare easier access to support in caring for a household member who is sick than in other needs, such as getting a job, loan, or credit. Data from the 2008 and 2010 ENIGH show that a greater percentage of formal than informal workers perceived access to these networks as "easy" or "very easy." Again, the more readily accessible types of support were, in order of importance, accompanying someone to a doctor's appointment, assistance with childcare, and helping someone who is ill. Less accessible were monetary loans and contributions to improve the neighborhood. The analysis showed that access to social networks was highly differentiated, and that people with more support from social networks were those with the highest income, those who were formally employed, and those who were self-employed. The people who were most isolated from support networks were the poorest, the informally employed, the unemployed or economically inactive, and unpaid workers (González de la Rocha, Moreno, and Escobar 2012; see Rabell and D'Aubeterre 2009 for similar findings). Other studies have shown that household structure may also limit access to social networks of support. Female-headed households, according to Chant (1997, 2007), González de la Rocha (1994), and Willis (1993), may have smaller social networks, which in turn makes them poorer. The literature cites different factors to explain the shortage of social networking among female-headed households: lack of ties with ex-partners' relatives, hostility and mistrust in the community (Chant 1997; Willis 1993), and female stigma associated with out-of-wedlock motherhood are some of them, as well as lack of time to spend on ". . .the cultivation of social contacts" (Willis 1993, 78) due to the fact that women in female-headed households are more involved in paid work than women in households with different domestic structures. In sum, female-heads are too busy as income providers and they have no time nor other resources left for networking (González de la Rocha 1994; Chant 1997).

The question is whether—in Mexico—unemployment, precarity, or informality in employment affect the strength of social ties, and how social ties relate to workers' labor instability, low wages, and lack of social security (Estrada 1996; Bazán 1999; González de la Rocha 1999, 2000, 2001; González de la Rocha and Villagómez 2006; Rabell 2009; Rabell and D'Aubeterre 2009; González de la Rocha, Moreno, and Escobar 2016). Lucía Bazán (1999) analyzed the social effects of the loss of a sole source of income and found that, above all, the unemployed lost social relations. After several months of unemployment, families had gone through a process of household atomization and disconnection from their former social support networks. Work is thus a source of structure as well as material and social well-being. The loss of employment modifies economic and social dynamics, to the detriment of social ties and support networks.[9]

In the course of a decade, from the mid-1980s to the mid-1990s, my own ethnographic work found evidence of significant change in the social relations of manual workers in Guadalajara, Mexico. In the 1980s, households with few social ties were seen as anomalous, but they came to be much more visible and less "atypical" with the growing precarity of labor markets. The economic crises of the 1980s spurred the expansion of informal protection networks: people who already maintained social relations of mutual support found themselves with the need to ask for more favors, especially of less needy relatives (González de la Rocha 1991; Velázquez Galindo 2013). However, as crises deepen, as was the case with the successive economic crises from 1982 and well into the 1990s, informal protection networks shrink (González de la Rocha 1991, 1999; Estrada 1995; Bazán 1999). That is, during processes of widespread impoverishment (precarity of employment, low wages, no social security), people's ability to reciprocate progressively deteriorates. This confirms Mingione's hypothesis (1994): networks of exchange depend on sufficient economic income. Moreover, as Pahl and Wallace (1985) affirmed, social relations and stable employment are closely related.

Mercedes González de la Rocha and Paloma Villagómez (2008) conclude that the precarity of employment leads to social isolation, but that other factors—such as old age and forced return migration—also contribute to this process. Cecilia Rabell and María Eugenia D'Aubeterre (2009) arrive at similar conclusions from other data: the factors with the greatest effect on social isolation (associated with not receiving help in situations of crisis) are: a) precarious socioeconomic condition; b) advanced age; and c) lack of close affective connections. A little more than half of those interviewed by Rabell and D'Aubeterre said that they received no social support in daily life. Households in the lowest quintiles are more likely to not receive social support, which contrast with households in the two highest quintiles. In addition, the greater the age of those interviewed, the higher the probability of reporting a lack of social support. The authors conclude that "the disparity in resources (time and money as fundamental assets) conditions participation in these exchanges. The lower the quintile, the less intense is the circulation of assistance" (Rabell and D'Aubeterre 2009, 94).

Apart from the social security offered by formal employment (available to a minority of the employed), precarious workers and their families lack the necessary resources to avoid the deepening of personal crises. Thus, as many of our studies have shown, individuals and families facing precarious, unstable, and poor living conditions cannot afford the costs of reciprocity (González de la Rocha 1999, 2000, 2001).[10] The deterioration of social ties appears as a result of the exhaustion of household resources and the downturn in household economies.

Academics, policy-makers, and development agencies have for decades now insisted on characterizing the world's poor as inherently *resourceful*, endlessly *capable* to adapt to precarity, and prodigiously *ingenious* at "solving away" the dangers of poverty through a quasi-natural ability to establish social relations and support networks. In response to these attitudes, we have argued that an insistence upon the resourcefulness of the poor or the endless capacity to respond, adapt, and continue reciprocating despite shrinking resources is factually false, ignorant of process, and perverse. Being part of social relations of mutual aid can, too, reach its limits (González de la Rocha and Villagómez 2006).

The Monetization and Commercialization of Favors

Rabell and D'Aubeterre (2009) proposed that time and money are the two fundamental resources that condition participation in social exchange. Time is crucial in the everyday "maintenance and reproduction of the household," "living labor" (domestic work, childcare, care of the sick), or what Nancy Folbre (2001) termed "labor invested in the economy of care," mainly women's labor. Money must be used to deal with transactions such as home repairs, paying debts, and buying food and other necessities that can be satisfied in the marketplace (Rabell and D'Aubeterre 2009). González de la Rocha, Martha Moreno, and Inés Escobar (2016) showed that favors based on the resource of time are more frequent and more accessible than those based on money. In other words, it is more common to give and receive favors when the currency put into action is time. By means of a confirmatory factor analysis (CFA) of survey responses to questions of access to different types of social support, the authors corroborated the hypothesis that time and money circulate as two kinds of currencies or key resources in the exchange of two types of social support. To show that the perception of favors or help received is closely related to variables associated with income, type of employment, and social deprivations,[11] we carried out a latent class analysis (LCA) on observations from this survey data for 2008, 2010, and 2012.

Based on this analysis, we constructed a typology based on household members' degree of confidence in the potential reception of help and whether this help depended on the availability of time or money. The aim was to find the types of households with higher scores of confidence to get access to social support and favors that circulate within social networks, and those with lower scores. Through latent class analysis we classified households into four strata or classes. The idea was to determine the social and economic characteristics of such households. The analysis elucidated greater confidence in general access to help as income increased, and employment benefits were also associated with increases in confidence levels (González de la Rocha, Moreno, and Escobar 2016). Regarding the variables of time and money, which we conceptualized as two distinct currencies (or circuits of exchange) mobilized in the exchange of two different types of help, we came to the following conclusion:

> The circuits are distinct because the currencies cannot be exchanged without complexities. The goods that circulate in the circuit of money cannot be mobilized with the currency of time. The currency of money does not operate in the circuit of time, which is essentially concerned with the exchange of care. As in the case of the Tiv circuits studied by Bohannan (1955), it might be expected that the exchange of the categories of goods and the categories of "currencies" that circulate in these two exclusive circuits would be possible only through the negotiation of moral principles and rules, because each of the circuits and goods is charged with separate and distinct moral loads. (González de la Rocha, Moreno, and Escobar 2016, 252–53)

Interest in the topic did not end with the publication of that article. Confirmation of our ethnographic findings through statistical methods aroused our *sociological imagination* (Wright Mills 2003). Of particular interest was the negotiation of moral principles and rules for situations where people find themselves obliged to use the currency of money in the circuit of care. This point emerged with particular force in recent interviews conducted in neighborhoods in the south of Guadalajara. Some excerpts from a case study illustrate what appears to be a newly significant phenomenon: the monetization or commercialization of favors. But before going into these excerpts, it is crucial to keep in mind that reciprocity and the provision of care within households and families and between them is based on conventional codes of familial and gendered altruism (Brickell and Chant 2010). As these authors argue, ". . .women's disproportionate share of the 'altruistic burden' within low-income households appears to be increasing rather than declining," despite rising female labor force participation in most countries of the Global South. The time devoted to providing care is mostly women's time, and women are expected by their household and family members, as well as by their neighbors and by society at large, to provide their time and effort to the caring for others in their daily routines and throughout their lives. Mothers, sisters, aunts, grandmothers, and female neighbors and friends conform to the circuits of care. The "feminization of responsibility and obligation" is a term coined by Chant to refer to the ". . .rising number of poor women of all ages [who] are not only working outside the home but continuing to perform the bulk of unpaid reproductive tasks for husbands, fathers, brothers and sons" (Brickell and Chant 2010, 148).

Esperanza is a 54-year-old woman who lives with her family in the municipality of Tlajomulco de Zúñiga, Jalisco. She has spent her life working, but to combine her reproductive labor—first as a mother and now as a grandmother—with waged work, she preferred to work "in homes" (as a domestic worker) over any other occupation. She barely managed to finish primary school, so she does not have the qualifications, nor the age, demanded by other jobs. Her husband has a job with benefits, including social security, enabling members of the nuclear family who have fallen ill to receive health and hospital care.

It was precisely on the topic of health that the idea of the monetization of care emerged. Esperanza was talking about an illness she had suffered from and that required surgery, including hospitalization for 12 days in central Guadalajara. Mexican public hospitals require the presence of a family member 24 hours a day to accompany the patient. Esperanza's husband and one of her daughters took turns doing this. Her husband spent the nights with Esperanza but had to leave early in the morning to go to work. When he left, Esperanza's teenage daughter, Lulú, replaced him. Esperanza explained, "I didn't have sisters, sisters-in-law, mother-in-law, or a mother, nothing, just those two. . . . Sometimes we asked them [relatives] to take care of us and they said no, that they didn't have time, or no, that they couldn't, and so forth. . . ." One of those days, Lulú had to study for a school exam and could not go to the hospital to be with her mother. Esperanza explained: "So I called my sister and I told her I was desperate, 'Come and take care of me, I'm desperate, I'll pay you.'"

Upon recalling her own wording and without being prompted, "Come and take care of me, I'm desperate, I'll pay you," Esperanza explained to me why she had offered to pay her sister for her care: "She didn't have enough for the bus fare. She told me, 'I don't have it.' That was when I told her 'I'll pay your bus fare, both ways.'" Her sister then agreed to come and take care of her in the hospital. When she arrived, Esperanza asked her sister if she had eaten breakfast, to a negative response: "I told her, 'Take this [money] and go have breakfast,' and she went. When she got back, I said to her, 'Just take care of me until 2 p.m., Lulú will get here between 2 and 3 and you can go.' My sister said 'Oh, okay.' Later Lulú got there and my sister said, 'I'm going now,' and I was like, 'Alright then' and 'Take this [money].'. . . . My sister said 'No, of course not.'. . . . But I insisted, 'No, seriously, take it, come on, I'm giving you some money, I'm going to pay you, like they [patrons] say, *for the day*.' I told her, 'I'm not giving you much because I don't have money either. . . . take it, if only for the bus.' I gave her like 80 pesos, plus what I gave her for breakfast.' And she said 'Okay,' and left."

Esperanza ended up paying her sister for the bus fare, for her breakfast, and a kind of daily wage: "for the day." She finds it strange that her sister accepted the offer of payment: "It surprised me that she accepted the money because it's not something you do with a sister." But reciprocity works in two directions: when favors are exchanged and when they are refused. In Esperanza's case, she had stopped offering help to her sisters long before her hospitalization because she felt they failed to reciprocate: "No, they never take care of me, they never took care of me, I asked them to do me favors but they wouldn't. . . . It feels bad that they won't come to take care of a member of their family. . . . So, I won't either."

Indeed, Esperanza feels estranged from her sisters as a result of their failure to reciprocate. The offer to pay for her sister's care came as a knee-jerk response to this estrangement, but it still confused her.

Reciprocity in the exchange of favors is affected in contexts of precarious employment or limited income. Esperanza forms part of a household with social security thanks to her husband's protected employment, which could seem to contradict the argument that the erosion of ties of support results from precarity. However, the crucial element within this case study is the insecurity felt by Esperanza's sister, for whom money is scarce and employment precarious. Esperanza's sister, in contrast to Esperanza, engages in sporadic, low-paid, and casual labor; receives no contribution from another provider; and lives on what-ever one of her married children can give her. Her living conditions do not allow her to use her resources on transportation to help her sister in the hospital. She does not have the means to cover the cost of breakfast or lunch away from home. She may have the time but not the money to cover the costs associated with doing her sister a favor and, for that reason, although she went through the motions to suggest that she did not want to take the money, she ended up taking it. Because she accepted money in exchange for care, and because she is not and has not been in a position to support her sister without payment, she has been progres-sively excluded from Esperanza's network of support. Once excluded, her vulner-ability only increases.

In another case, one perhaps less obvious but analytically similar, the narrator of the story considers a moral problem. José, a construction worker specialized in painting walls, knows a young couple who have just had their third child. The young mother was still in the hospital when her husband asked his own mother for help in taking care of the other two children while he was at work. Would she care for her grandchildren while their mother was in the hospital? Could she care for them afterward, while their mother recovered and readapted to caring for a newborn baby? The mother (of the husband) refused, saying that she had already raised her own children and that she did not have the time or strength to take charge of two grandchildren. José finished telling the story in a tone of alarm: "The woman didn't want to take care of her own grandchildren! The couple had to pay someone else to take care of them!"

Conclusion: Family Morality and the Limits of the Market

Social life is entangled with economic life (Zelizer 2005). Indeed, as I have argued here, social networks thrive among the better-off and increasing poverty erodes them (González de la Rocha 1999, 2001). Reciprocity and trust are deter-minant qualities for socioeconomic exchange, help, and favors to take place, but social exchange requires economic resources. Contrary to other forms of exchange, however, social exchange does not belong to the market.

José's alarm at the grandmother's refusal is similar to Esperanza's surprise when her own sister accepted payment for taking care of her in the hospital. Both related their stories as noteworthy and made their discomfort explicit: the woman who took payment to care for a family member and the woman who refused to care for her grandchildren transgressed expectations and norms, including female altruism (Brickell and Chant 2010; cf. Rodgers 2007). *You don't do that with a sister (or a son).* José's astonishment lies in the fact that the grandmother refused to care for her grandchildren, her son's children, "blood of her blood," and her refusal forced the young family to pay for care. José's position is representative of that of others, as it is a matter of socially sanctioned norms and values. If someone has no intimates or close relations to help out, he or she must pay for the service. However, exchanging money for the service of care is understood as something that happens among strangers. If one has family, the provision of care is expected to flow freely among family members because caregiving and mutual support are considered familial obligations. As Folbre (2001) puts it, the moral values of the family are made up of a combination of socially constructed notions and practices of love, obligation, and reciprocity. It is mostly women who in the bosom of the family take care of others. They are the ones who provide the goods and services their families and households need on an everyday basis or in special circumstances. They do so and are socially expected to do so altruistically or in exchange for gratitude and delayed reciprocity, not money. Zelizer is right to argue that plenty of economic activity goes into creating, defining, and sustaining social ties. She sheds light on the discussion by observing, however, that the mingling of intimate life and economic activities is based on their moral and socially enforced distinction: ". . .crucial distinctions among different combinations of relations, transactions, and payment media defend those distinctions with moral practices and put pressure on participants to respect relevant moral and legal codes" (2005, 12–13).

Folbre argues that the market has clearly and decisively expanded into our lives.[12] One of the implications of this process, she writes, is that individuals are ideologically stimulated to satisfy their own interests, often at the expense of caring for others. In other words, the observable commodification of life is not exclusive to precarious and poor households, as it clearly transcends class. Folbre warns us about how ". . .the expansion of an economy based on self-interest might weaken moral sentiments" in general (Folbre 2001, xiii). And yet, for Folbre, collective life and social reproduction require time and money, and those who cannot afford their costs are unable, not just unwilling, to maintain the social ties constituted by social exchange. In the cases discussed here, withdrawal from collective processes of care and reproduction based on reciprocity and the increasing commodification of favors have more to do with people's incapacity than their refusal. Diminished resources and hard socioeconomic contexts are the determining factors pushing commodification processes over and above the adoption of a given ideology; after all, people understand these events as morally wrong even if they necessarily engage in them.

Is the commodification of family life, or the commercialization of favors relating to care, the possible result of women's increasing participation in wage work, as Folbre suggests? She argues that, to the extent that employment opportunities for women have increased, so has the money they would lose in devoting time to care. This translates, in Folbre's economistic thinking, into higher costs of care—care costs more because women lose wage income when they spend time providing it. As a result, more people now lack the care they need, especially children, the elderly, and other dependent groups (Folbre 2001). If women lose wage income in taking care of children and the elderly and are therefore not willing to do it, they have the following options: a) pay a relative, normally a woman in the kin network (as Esperanza did); b) pay someone to perform a service (as in the case described by José) so that care can be provided at home, but by a person without ties of kinship (nannies, domestic workers, specialized caregivers); c) pay for institutional care (daycare, nursing homes, retirement homes); d) leave dependent household members with friends, relatives, or neighbors (without payment); or e) leave dependents without supervision or the care they need (which is sometimes quite specialized).

Changes in the collective practices of care, however, are not solely explicable by the rising cost of care as future (female) income forfeited. They are also tied to the ways in which time and money constitute fundamental and increasingly rare resources in the creation and maintenance of relationships of social exchange for the world's precarious majorities. Moreover, the transformation and commodification of social reproductive practices present moral dilemmas that individuals, households, and kinship groups often fail to successfully manage, leading to the further erosion of social ties.

As shown, time and money are the two most important inputs in the flow of favors. They are distinct currencies for the exchange of two distinct circuits of exchange, those essentially economic or monetary and those involving time to enact and practice care. Because each circuit is marked by distinct norms and values, the currencies are not interchangeable (such as using money in the circuit of care) unless the moral norms and values of the family are negotiated or transgressed. Indeed, the cases of Esperanza and José demonstrate that the use of the currency of money in the care circuit is not free of complexities, and the negotiation of moral norms and principles is evident. As time and money become increasingly scarce resources for most people, especially low-income working families with few or no social security benefits, people and groups are forced into double binds. For this reason, and following Folbre (2001), the quantity and the quality of care are under growing economic pressure.

To recall Devereux and his analysis of the gradual erosion of the moral economy, the deterioration of the social networks through which nonmarket transactions flow is a product of the intensification of poverty. The expansion of networks of informal protection at the start of crises contrasts with their contraction as crises deepen (Devereux 1999). The gradual erosion of the moral economy means that people are losing the ability to harness informal safety nets to cushion or protect themselves in the process of economic crises.

If caring for a sick relative is for sale and socially treated as a commodity, as the cases of Esperanza and José describe, those with access to the "good" of care are those who have the resources to pay for it. If everything is for sale, life becomes increasingly difficult for those with limited means (Sandel 2012). If money is the only medium for obtaining goods and services, its possession creates categorical differences in people's capacity to enjoy basic well-being, such as care. If care and company are for sale, those who have no resources cannot but resign themselves to loneliness and abandonment.

By putting a price on things (as in the case of favors), we run the risk that the values of the market will displace or transfigure nonmarket values (Sandel 2012). This point is crucial in understanding Esperanza's surprise and discomfort and José's astonishment and shock. For them, the values of the family are not market values; care in the bosom of the family is not a commodity. By putting favors up for sale, as Esperanza's sister felt forced to, the nonmarket values of the family are perceived to be corrupted. Esperanza and José, in their awe and confusion at what they see as a crisis in family care, are reaffirming values, moral concepts, and socially sanctioned ways of acting. They, like Folbre (2001), value family life as a structure of affection, obligations, and reciprocities, and, like Sandel (2012), believe that the market should be kept at a distance from family life.

In this context, where care among relatives is for sale, a paradox emerges. Those who have the least, been hurt, made precarious, and excluded by the market economy are pushed into adopting survival strategies that assign market prices to survival and reaffirm the market economy's expansion. In so doing, however, people violate the moral covenant of reciprocity and further exclude themselves from the circuits of social exchange on which their very existence depends. In this context, the upholding of moral values is a luxury few can afford.

Notes

1. Favors understood as help and mutual assistance, which the literature has documented as elements of support systems that are not part of market relations.

2. Case study from the author's fieldwork in Mexicali, Baja California, as part of the research project "Social Isolation in Urban Contexts," sponsored by the Mexican Secretary of Social Development.

3. Her weekly salary in 2004. With an average inflation rate of 4.22 percent from 2004 to 2019, Ciria's weekly salary would be, today, 1.301 Mexican pesos (68.23 dollars at a rate of 19.07 pesos per dollar).

4. Besides social security, her other benefits include a year-end bonus (*aguinaldo*), profit-sharing (*utilidades*), paid vacation, and a seniority bonus, but there is no union. She has signed two contracts with the factory in the 15 years she has worked there, and the second one has been in effect for many years. She knows that this company is unusual: many others in Mexicali hire workers for six months at a time and lay them off without even considering their seniority.

5. INEGI. 2016. Indicadores de Ocupación y Empleo, cuarto trimestre de 2016. Available from www.inegi.org.mx.

6. Ibid.

7. Módulo de Condiciones Socioeconómicas de la Encuesta Nacional de Ingresos y Gastos de los Hogares (MCS/ENIGH) 2008, 2010.

8. Encuesta de Familia y Vulnerabilidad en México (ENFAVU) 2006.

9. See Jahoda (1981) for a classic assessment of the loss of a sole source of income and its implications for social life. Employment, as the author points out, promotes social contact and collective purposes (among other categories of experiences).

10. In *Reciprocity under Threat: One More Cost of Urban Poverty*, I argue that the scarcity of economic resources hinders the exchange of favors (González de la Rocha 1999). When friends, relatives, and neighbors are just as poor as the person in need of support, they cannot help one another. The lack of steady income interferes with social exchange.

11. Social deprivations refer to the lack of compliance of the social rights established by the law (General Law of Social Development or *Ley General de Desarrollo Social*): access to food, education, health care, social security, basic housing services, and quality of housing.

12. See also Sandel (2012) for a view on the expansion of mercantile values to dimensions of life that once stood apart from the monetary economy.

References

Anderson, Michael. 1971. *Family structure in nineteenth-century Lancashire*. Cambridge: Cambridge University Press.

Anderson, Michael. 1980. *Approaches to the history of the western family 1500–1914*. London: The MacMillan Press Ltd.

Ariza, Marina. 2017. Escenarios migratorios, familias y hogares en el México contemporáneo. In Jéssica Nájera, Brígida García and Edith Pacheco (eds.), *Hogares y trabajadores en México en el siglo XXI*. Mexico City: El Colegio de México.

Bähre, Erik. 2007. Reluctant solidarity. Death, urban poverty and neighbourly assistance in South Africa. *Ethnography* 8 (1): 33–59.

Bazán, Lucía. 1998. El último recurso: Las relaciones familiares como alternativas frente a la crisis. PhD diss., LAS, Chicago.

Bazán, Lucía. 1999. *Cuando una puerta se cierra cientos se abren. Casa y familia: los recursos de los desempleados de la refinería 18 de Marzo*. Mexico City: CIESAS

Bohannan, Paul. 1955. Some principles of exchange and investment among the Tiv. *American Anthropologist* 57 (1): 60–70.

Brickell, Katherine, and Sylvia Chant. 2010. "The unbearable heaviness of being": Reflections on female altruism in Cambodia, Philippines, The Gambia and Costa Rica. *Progress in Development Studies* 10 (2): 145–59.

Chant, Sylvia. 1997. *Women-headed households: Diversity and dynamics in the developing world*. Basingstoke: Macmillan.

Chant, Sylvia. 2007. *Gender, generation and poverty. exploring the "feminisation of poverty" in Africa, Asia and Latin America*. Cheltenham: Edward Elgar.

Devereux, Stephen. 1999. "Making less last longer": Informal safety nets in Malawi. IDS Discussion Paper 373, Institute of Development Studies, England.

Estrada, Margarita. 1995. En el límite de los recursos. El efecto de la crisis de 1995 en familias de sectores populares urbanos. In *Familias en la crisis*, ed. Margarita Estrada Íñiguez, 43–59. Mexico City: CIESAS.

Estrada, Margarita. 1996. Después del despido. *Desocupación y familia obrera*. Mexico City: CIESAS.

Folbre, Nancy. 2001. *The invisible heart. Economics and family values*. New York, NY: The New Press.

García Guzmán, Brígida. 2009. Los mercados de trabajo urbanos de México a principios del siglo XXI. *Revista Mexicana de Sociología* 71 (1): 5–46.

González de la Rocha, Mercedes. 1986. *Los recursos de la pobreza. Familias de bajos ingresos de Guadalajara*. Guadalajara: El Colegio de Jalisco, CIESAS and SPP.

González de la Rocha, Mercedes. 1991. Family wellbeing, food consumption, and survival strategies during Mexico's economic crisis. In *Social responses to Mexico's economic crisis of the 1980's*, eds. Mercedes González de la Rocha and Agustín Escobar Latapí, 115–27. La Jolla, California: Center for U.S.-Mexican Studies, UCSD.

González de la Rocha, Mercedes. 1994. *The resources of poverty. Women and survival in a Mexican city*. Oxford: Basil Blackwell.

González de la Rocha, Mercedes. 1999. La reciprocidad amenazada: Un costo más de la pobreza urbana. In *Hogar, pobreza y bienestar en México*, Rocío Enríquez (coord.), 13–36. Guadalajara: Instituto Tecnológico de Estudios Superiores de Occidente.

González de la Rocha, Mercedes. 2000. Private adjustments: Household responses to the erosion of work. Conference paper series 6. New York, NY: UNDP.

González de la Rocha, Mercedes. 2001. From the resources of poverty to the poverty of resources? The erosion of a survival model. *Latin American Perspectives* 28 (4): 72–100.

González de la Rocha, Mercedes, Martha Moreno, and Inés Escobar. 2012. *Trabajo, modos de subsistencia y vida social en México*. [*Moving jobs to the center stage in Mexico*]. Case study for the World Development Report 2013. Washington, DC: World Bank.

González de la Rocha, Mercedes, Martha Moreno, eand Inés Escobar. 2016. Empleo e intercambio social en México. *Perfiles Latinoamericanos* 24 (47): 225–58.

González de la Rocha, Mercedes, and Paloma Villagómez. 2006. Espirales de desventajas: pobreza, ciclo vital y aislamiento social. In *De la pobreza a la exclusión: continuidades y rupturas de la cuestión social en América Latina*, ed. Gonzalo Saraví, 137–66. Buenos Aires: CIESAS/Prometeo.

González de la Rocha, Mercedes, and Paloma Villagómez. 2008. ¿Encuesta o etnografía? Avances y tropiezos en el estudio del intercambio social. In *Método científico y política social. A propósito de las evaluaciones cualitativas de programas sociales en México*, eds. Fernando Cortés, Agustín Escobar, Mercedes González de la Rocha, 297–373. Mexico City: El Colegio de México.

Jahoda, Marie. 1981. Work, employment, and unemployment. Values, theories, and approaches in social research. *American Psychologist* 36 (2): 184–91.

Klinenberg, Eric. 2002. *Heat wave. A social autopsy of disaster in Chicago*. Chicago, IL: University of Chicago Press.

Laughlin, Charles D. 1974. Deprivation and reciprocity. *Man* 9:380–96.

Lis, Catharina. 1986. *Social change and the labouring poor: Antwerp, 1770–1860*. New Haven, CT: Yale University Press.

Lomnitz, Larissa. 1977. *Networks and marginality*. New York, NY: Academic Press.

Lomnitz, Larissa, and Marisol Pérez Lizaur. 1993. *Una familia de la élite mexicana, 1820–1980. Parentesco, clase y cultura*. Mexico City: Alianza Editorial.

Mauss, Marcel. 2000. *The gift: Forms and functions of exchange in archaic societies*. New York, NY: Norton.

Mingione, Enzo. 1994. Sector informal y estrategias de sobrevivencia: hipótesis para el desarrollo de un campo de investigación. In *Solidaridad y producción informal de recursos*, René Millán (comp). Mexico City: IIS/UNAM.

Montes de Oca, Verónica. 2004. Envejecimiento y protección familiar en México: límites y potencialidades del apoyo en el interior del hogar. In *Imágenes de la familia en el cambio de siglo*, Marina Ariza y Orlandina de Oliveira (coords.), 519–63. México: Instituto de Investigaciones Sociales/UNAM.

Narayan, Deepa, Robert Chambers, Meera K. Shah, and Patti Petesch. 2000. *Voices of the poor. Crying out for change*. Washington, DC: The World Bank.

Pahl, Raymond Edward, and Claire Wallace. 1985. Household work strategies in economic recession. In *Beyond employment: Household, gender and subsistence*, eds. Nanneke Redclift and Enzo Mingione, 189–227. Oxford: Basil Blackwell.

Pearson, Ruth, Ann Whitehead, and Kate Young. 1984. Introduction: The Continuing Subordination of Women in the Development Process. In *Of Marriage and the Market. Women's subordination internationally and its lessons*, 2nd ed., eds. Kate Young, Carol Wolkowitz and Roslyn McCullagh, ix–xix. London: Routledge & Kegan Paul.

Rabell Romero, Cecilia. 2009. Introducción. In *Tramas familiares en el México contemporáneo. Una perspectiva sociodemográfica*, Cecilia Rabell Romero (coord.), 9–38. Mexico City: El Colegio de México.

Rabell Romero, Cecilia, and María Eugenia D'Aubeterre. 2009. ¿Aislados o solidarios? Ayudas y redes familiares en el México contemporáneo. In *Tramas familiares en el México contemporáneo. Una perspectiva sociodemográfica*, Cecilia Rabell Romero (coord.), 41–95. Mexico City: El Colegio de México.

Rivera González, José Guadalupe. 2005. Alcances y límites de las redes de reciprocidad entre un grupo de familias de sectores medios en la ciudad de México. *AIBR, Revista de Antropología Iberoamericana* 43.

Rivera González, José Guadalupe. 2006. Crisis y refuncionalización de las redes de reciprocidad familiares: el caso de sectores medios en la Ciudad de México. *Economía, sociedad y territorio* 4 (21): 87–118.

Rodgers, Dennis. 2007. "Each to their own": Ethnographic notes on the economic organisation of poor households in urban Nicaragua. *The Journal of Development Studies* 43 (3): 391–419.

Sandel, Michael J. 2012. *What money can't buy. The moral limits of markets*. New York, NY: Farrar, Straus and Giroux.

Velázquez Galindo, Yuribia. 2013. Interdependencia y economía de dones. La "ayuda" (quipalehuiya) como forma económica básica entre los nahuas, México. Antípoda. *Revista de antropología y arqueología* 17:175–201.

Willis, Katie. 1993. Women's work and social network use in Oaxaca City, Mexico. *Bulletin of Latin American Research* 12 (1): 65–82.

Wright Mills, Charles. 2003. *La imaginación sociológica*. 3rd ed. México: Fondo de Cultura Económica.

Zelizer, Viviana A. 2005. *The purchase of intimacy*. Princeton, NJ: Princeton University Press.

Walking a Tightrope: Using Financial Diaries to Investigate Day-to-Day Financial Decisions and the Social Safety Net of the Financially Excluded

Financially vulnerable, low-income individuals are more likely to experience financial exclusion as they are unable to access financial services that meet their needs. How do they cope with economic instability, and what is the role of social networks in their coping strategies? Using financial diaries, we explore the day-to-day monetary transactions (n = 16,889) of forty-five low-to-moderate income individuals with restricted access to mainstream lending in Glasgow, UK, over a six-month period. Our sample includes users of microcredit and financial advice, as well as nonusers of these services. Findings reveal that informal lending to avoid the pernicious effects of short-term illiquidity was pervasive among these individuals. However, taking informal loans often strains valuable social capital and keeps people from building up a formal credit footprint. Our findings suggest that financially vulnerable populations would benefit from policies that focus on alternative financial mechanisms to help stabilize income-insecure individuals in the short-term.

Keywords: financial exclusion; poverty; social networks; financial diaries; microcredit; RoSCAs; informal finance

The ability to access and use financial services that are appropriate to one's needs is essential for a healthy financial life (Morduch and Siwicki 2017). Changes in the nature of work and employment insecurity (Friedman 2014), among other factors, such as welfare policies, are contributing to high month-to-month income volatility (Farrell and Greig 2016;

By
OLGA BIOSCA,
NEIL MCHUGH,
FATMA IBRAHIM,
RACHEL BAKER,
TIM LAXTON,
and
CAM DONALDSON

Olga Biosca is a reader in social business and microfinance in the Yunus Centre for Social Business and Health at Glasgow Caledonian University. She has published on social and financial exclusion, microcredit, and income and health inequalities.

Neil McHugh is a reader in the Yunus Centre for Social Business and Health, Glasgow Caledonian University. His research focuses on various aspects of distributive justice, including, for example, microcredit and eliciting social values in the context of health resource allocation.

Correspondence: olga.biosca@gcu.ac.uk

DOI: 10.1177/0002716220921154

Hannagan and Morduch 2016; Hills, McKnight, and Smithies 2006). Those for whom incomes are low particularly struggle to manage increasing short-term income fluctuations; restricted access to high-quality and affordable financial services frequently combine with a lack of assets and savings that limit their ability to stabilize consumption over time (Morduch and Schneider 2017; Tomlinson 2018), therefore increasing financial insecurity and vulnerability. One way in which low-income individuals may deal with this insecurity is reliance on the help of family and friends. There is a strong association between social capital (in the form of private social networks) and individuals' insurance against income volatility (Pericoli, Pierucci, and Ventura 2015). The nature and extent of social networks can determine the ability to access a combination of formal and informal credit sources to manage income fluctuations more effectively (Lenton and Mosley 2013; Siwicki 2019).

While the literature has highlighted the problem of income volatility for those on the verge of financial exclusion, who are unable to access affordable financial products and services that meet their needs, as well as their reliance on personal networks (see the introduction to this special issue), empirical evidence about the relative importance of social networks and other strategies in households' financial management is scarce. Yearly population surveys, such as the Scottish Household Survey, allow us to observe which financial instruments people are using; however, little is known about how informal strategies are used to cope with dips in income or peaks in expenditure. Traditional studies of financially excluded individuals in the UK, using surveys, bank account records, or in-depth interviews are also not frequent enough to capture the detail of individuals' financial management strategies or the underlying rationales for their behavior.

This article discusses the day-to-day financial management of people with low-to-moderate income, living below the UK median household income threshold, and their experiences of using social capital to smooth consumption, by analyzing their financial diaries maintained over a six-month period. Our aim is to explore in depth how financial insecurity and income and expenditure volatility affect decision-making. Our research objectives are:

Fatma Ibrahim is a PhD candidate at the Yunus Centre for Social Business and Health, Glasgow Caledonian University. Her research focuses on the connection between money management strategies and health in vulnerable populations, particularly refugees.

Rachel Baker is professor of health economics and director of the Yunus Centre for Social Business and Health at Glasgow Caledonian University. She has published on a range of topics, broadly linked by her interest in researching issues relating to public values, resource allocation, and health and well-being.

Tim Laxton is a PhD candidate at the School of Health and Life Sciences at Glasgow Caledonian University.

Cam Donaldson holds the Yunus Chair in Social Business and Health at Glasgow Caledonian University, where he is also pro vice chancellor research. Over a 35-year period, Cam has published more than 250 peer-reviewed articles in medical, public health, health policy, and economics journals.

NOTE: This work was supported by the Chief Scientist Office (CSO) Scotland (FinWell – ref. CZH/4/1095).

1. To generate detailed financial data using diaries over a six-month period with individuals with low-to-moderate income to observe if and how they cope with financial instability.
2. To examine the extent to which formal and informal social capital-based financial instruments are used, how these financial networks are mobilized and operationalized, and how their use is managed and negotiated in the context of everyday lives of the financially excluded.

In the next section, we discuss the relationship between income volatility, financial exclusion, and the use of social capital to smooth consumption. We then describe our data and the financial diary methodology. Our results show the major role that social networks play in the lives of our diarists and offer insights about how these are used to deal with life events such as job loss, bereavement, or divorce. Finally, the discussion and conclusion section outlines the need to provide individuals living on the verge of financial exclusion with more effective and affordable services to prevent the damage of individuals' already limited social networks. Our findings suggest that financially vulnerable individuals would benefit from anti-poverty policies that focus on helping them to better cushion for life events.

Background

Recent studies have highlighted the importance of (increasing) short-term income volatility on the lives of the low-to-moderate income groups of the population. While high month-to-month income fluctuations have been observed in both the UK (Hills, McKnight, and Smithies 2006; Tomlinson 2018) and the United States (Farrell and Greig 2016; Hannagan and Morduch 2016), short-term stability is essential for financial security and intergenerational economic mobility (Morduch and Schneider 2017; Siwicki 2019). Individuals can achieve short-term financial stability, defined as having the means to cope with everyday shocks, while still progressing toward financial goals (Morduch and Siwicki 2017), mainly through: (a) income regularly exceeding expenses, (b) savings, (c) credit, and (d) social networks (Siwicki 2019).

In 2017, half of the UK adult population showed characteristics of potential financial vulnerability, such as limited financial resilience; low financial capability; suffering a health-related problem that affects a person's day-to-day activity; or a recent life event, such as redundancy or job loss, unexpected reduction in working hours, bankruptcy, relationship breakdown, serious accident or illness, bereavement, or becoming the main carer of a close family member (Financial Conduct Authority 2018). This vulnerability is more acute for the low-to-moderate income group, aggravated by low income and irregular unreliable pay combined with frequent expenditure peaks (Financial Conduct Authority 2018; Tomlinson 2018). For this poorer population group, high-quality, flexible, and affordable financial services, such as saving or credit products, are essential to manage uncertainty and better cope with both fairly predictable and unexpected everyday challenges. However, an estimated 1.3 million UK adults did not have a bank account in 2017 (Financial Conduct Authority 2018), and around half the population experience more nuanced forms of financial exclusion in that they are unable to access or use mainstream financial services that are appropriate to their needs (e.g., a lack of home contents insurance or savings accounts, which in turn limits access to other products such as mainstream credit) (Bunyan, Collins, and Torrisi 2016). Financial exclusion is a dimension of social exclusion (Wilson 2012), and unequal access and use of financial services have been linked to income and socioeconomic inequality and poverty (Affleck and Mellor 2006; Beck and Demirgüç-Kunt 2008). Economic theory and empirical evidence indicate that inclusion in financial systems can enhance individual welfare through: (a) improved risk-management, consumption smoothing, and cushioning against "asset-depleting" strategies after an economic shock; and (b) efficient allocation of capital, partly by allowing access to riskier, potentially highly profitable, investments (Honohan 2008).

Poorer communities in the UK are historically more likely to experience financial exclusion with limited options (particularly of saving and credit products) available to them. To help fill this void, UK and Scottish governments have actively encouraged the development of credit unions and community development finance institutions (CDFIs)—which have emerged as an affordable alternative to high-cost, subprime lending and mainstream banks—to help tackle financial exclusion (Lenton and Mosley 2013; McHugh, Baker, and Donaldson 2019; McHugh et al. 2014; McKillop, Ward, and Wilson 2007). Credit unions have traditionally focused on the provision of savings products while some CDFIs offer microcredit: small, fast, affordable loans that do not require collateral or credit history. However, these organizations do not exist at the scale needed to address exclusion, and pockets of the population remain underserved (Bunyan, Collins, and Torrisi 2016). In the absence of providers that can help individuals to smooth their income and prevent illiquidity, the poor rely primarily on a host of informal credit providers (Collins et al. 2009; Siwicki 2019).

The economic development literature has traditionally argued that social capital, in terms of social networks, positively impacts consumption smoothing (Townsend 1994; de la Rocha 2001, 2006), and the same argument has recently been made for the UK (Pericoli, Pierucci, and Ventura 2015). Individuals with higher social capital are likely to be able to smooth their consumption by drawing on cash transfers from relatives and friends or in-kind exchanges. At the same time, experimental evidence has found that risk-pooling in groups of microcredit borrowers increases with higher social interaction (Feigenberg, Field, and Pande 2013). However, income and asset-poor individuals are also usually network poor—their personal networks include mostly resource-poor people in terms of knowledge, wealth, skills, power, and information—so the extent to which they can benefit from social networks is limited (Van Eijk 2010; de la Rocha 2006).

Our study analyzes high-frequency financial transaction data of forty-five financial diaries, including subjective rationales and field notes, which were collected monthly over six months from financially excluded individuals in Glasgow. The most populous city in Scotland was considered ideal to undertake this study as it has traditionally been one of the most socioeconomically deprived in the UK; home to the ten most deprived neighborhoods in Britain (Stewart et al. 2018) with extreme health inequalities between the richest and poorest being well documented (Marmot 2007). Glasgow also has more varied and complex financial products and services for low-income groups when compared to other UK cities. The high frequency of financial diaries, repeated interaction with diarists, and the consequent building of rapport and trust between the research team and the participants enabled us to develop a detailed understanding of individual coping strategies, including the financial role of social networks in the lives of the financially excluded.

Data and Methods

Sampling

To gain access to individuals on the verge of exclusion, sampling was focused on users of nonmainstream financial products (Wilson 2012), such as microcredit and financial advice, as well as on a group of individuals with similar socioeconomic characteristics who were nonusers of these financial products. The sample was recruited through client referrals of a number of service providers working with our target population in Glasgow: (1) Grameen in the UK—a microfinance institution (MFI) that supplies microloans to individuals to undertake productive ventures; loans are distributed via group lending, which involves borrowers organizing themselves into groups of five; (2) Scotcash—a not-for-profit social enterprise offering personal microloans and inclusive services such as assistance to open basic and savings bank accounts and financial advice; (3) Glasgow Central Citizens Advice Bureau (CAB)—a publicly funded charity offering financial advice; (4) Money Advice Scotland (MAS)—an umbrella organization that promotes the development of free, independent, impartial, and confidential debt advice and financial inclusion; and (5) Glasgow Housing Association (GHA)—a not-for-profit organization and Scotland's largest social housing and property management group. GHA works in close partnership with both Scotcash and CAB, and its clients are in a similar financial situation as CDFI clients and financial advice user groups.

A qualitative sampling frame was applied for referral organizations and a purposeful sampling strategy was adopted to maximize variation in terms of individuals': (a) participation in financial inclusion programs—business microcredit (n = 16), personal microcredit (n = 10), money advice (n = 9), and nonusers of such initiatives (n = 10); (b) sociodemographic characteristics such as age, gender, ethnicity, and household composition; (c) disability and health status; and (d) neighborhoods in and around Glasgow. Despite our offering incentive payments that paid the highest on completion of all six diaries, due to the sensitivity of the data collected, recruitment and retention were challenging. Snowball sampling, i.e. referrals from study participants, was also used to complement referrals from organizations. Attrition was 21 percent and 45 diarists (out of 57)

TABLE 1
Demographic Characteristics of Diarists, by Group (%)

	Business microloan (n = 16)	Personal microloan (n = 10)	Financial advice (n = 9)	Nonusers (n = 10)	Total (n = 45)
Female	75	60	78	50	67
Disabled / Long-term sick	19	60	44	30	36
Employed / Self-employed	75	0	56	30	44
On means-tested benefits	75	90	89	80	82
Ethnicity					
White British	19	90	100	60	60
African	56	0	0	30	27
Other	25	10	0	10	13
Age groups					
20-35	19	40	11	30	24
36-45	56	10	44	30	38
46-55	19	40	22	30	27
>55	6	10	22	10	11
Household composition					
Lone parent w/ dependent children	50	40	56	0	38
Couple w/ dependent children	25	10	22	50	27
Single	0	50	22	50	27
Separated / Widowed	19	0	0	0	7
Family abroad	6	0	0	0	2

were included in the analysis. The study was approved by the Ethics Committee of Glasgow School for Business and Society, Glasgow Caledonian University.

Table 1 presents descriptive statistics of sociodemographic characteristics of the participants who completed four or more financial diaries (n = 45). All research participants were on low-to-moderate incomes, with the majority (82 percent) receiving means-tested welfare benefits. All participants were financially vulnerable so they had at least one of the following characteristics: limited financial resilience; low financial capability; a long-term health condition or disability; or experienced a recent serious life event, such as job loss, relationship breakdown, illness, bereavement, or becoming the main caretaker for a family member (Financial Conduct Authority 2018).

Diaries and interviews

Monthly financial diaries were administered with forty-five diarists living in and around the city of Glasgow. Financial diaries are systematic records of all daily income and expenditure transactions, as well as gifts, assets, and liabilities, aimed at understanding the money management strategies of low-income populations over time (Collins et al. 2009). Originally applied in developing countries, this method has recently been used in advanced nations such as the United States (Morduch and Schneider 2017) and, for the first time with this study, in the UK (McHugh, Biosca, and Donaldson 2017). Similar to the U.S. Financial Diaries (Morduch and Schneider 2017) and Portfolios of the Poor (Collins et al. 2009), in Glasgow the term *diaries* is used to reflect the high-frequency of data collection and not the diarists logging transactions themselves. Through diary data, we explore the financial lives of low-to-moderate income, financially vulnerable individuals, including unique information on behavior and use of financial products. Additionally, information about individuals' financial transactions were used as prompts to generate qualitative data in relation to participants' lives, social networks, life events, and periods of difficulty.

Phased data collection took place from February 2016 until March 2017. Diaries were constructed through 306 diary-interviews that took place in participants' homes or workplaces or universities every month. The aim was to collect diaries over a six-month period; however, the duration of data collection varied across participants: four-month diaries (n = 3), six-month diaries (n = 39), and seven-month diaries (n = 3). A baseline questionnaire was administered to collect information on demographic and socioeconomic characteristics of the participants, including information on social capital, financial knowledge and behavior, level and sources of income, and coping strategies, among others. This initial information enabled the construction of a profile for each participant. A similar questionnaire was administered at the end to assess changes in financial lives. The financial transactions (n = 16,889) were recorded and captured in a database adapted from an instrument developed by Microfinance Opportunities.[1] The predefined variables captured for each transaction were: purpose, amount (in £), direction of transaction (outflow/inflow), method of payment (cash, card, financial transfer, etc.), and channel (in person/online/phone). The database also had an open "additional comments" section. For financial transactions, we coded predefined details of the organization or individual involved in the transaction. For example, for informal finance exchanges, we coded the relationship between the individual and the diarist (relative, friend, etc.) and their gender. The data were then exported into Stata software for quantitative descriptive analysis.

Several mechanisms were put in place to control the quality of the diary data. To minimize recall bias, participants were sent weekly reminders in addition to being visited monthly to collect diaries. Diarists' bank statements and receipts were also frequently provided and cross-checked with reported transactions. Inconsistencies in income and savings against expenditure, as well as other misreporting errors, were tracked and addressed on subsequent visits to the diarist. Data on cash-in-hand and savings were used to assess any margins of error between sources and uses of funds, with their causes explored with diarists.

To systematically collect information with a high level of detail and consistency across diarists, and also due to the limited English language and literacy skills of some diarists, three skilled researchers were responsible for recording every income and expenditure transaction that was annotated by the diarists or appeared in bank statements during the preceding month, as well as assets, liabilities, and life events. Subjective comments on each transaction were recorded in the database, such as, for example, the motivation behind asking for a loan.

Our research team also used the diaries to inform qualitative questions based on financial transactions that were recorded in the form of field notes and then collated in "life event sheets" for each diarist (life events occurring in between data collection points). This information was used to understand the reasons behind participants' financial behavior that could not be observed by analyzing income and expenditure patterns alone—for example, why and how they used informal lending. One of the main advantages of the financial diary method was the high levels of trust that developed between researchers and participants through ongoing engagement. In these diary-interviews, diarists shared perceptions and personal details of their lives that were often crucial for the interpretation of the quantitative data.

Data analysis

A mixed-methods approach was used to analyze diary data. First, the descriptive statistics of monthly income and expenditure transactions were examined for each diarist; transactions capturing the use of different financial products—regulated and nonregulated by the Financial Conduct Authority (FCA)—and their association with participant's characteristics and key events and shocks (identified through the qualitative data) were explored. Second, we purposely sampled individual cases based on intensity and diversity of financial products used and analyzed the selected cases using corporate finance tools (cash flow statements and monthly balance sheets). Finally, the quantitative interpretation of the results was combined with the qualitative individual stories collected in life event sheets, researcher field notes, and diarist notes on financial transactions, to provide context into diarists' (financial) lives and rationales for their financial behaviors (Collins et al. 2009). Pseudonyms are used to maintain diarists' anonymity.

Results

The financial diaries of our forty-five participants reveal the intricate financial management strategies used either to cope with periods of cash illiquidity or for investment purposes. This complexity is better understood through the analysis of participants' perceptions of their financial lives and accounts of their decision-making processes. Diarists needed to use sophisticated money management strategies mainly due to their general economic insecurity, precarious employment, and frequent month-to-month income and expenditure swings.

Managing day-to-day finances

In the context of low, but also unstable income streams, finance was crucial for diarists to smooth consumption patterns. As shown in Table 2, finance-related

TABLE 2
Distribution of Transactions (Incoming and Outgoing) per Category

Category	Frequency	Percent
Food	4,359	25.82
Entertainment	2,141	12.68
Financial	1,758	10.41
Benefits	1,287	7.62
Bills	1,283	7.6
Transport	1,059	6.27
Household	1,035	6.13
Gift	562	3.33
Clothing	540	3.2
Employment income	445	2.64
Miscellaneous	415	2.46
Housing	268	1.59
Taxes	245	1.45
Business	238	1.41
Incentives for research participation	231	1.37
Gambling	223	1.32
Other	792	4.69
Total	16,881	100

transactions—those including credit, savings, insurance, and other financial services—were the third most frequent overall (10 percent, n = 1,758), after groceries (26 percent, n = 4,359) and entertainment (13 percent, n = 2,141). In terms of total value, finance-related transactions were also third (£129,741), after benefits (£225,001), and employment income (£133,504). On average, diarists were making decisions related to financial services such as buying insurance or taking out or paying back a loan approximately every other day, with most of these transactions being related to credit (72 percent), followed by insurance (12 percent), and savings (8 percent). Only four diarists in our sample did not have a current loan (9 percent). Furthermore, a majority of participants (80 percent, n = 36) were simultaneously using at least two types of financial providers during the study, both FCA-regulated and nonregulated. Over the data collection period, study participants were using three credit products on average and one diarist was found to be managing eight loans simultaneously.

In our sample, managing multiple loans was associated with a lack of access to mainstream financial products; even if all diarists had a bank account, they were experiencing nuanced financial exclusion. Most of our participants could not borrow from mainstream financial institutions because of low salaries, unstable employment, part-time or self-employment, having a poor credit history or being "credit invisible," i.e., not having a credit history. Those diarists who did not have a bank loan or a low-cost mortgage were more likely to be managing a portfolio

TABLE 3
Financial Instruments Used, by Group (%)

Financial instruments	Business microloan (n = 16)	Personal microloan (n = 10)	Financial advice (n = 9)	Nonusers (n = 10)	Total (n = 45)
Microcredit	100	100	0	0	58
Relatives and friends	38	50	44	10	36
Overdraft	38	30	44	20	33
Credit card	38	0	56	20	29
Rent-to-own	38	20	11	10	22
Student loans	25	0	11	30	18
Menage (RoSCA)	25	0	22	10	16
Credit union	19	10	11	10	13
Store card	25	10	0	0	11
Mortgage	6	10	22	10	11
Car loan	19	0	0	10	9
Catalogue	6	0	22	10	9
Pawn	6	10	11	10	9
Bank loan	19	0	0	0	7
Doorstep[a]	6	0	11	0	4

a. A doorstep loan, also called a home credit loan, is a form of home-collected high-cost credit.

of regulated subprime loans (rent-to-own, car loans, pawn brokers, catalogue, doorstep, etc.), coupled with informal loans from relatives and friends. The wide range of financial providers used as well as the percentage of diarists using them at baseline is shown in Table 3.

Throughout the diaries, the role of relatives and friends in assisting with financial instability and helping prevent illiquidity among our sample of individuals was central (see Table 3). This is corroborated by baseline data: when participants were asked what they would do if they had a financial emergency and needed £1000 in a hurry, nearly half of the sample (n = 18) replied they would turn to a relative or friend. The next most common response was "I wouldn't be able to cope," selected by one third (n = 15) of diarists. Only 9 percent (n = 4) of diarists would be able to use savings to cover the emergency expenditure. Instead we observed how diarists mobilized their social networks not only as a coping strategy after a life event or shock but also, more generally, during relatively longer periods of difficulty and financial instability. The six months of coded financial data show, for most diarists, extensive and strategic use of social capital as a safety net. Personal and organizational social networks were mobilized and created to access loans through three main financial mechanisms: (i) nonregulated informal loans, (ii) rotating credit and savings associations (RoSCAs), and (iii) FCA-regulated group microfinance.

TABLE 4
Informal Transactions over Six Months, by Group

Informal transactions	Business microloan	Personal microloan	Financial advice	Nonusers	Total
Average frequency	12	16	29	4	12
Minimum frequency	1	1	2	1	1
Maximum frequency	34	35	80	12	80
Percentage of informal overall credit transactions (frequency)	29%	36%	70%	54%	47%
Average amount (£)	1386	879	851	364	870
Minimum amount (£)	50	90	338	20	20
Maximum amount (£)	3922	2303	1578	853	3922
Average amount per transaction (£)	116	55	29	91	72
Number of diarists reporting informal transactions	15	8	5	6	34
Total number of diarists	16	10	9	10	45

Informal mechanisms for managing short-term illiquidity: Rich in friends, poor in nothing?

From all credit transactions recorded, those related to loans with family and friends were the most frequent (34 percent), followed by those with rent-to-own organizations (14 percent). When possible, illiquidity situations were managed through family and friends because participants valued that informal loans were relatively easy to access, fast, small, and repayment was flexible. Table 4 shows that 34 diarists (76 percent) reported at least one informal transaction during the study period (4 diarists did not use any form of credit and 7 used other forms of credit but not informal). The average number of informal transactions during the study period was 12, with one diarist reporting 80 informal transactions during a six-month period. Table 4 also shows that nearly half (47 percent) of the credit transactions reported during the study were informal, with the importance of informal finance depending on access to other more formal forms of credit. For example, microcredit users rely on other credit forms, while recipients of financial advice and nonusers rely mainly on informal sources.

During the six months of data collection, transactions reveal that most diarists repeatedly relied on a person or a small group of very close people of similar socioeconomic characteristics who usually lived nearby. Examples of this are Sabrina and Uma, who were both immigrant single mothers with young families, in their forties, combining part-time employment and self-employment. They were also neighbors and, like many of our diarists, they relied on each other frequently for financial support. Financial transactions between them are an example of how our diarists borrowed or lent money to peers; most of their transactions were small (sometimes only

£5) and via electronic transfer as the money needed to reach the bank account fast as it was usually to pay a direct debit or standing order of a bill coming through the following day. Overall, informal loan transactions were slightly more than £70 on average (see Table 4), frequently repaid in less than a week and used to cover short-term cash shortages. Table 4 shows that, on average, £870 was exchanged informally by each participant using informal finance during the six months (n = 34), with some reporting figures as low as £20 and others close to £4,000.

Informal loans were also interest free, but most diarists perceived costs in terms of having to reciprocate to ensure the link remained a reliable source for future needs, even when their own economic situation was insecure. One of the consequences of this tension was that 73 percent of diarists (33 out of 45) used others' credit cards and catalogue subscriptions as a form of payment or to lend to others at least on one occasion during the study. For example, Rebecca, a 21-year-old single mother from Glasgow used her mothers' credit card repeatedly during the study period, paying back the outstanding balance (around £100) every month. This was effectively used as a credit line depending on the needs: urgent household repairs, furniture for a new flat, social activities, soft-play sessions for her toddler and other general (but essential) day-to-day expenses. This behavior poses important risks to an already vulnerable group in two ways. First, it might affect their/others' credit scores and contribute to deepening financial exclusion in poorer communities. Second, if the borrower is not able to pay back on time to the person who has taken debt on their behalf, they risk losing their already limited social support network. We found that the repayment schedules of informal financial arrangements were frequently not discussed between lender and borrower at the time that the exchange took place. While for repeated transactions between friends, distinguishing between a loan and a gift was straightforward, some diarists found it difficult, in particular if it was a new lender/borrower or in situations where the borrower was perceived to be struggling.

Not all of the diarists in the study had a core network to support them financially. This is in line with the argument in the literature that people in poverty have smaller support networks (Van Eijk 2010). Additionally, even when available, support networks were frequently income and asset poor, which posed additional constraints. Throughout his financial diaries, Paul—a 53-year-old Scottish male from Easterhouse, one of the most deprived areas in Glasgow—and his sister transferred money back and forth to cushion against illiquidity. Paul's sister was the only person who provided a safety net for him, but Paul was aware that his sister, a pensioner, could not always help as she had her own financial problems. For most research participants, borrowing from family and friends was perceived as a last resort and they were reluctant to do so: they knew it was a lot to ask from people also living in difficult circumstances but, lacking access to alternative forms of finance, they perceived they had no choice.

Parties are not just about fun: Amina's safety net

To show the complexity of financial management strategies used by our diarists, we present the case of Amina. Amina is a single mother of a toddler and a baby

FIGURE 1
Amina's Aggregate Personal and Business Income and Expenditure, Monthly

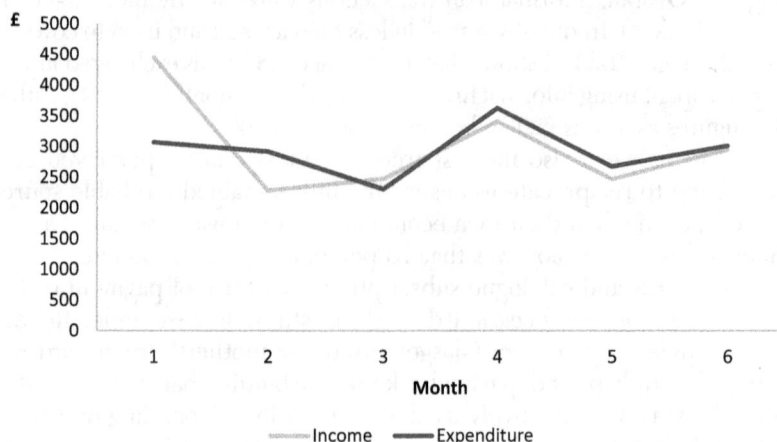

born during the study (month 4). She is originally from West Africa but has been living in the UK for almost 20 years. She is self-employed and runs a clothes shop in central Glasgow. When she became a study participant, Amina was five months pregnant. She had been unable to work since the start of the pregnancy and this was severely affecting her life. Income from the shop she owned had lowered substantially during her pregnancy months. Suffering from pains and discomfort, she was not physically fit to work the hours required to make the shop profitable. However, she did not want to close the shop down as she felt she could make it profitable again after delivering her second child and going back to work. This was her only source of income and she wanted to be self-employed. Given that business income kept decreasing until after she delivered her baby in month four of the diaries, Amina was constantly thinking about strategies to cope with the decrease in her income and the expenditure associated with a new baby. When we met her, she had just taken a business microloan to buy stock for her shop for when she could return to work. However, the productive nature of this loan did not help her with managing illiquidity.

Figure 1 includes Amina's total personal and business income and expenditure every month during the study. During these months, she had been carefully pondering which expenses were necessary and which could be postponed and matched to her income. To cope, she had already taken small loans from subprime lenders as well as her core informal network. Lacking access to other credit options, she thought of a plan. Even though she was not feeling physically up to it, Amina organized a big party for her newborn. She knew that, for cultural reasons, relatives and friends would help with food, drinks, favors, and organizing the party. Amina's monthly budget for month four, shown in Table 5, reveals that for this party she not only managed to persuade friends and relatives to lend her money (£600) to stabilize her situation (diversifying sources of flexible free

TABLE 5
Amina's Monthly Budget for Month 4 (in £)

Sources of funds	3423	Uses of funds	3622
Housing benefit	315	Rent	315
Business revenue	235	Council tax	30
Tax credit	1385	Council tax arrears	17
Child benefit	140	Electricity and gas	50
JSA	33	Electricity arrears	50
Loan from family/friends	*600*	Landline and internet	100
Gifts for new baby	*700*	Mobile phone	10
GCU incentives	15	Groceries	230
		Childcare	570
		Insurance	62
		Baby (car seat, nappies, etc.)	445
		Baby party	*224*
		Toiletries	26
		Lottery	32
		Loans to family/friends	420
		Rent-to-own	108
		Subprime credit card	60
		Doorstep loan	192
		Business operational expenses	232
		Business tax	51
		Business loan	198
		Business rent	200

loans), but she also spent less (£224) than she received as gifts (£700), making a £476 profit. In the end, this strategy of organizing a party, which may seem irrational for an outsider given Amina's economic situation, was more effective than any of her alternatives: it was faster, she made a profit, and had a flexible repayment schedule adapted to her needs and health problems. Amina found a strategy to capitalize on her extended network when she had no other options left to stabilize her economic situation.

Savings for a purpose: join a menage

Another relationship-based financial instrument, used by seven of our forty-five diarists, were RoSCAs, popularly known as "moneyrounds" or, in Scottish Gaelic, "menage." This is a traditional unregulated financial mechanism of saving and credit, which, in its simplest form, consists of a group of individuals who come together and make regular cyclical contributions to a common fund, which is then given as a lump sum to one member in each cycle. These are prevalent in developing country contexts (Ambec and Treich 2007) and have been observed in immigrant populations in advanced countries such as the United States and the UK (Light and Pham 1998). In our study, three out of seven of the diarists who used RoSCAs at some point during the study were Scottish. The majority of users were single mothers; all menage participants were female, except for one single young man who was introduced to menage by his mother as a means of saving to pay for accumulated arrears. RoSCAs were mainly used as a means to save lump sums of money that users perceived they could not have saved otherwise. Menage users had clear objectives for their participation (for example, paying car-related expenses—insurance, MOT, road tax—traveling to visit family, or buying Christmas presents). The menages we encountered in the study were not continuously operating; some were only mobilized when an individual of the core network (group of close friends) or members of the church congregation experienced a life event that had financial implications, such as weddings, bereavement, partnership breakups, or an emergency. In this case, the groups were mobilized as a safety net to quickly raise a lump sum of money that diarists would not be able to borrow from individuals in their network. Menage users perceived additional advantages over more "structured" savings products that they could access in the market; like with informal loans, the trust between members allowed for additional flexibility. On emergency occasions when money was tight, individuals could negotiate with the member getting the lump sum and defer payment or even default if it had not been their turn yet; the only consequence of this being the defaulted money would be deducted when their payment was due. The amount paid into menages by Scottish participants was modest (around £10/month), while the more sophisticated ones, run electronically by immigrants living across the country, were up to £200/month (which were doubled-up to £400 by taking two rounds). These differences are likely due to the reasons behind financial exclusion for the two populations. While Scots lacked access to mainstream financial services because of their low incomes and poor credit records, immigrants frequently did not have credit histories, which made them "credit invisible." The duration of the menages varied depending on the number of members (up to fifteen members). The highest amount of money paid in a moneyround to a participant was £3,000. These financial mechanisms operated on the basis of trust and participants were selected carefully: all menage participants could veto a potential new entrant and, to minimize risk, new entrants' turn to receive the money came last or close to last. Gender, marital status, having children, race, and religion were all mentioned as selection criteria. For example, one menage was exclusively for single mothers and another only for families with children. In the words of one of the Southeast Asian menage participants: "You don't handle money with white people, you rather keep your business with your own people." The definition of "own people" was broad and the menage included African and Asian first- and second-generation immigrants.

Capitalizing on social networks: Microcredit for business

Self-employed participants were able to capitalize on and expand their core social networks by accessing business microcredit. The financial product offered by Grameen in the UK required that prospective borrowers formed groups of five people to meet every week for loan repayment. If someone in the group defaulted on their loan, the group would be dissolved and no further loans provided. The selection of the group members was based on trust so all group members needed to be in the core network of another group member. The group meetings and trust relationships were generally associated with higher flexibility and pooling of resources. Frequently, diarists who were members of one of these Grameen in the UK groups would pay for each other's installments if one of them could not afford to pay that week. In turn, they received (and expected) reciprocal behavior from group members. This additional flexibility provided by the social network cushioned participants against defaulting on their loans and compensated for a relatively rigid microcredit product design.

Discussion and Conclusion: Until Debt Do Us Part?

This study has shown the crucial role that relatives and friends play in the everyday finances of relatively poor, financially excluded individuals. Social networks are mobilized in different ways to manage cash flows and avoid the pernicious effects of short-term illiquidity. However, this can result in the networks of the more vulnerable, frequently small and also resource-poor, being damaged because of financial matters. While the importance of social exchange between neighbors, relatives, and friends as a survival strategy for the low-income population resonates well with the development literature, some authors have highlighted that being excluded from, for example, the labor market will affect the financial and social resources of individuals and, subsequently, their ability to be part of a relationship of reciprocity (de la Rocha 2006). This article builds on this by exploring the association between financial exclusion and social networks. The alternatives for the financially excluded are few or nonexistent. Our results confirm the importance in the UK of credit over savings to cope with financial insecurity (Hood, Joyce, and Sturrock 2018), with only 22 percent of UK adults not holding credit of any kind in 2017 (Financial Conduct Authority 2018). These results also align well, given the sociodemographic characteristics of our participants, with the fact that 24 percent of UK adults had less than £1,000 as a savings buffer in 2017 (Financial Conduct Authority 2018). Other forms of finance, mainstream and subprime, are found to be complementary to those provided by social networks. Individuals end up managing a portfolio of loans and making continuous financial decisions, which are particularly complex in terms of their relatively large amounts, their future implications, and because they cannot be easily reversed. These findings have implications for the nature of social networks, policy, and practice.

Social networks can provide credit in times of need and lead to increased participation in risk-pooling within formal and informal institutions, such as microcredit group lending and RoSCAs. Repeated interactions between members, through use of these financial products, create more space for solidarity and flexible arrangements. However, this sophisticated use of social networks can have detrimental effects on already low levels of social capital in these communities and increase individuals' exclusion from mainstream finance.

The pervasiveness of social networks for financial stability has the potential to alter the qualitative nature of the individuals' relationships. Instead of drawing on friends and family occasionally or in an emergency, our data suggest that informal lending is common and well-established. If money comes to define relationships, the relationship can be put under pressure. A further unintended consequence is that individuals do not have the opportunity to build up their formal credit footprint and will more likely remain "credit invisible." Thus, despite having sophisticated financial management skills, these individuals will continue to be excluded from the mainstream and unable to access financial products and services, such as mortgages and insurance products, which could enhance their life.

Policy and practice: What should be done?

Our financial diary data highlight that low-to-moderate income individuals living on the verge of financial exclusion do not always have enough cash to cover their basic needs, and they turn to (in)formal lending to manage their financial (in)stability. Indeed, individuals' financial lives are so complex that diarists are making financial-related decisions approximately every other day, which represents a significant cognitive burden.

This article reveals that social networks, instead of the state, operate as the main safety net of financially excluded individuals. The importance of social networks for financial stability, even in advanced economies such as the UK, indicates that (a) the design of the current welfare system does not cope well with growing income volatility and financial insecurity, and (b) there is a gap in the provision of credit. Policy can respond to this by tackling the bigger, systemic issue of meeting basic needs and providing better cushioning for financial instability or responding to the gap in the provision of finance. Our focus here is on ways to address the latter issue.

One way to reduce the reliance on social networks is to promote "alternative" economic spaces that prioritize the interests and well-being of their users, such as CDFIs (McHugh, Baker, and Donaldson 2019). However, the government needs to support these institutions, as it is difficult to sustainably offer financial products to low-to-moderate income individuals (Wilson 2012). To succeed, these financial inclusion policies need to be part of a more general policy agenda to address growing levels of financial insecurity in different income levels of the population. The reliance on social networks also conditions how relationships are understood in poorer communities and incentivizes individual behaviors that can harm social networks and promote financial exclusion even further. Alternative high-quality, affordable, fast, safe, and flexible financial products that allow individuals to build up credit histories are required to help the financially insecure. These should be combined with anti-poverty policies that are better adapted to the needs of those who do not have enough slack to cope with the ups and downs of everyday life.

Note

1. Microfinance Opportunities is a global non-profit committed to understanding the financial realities of low-income households. See https://www.microfinanceopportunities.org/.

References

Affleck, Arthur, and Mary Mellor. 2006. Community development finance: A neo-market solution to social exclusion? *Journal of Social Policy* 35 (2): 303–19.
Ambec, Stefan, and Nicolas Treich. 2007. Roscas as financial agreements to cope with self-control problems. *Journal of Development Economics* 82 (1): 120–37.
Beck, Thorsten, and Asli Demirgüç-Kunt. 2008. Access to finance: An unfinished agenda. *The World Bank Economic Review* 22 (3): 383–96.
Bunyan, Sabrina, Alan Collins, and Gianpiero Torrisi. 2016. Analysing household and intra-urban variants in the consumption of financial services: Uncovering "exclusion" in an English city. *Journal of Consumer Policy* 39 (2): 199–221.
Collins, Daryl, Jonathan Morduch, Stuart Rutherford, and Orlanda Ruthven. 2009. *Portfolios of the poor: How the world's poor live on $2 a day*. Princeton, NJ: Princeton University Press.
de la Rocha, Mercedes. 2001. From the resources of poverty to the poverty of resources? The erosion of a survival model. *Latin American Perspectives* 28 (4): 72–100.
de la Rocha, Mercedes. 2006. Vanishing assets: Cumulative disadvantage among the urban poor. *The ANNALS of the American Academy of Political and Social Science* 606 (1): 68–94.
Farrell, Diana, and Fiona Greig. 2016. Paychecks, paydays, and the online platform economy: Big data on income volatility. JP Morgan Chase Institute ID 2911293. Rochester, NY: Social Science Research Network. https://papers.ssrn.com/abstract=2911293.
Feigenberg, Benjamin, Erica Field, and Rohini Pande. 2013. The economic returns to social interaction: Experimental evidence from microfinance. *The Review of Economic Studies* 80 (4): 1459–83.
Financial Conduct Authority. 2018. The financial lives of consumers across the UK: Key Findings from the FCA's Financial Lives Survey 2017. Availble from https://www.fca.org.uk/publication/research/financial-lives-consumers-across-uk.pdf.
Friedman, Gerald. 2014. Workers without employers: Shadow corporations and the rise of the gig economy. *Review of Keynesian Economics* 2 (2): 171–88.
Hannagan, Anthony, and Jonathan Morduch. 2016. Income gains and month-to-month income volatility: Evidence from the U.S. financial diaries. In *Economic mobility: Research and ideas on strengthening families, communities and the economy*. St. Louis, MO: Federal Reserve Bank of St. Louis.
Hills, John, Abigail McKnight, and Rachel Smithies. 2006. Tracking income: How working families' incomes vary through the year. Centre for Analysis of Social Exclusion reports (32). London: London School of Economics and Political Science. Available from http://sticerd.lse.ac.uk/case.
Honohan, Patrick. 2008. Cross-country variation in household access to financial services. *Journal of Banking & Finance* 32 (11): 2493–2500.
Hood, Andrew, Robert Joyce, and David Sturrock. 2018. *Problem debt and low-income households*. London: The Institute for Fiscal Studies. Available from https://www.ifs.org.uk/publications/10336.
Lenton, Pamela, and Paul Mosley. 2013. Financial exit routes from the "poverty trap": A study of four UK cities. *Urban Studies* 51 (4): 744–62.
Light, Ivan, and Michelle Pham. 1998. Beyond creditworthy: Microcredit and informal credit in the United States. *Journal of Developmental Entrepreneurship* 3 (1): 35–51.
Marmot, Michael. 2007. Achieving health equity: From root causes to fair outcomes. *The Lancet* 370 (9593): 1153–63.
McHugh, Neil, Rachel Baker, and Cam Donaldson. 2019. Microcredit for enterprise in the UK as an "alternative" economic space. *Geoforum* 100 (March): 80–88.
McHugh, Neil, Olga Biosca, and Cam Donaldson. 2017. From wealth to health: Evaluating microfinance as a complex intervention. *Evaluation* 23 (2): 209–25.

McHugh, Neil, Morag Gillespie, Jana Loew, and Cam Donaldson. 2014. First Steps towards self-employment – microcredit for enterprise in Scotland. *Scottish Affairs* 23 (2): 169–91.

McKillop, Donal G., Anne-Marie Ward, and John O. S. Wilson. 2007. The development of credit unions and their role in tackling financial exclusion. *Public Money and Management* 27 (1): 37–44.

Morduch, Jonathan, and Rachel Schneider. 2017. *The financial diaries: How American families cope in a world of uncertainty*. Princeton, NJ: Princeton University Press.

Morduch, Jonathan, and Julie Siwicki. 2017. In and out of poverty: Episodic poverty and income volatility in the US financial diaries. *Social Service Review* 91 (3): 390–421.

Pericoli, Filippo, Eleonora Pierucci, and Luigi Ventura. 2015. The impact of social capital on consumption insurance and income volatility in the UK: Evidence from the British Household Panel Survey. *Review of Economics of the Household* 13 (2): 269–95.

Siwicki, Julie. 2019. Short-term financial stability: A foundation for security and well-being. Aspen Institute Financial Security Program. Aspen CO: The Aspen Institute. Available from https://assets.aspeninstitute.org/content/uploads/2019/04/Short-Term-Financial-Stability_Report.pdf.

Stewart, Joanna, Mark Livingstone, David Walsh, and Richard Mitchell. 2018. Using population surfaces and spatial metrics to track the development of deprivation landscapes in Glasgow, Liverpool, and Manchester between 1971 and 2011. *Computers, Environment and Urban Systems* 72 (November): 124–33.

Tomlinson, Daniel. 2018. Irregular payments: Assessing the breadth and depth of month to month earnings volatility. Resolution Foundation Report. https://www.resolutionfoundation.org/publications/irregular-payments/.

Townsend, Robert. 1994. Risk and insurance in village India. *Econometrica* 62 (3): 539–91.

Van Eijk, Gwen. 2010. Does living in a poor neighbourhood result in network poverty? A study on local networks, locality-based relationships and neighbourhood settings. *Journal of Housing and the Built Environment* 25 (4): 467–80.

Wilson, Therese Ann. 2012. Supporting social enterprises to support vulnerable consumers: The example of community development finance institutions and financial exclusion. *Journal of Consumer Policy* 35 (2): 197–213.

Relationships Stretched Thin: Social Support Mobilization in Poverty

By
MIRANDA J. LUBBERS,
HUGO VALENZUELA
GARCÍA,
PAULA ESCRIBANO
CASTAÑO,
JOSÉ LUIS MOLINA,
ANTÒNIA CASELLAS,
and
JORGE GRAU REBOLLO

Research on how the poor "make ends meet" typically shows that they are able to do so by relying on dense support networks of family and close friends. Recent research suggests, however, that these networks play a limited role. This article examines the role of informal networks in how sixty-one households in Barcelona, Spain, cope with poverty. We use a mixed-methods design that combines structured network delineation with semistructured interviews about the processes of support mobilization. Findings show a great variation in network size and resource capacity among households and in the kinds of ties that offer support. Social support was regarded as essential among members of poor households, but mobilized networks were often insufficient for covering even the most basic needs, and prolonged network mobilization could cause strain and long-term conflict. This analysis suggests that support networks may help people to cope with income volatility while simultaneously increasing the potential for social exclusion and isolation.

Keywords: personal networks; social support; poverty; reciprocity; relational work; disposable ties

Past research in poor urban communities has shown that individuals and families struggling to get by rely on the informal support of relatives and close friends (Adler de Lomnitz 1977; Domínguez and Watkins 2003; Edin and Lein 1997; Stack 1974). Detailed ethnographic accounts revealed that money, goods, and

Miranda J. Lubbers is an associate professor in the Department of Social and Cultural Anthropology at the Universitat Autònoma de Barcelona (Autonomous University of Barcelona). Her research interests include social networks, social exclusion, poverty and livelihood strategies, and social cohesion.

Hugo Valenzuela García is an associate professor in the Department of Social and Cultural Anthropology at the Universitat Autònoma de Barcelona. His main field of interest is economic anthropology, and he has recently worked on poverty and livelihood strategies, as well as social networks and exclusion.

Correspondence: mirandajessica.lubbers@uab.es

DOI: 10.1177/0002716220911913

services were frequently exchanged through geographically bounded, dense, and durable kin-based networks, which allowed families to survive economic deprivation (Adler de Lomnitz 1977; Stack 1974). While this literature emphasized the importance of social support for low-income families, González de la Rocha (2007) warned that it had inadvertently created a "myth of survival," depicting the personal networks of the poor as "a cushion against the impact of economic change, and an asset that the poor can always turn to in case of need" (p. 47). Further, in the context of an economic recession, changing family structures, and an erosion of welfare states, she questioned whether the poor still benefited from support networks (cf. Roschelle 1997; see also the introduction to this volume by Lubbers, Valenzuela, and Small) and suggested a change in focus from the "resources of poverty" to the "poverty of resources" (González de la Rocha 2001). In line with her suggestion, various studies have shown the relative isolation and network poverty of low-income individuals (e.g., Menjívar 2000; Offer 2012).

A question that remains open, however, is why some studies show that social networks help individuals to cope with poverty while others observe a radically different reality (see introduction to the volume). To better understand how informal networks function under economic stress, we argue that scholars need to go beyond static descriptions of the association between poverty and received or available support to focus on the network mechanisms[1] underlying this association. Understanding how networks are shaped and how they are mobilized in times of need can help us to explain the varying levels of support obtained by people experiencing poverty.

This article focuses on the role that informal networks play in coping with poverty in a contemporary urban context. It examines the extent to which the

Paula Escribano Castaño is a PhD student in the Department of Social and Cultural Anthropology at the Universitat Autònoma de Barcelona. Her research interests include livelihood strategies in rural areas, neo-peasantry and self-sufficiency, and public policies and environmental values in Western societies.

José Luis Molina is a professor in the Department of Social and Cultural Anthropology at the Universitat Autònoma de Barcelona. Personal networks, migration, and livelihood strategies are among his research interests.

Antònia Casellas is an associate professor in the Geography Department at the Universitat Autònoma de Barcelona. Her research interests include urban governance, impacts and vulnerability of global change, and community economies.

Jorge Grau Rebollo is an associate professor in the Department of Social and Cultural Anthropology at the Universitat Autònoma de Barcelona. His research interests include family and kinship, childrearing, and social vulnerability.

NOTE: We are especially grateful to the study's respondents for their participation and openness. Furthermore, we thank Isabel Ferràndiz, Eduard Sala, Mercedes Vázquez, and Marta Lobato who assisted with the data collection; and Mario Small for his valuable feedback on an earlier draft. The article further benefited from anonymous peer review. The research leading to these results has received funding from RecerCaixa (Award no. 2015ACUP 00145). The contents of this article are the responsibility of the authors and do not necessarily reflect the views of the RecerCaixa program.

personal networks of the poor are supportive and the processes through which support is mobilized. To do this, we first identify, from the extant literature, three mechanisms that govern the constitution and mobilization of networks and discuss how these mechanisms can generate different outcomes of support under economic stress. We also consider that individual agency, in the form of relational work (Zelizer 2005), may counteract these structural and normative mechanisms. This theoretical framework has guided our empirical research with sixty-one households in Barcelona, Spain, that were experiencing economic hardship. By combining semistructured interviewing and structured network delineation, we can simultaneously study mechanisms and outcomes.

Data were collected in Barcelona in 2017, in the aftermath of the economic crisis, when poverty, unemployment, and eviction had skyrocketed in Spain. As a Mediterranean welfare state that considers welfare provision primarily a family responsibility (e.g., Flaquer 2000), Spain has a much more limited social security system than Nordic and conservative European welfare states. Therefore, personal networks are believed to play a vital, protective role (cf. Lumino et al. 2017). The current case is thus particularly interesting for studying social support mobilization among the poor, as it combines high needs and low state provision. The next section presents our theoretical framework. Subsequently, we describe our data, methods, and results, and then conclude with a summary and a discussion of implications.

Social Networks and Support Mobilization in Situations of Poverty

Social support—the "emotional, informational, or practical assistance from significant others, such as family members, friends, or coworkers" (Thoits 2010, S46)—is embedded in an individual's personal network, that is, the set of social relationships surrounding a person (e.g., relatives, friends, colleagues, neighbors; McCarty et al. 2019). From the personal network literature, we have deduced three mechanisms governing the constitution and functioning of personal networks that, when applied to persons experiencing poverty, put into question the level of social support they can obtain.

First, the composition of personal networks is profoundly shaped by *social foci*, that is, entities of different types (e.g., organizations, neighborhoods, individuals) around which joint activities of individuals are organized (Feld 1981). Particularly, participation in routine organizations (e.g., workplaces, schools, churches, sports clubs; Small 2009) creates meeting opportunities for starting and maintaining relationships. Common causes of poverty are associated with withdrawal from foci: losing one's job tends to cut off workplace ties, divorce creates ruptures with in-laws and shared friends, and severe illness reduces social participation more amply (e.g., Wrzus et al. 2013). The lack of resources caused by poverty (e.g., a car, club memberships) may further inhibit participation in leisure activities (e.g., Van Eijk 2010). These processes of exclusion may explain the observation that people in poverty have *smaller networks* (e.g., Böhnke and Link 2017; Marques 2012; Campbell,

Marsden, and Hurlbert 1986) than people with higher incomes. However, studies typically measure network size based on available or activated support; therefore, an alternative explanation for this finding is that a smaller set of network members are activated for support (E. Smith, Menon, and Thompson 2012).

Second, network composition is governed by *homophily*, that is, the tendency of individuals to associate with people who are similar to themselves in attributes such as sex, race, education, and social class (McPherson, Smith-Lovin, and Cook 2001). Homophily is partly induced by social foci, which often attract people with similar attributes, but individuals are also believed to prefer association with people like themselves (Byrne 1971) and to avoid dissimilar people (the latter is called *heterophobia* [Wimmer and Lewis 2010] or *repulsion* from dissimilar others [Skvoretz 2013]). Income homophily can be detected in networks if it is more salient than other forms of homophily or if income is strongly correlated with more salient attributes (e.g., race; Blau 1977). For people experiencing poverty, income homophily limits the material and financial support that their networks can provide (e.g., Harknett and Hartnett 2011).

Third, exchanges in informal networks are regulated by *norms of obligation, reciprocity, autonomy, and equity* (Portugal 2009; Jacobson 1987) that favor the emergence of long-term cooperation by promoting moral values of loyalty and fairness. The precise norms vary with the type of ties, creating tie-specific scripts of expectations, obligations, and types of transactions that are considered appropriate (e.g., Zelizer 2005). In particular, durable kinship ties are universally associated with an internalized sense of *obligation* to help one another (Curry, Mullins, and Whitehouse 2019) and with generalized (i.e., multilateral) and deferred *reciprocity*:

> Mediated between affections and trust, reciprocity between family members often takes place on a "lifetime scale" and transforms help into a sort of "long-term credit" which does not need to be repaid immediately, nor to be symmetrical: the counter-gift can come much later or even be destined for another person. (Portugal 2009, 61)

The more fleeting nonkin relationships, in contrast, are less obliged to help and are based on a narrower norm of balanced (i.e., bilateral), short-term reciprocity (Nelson 2000). In other words, it is less expected that people lend money or give material help to their friends, acquaintances, neighbors, or colleagues in need; but if they do, they expect the favor to be returned to them within a relatively short period of time. Yet among kin, balanced reciprocity also reigns alongside generalized reciprocity (Portugal 2009): about half of the economically distressed individuals who receive support from their families also provide it to them (Hogan, Eggebeen, and Clogg 1993). Even gifts obey this norm of give-and-take, as they usually incur an obligation of a reciprocal gift in reasonable time (Mauss 1923/1990; Sahlins 1972). Thus, despite its positive connotations for network cohesion, the norm of reciprocity becomes an expectation that people in poverty cannot always meet, limiting the mobilization of social support (Komter 1996; Offer 2012). Furthermore, support mobilization is potentially limited by the norm of *autonomy*, which implies that households are supposed to function as independent units. We focus on the norm of *equity*[2] only insofar that special conditions are considered that may form exemptions from these norms, for instance, for lack of money or time (Jacobson 1987; Portugal 2009).

In sum, based on these three mechanisms, we expect that the support networks of people in poverty are smaller and resource scarce and that network norms impede social support mobilization in times of poverty. As others have indicated, informal networks may be able to mitigate economic scarcity and function as "safety nets" at the micro level, but at the macro level, they may amplify social inequality, producing *cumulative disadvantage*: those who most need the support of their networks do not have it (DiMaggio and Garip 2012; Offer 2012).

A full understanding of how networks work requires not only an analysis of network structure and an understanding of meso-level norms, but also of people's agency within that structure, or *relational work* (Zelizer 2005), that is, "the creative effort people make establishing, maintaining, negotiating, transforming and terminating interpersonal relations" (Zelizer 2012, 149). This relational work could counter the assumed negative consequences of the network mechanisms outlined above.

First, people may intentionally create relationships with others they believe can support them (Lin 2001). For example, Desmond (2012) observed that people in chronic poverty often no longer obtained support from their families, and therefore they established new social relationships accelerating the process of developing intimacy. Once formed, these bonds provided all kinds of resources, but they were usually not long-lived (hence his label *disposable ties*). Nevertheless, this strategy, characterized by the rapid creation, development, and discontinuation of the social ties, allowed households in deep poverty to get by on a day-to-day basis.

Second, individuals may employ tactics during support mobilization to improve the likelihood of obtaining help. Wherry, Seefeldt, and Alvarez (2018) found that potential *lenders* engage in *obfuscatory relational work* (cf. Rossman 2014), that is, the performance of face-saving strategies to deny a loan to close relationships, without breaking morality-laden norms of obligation or reciprocity. Strategies included stretching out the time to deliver the loan and offering a different type of help than what was asked in the hope that the help seeker would reconsider. We examine whether help seekers enact similar tactics that improve the likelihood of obtaining support.

Our Research

Data were collected within the framework of a research project about personal networks and poverty.[3]

Sample

The project selected both (1) clients of the organizations that we focused on in our study: two charity organizations, a foundation for labor reinsertion, and an organization for evicted people that was started by others who had themselves been evicted; and (2) respondents not linked to these entities. For the first group, we drew an institutional sample from the organizations; while for the second, we used chains of references. Criteria for case selection included residence in the metropolitan area of Barcelona, 18 years or older, and being income poor. Proxy questions were used to probe qualification for this latter requirement, whereas more detailed questions about the household economy were asked during the structured interview. The diversity of the sample was maximized in terms of gender, age, household composition, nationality, locality, and employment status. Data were collected between January 16 and August 31, 2017.

The sample consists of sixty-one persons, forty women and twenty-one men, with an average age of 46.9 years (SD = 11.6; range 19–80). Most were born in Spain (N = 50). Forty-nine households were located under the Spanish poverty threshold after social transfer,[4] also counting income from undeclared jobs; twelve were located above that level at the time of the interview. The latter happened, for example, when a low-income single mother and her children had moved in with her parents, and the (extended) household was no longer in poverty, or when the financial situation fluctuated from month to month, or when people just came out of a situation of poverty. We included these cases for the narratives, but not in the descriptive statistics. About half of the sample was unemployed (N = 32), twenty were employed, five retired, and four had other employment statuses. Seventeen respondents lived in households formed by a couple with children, fourteen were single, eleven single parents with children, eight lived in three-generation households (usually after returning to the parental house), five in a couple without children, and six in other types of households.

Instruments and procedures

Face-to-face, semistructured and structured interviews were conducted by a team of trained researchers, in Spanish and/or Catalan. Interviews lasted between 1.5 and 4 hours. The semistructured (conversational) part explored life histories; household practices; and the access, roles, and dynamics of formal and informal support, following an interview guide developed and pilot tested in the project. This part was tape recorded with consent from the respondents and fully transcribed. The software used for qualitative data analysis was Atlas.ti. We employed both an a priori coding scheme based on the research questions and open coding to include emerging themes.

For the structured (survey-style) part of the interview, a questionnaire was designed and implemented in the software Egonet (see McCarty et al. 2019), regarding the respondents, their households (e.g., composition, work intensity, income, and housing), and their social networks. For networks, respondents were presented with seventeen freelist "name generators," that is, questions to elicit a list of names of people outside the household (1) with whom respondents felt close and with whom they talked, went out, or had fun (socialization network; two questions); (2) who gave them and to whom they gave emotional, financial, material support; job information; and help with chores in the past year, as well as people who did

FIGURE 1
The Network of Yolanda

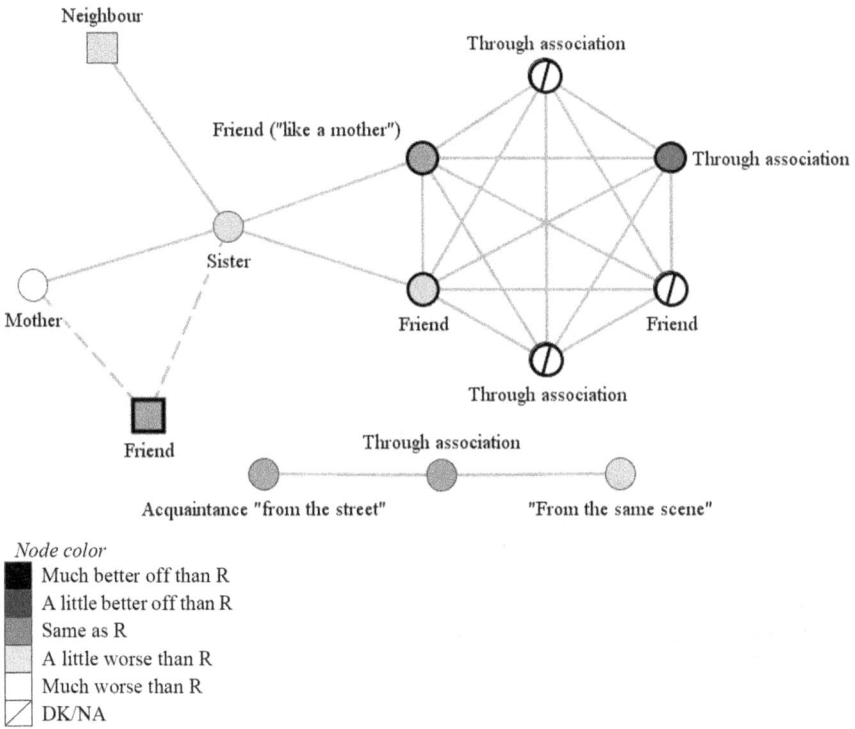

NOTE: Each node represents a network member. Respondents are not visualized because they are by default connected to all network members. Node color indicates the perceived relative economic situation (see key). Squares indicate nodes that have provided material or financial help to the respondent (R), while circles do not provide such help. Nodes with a thicker border are people with whom Yolanda feels close. Network members who are in contact are connected by a solid line; network members who hardly have connect are connected by a hyphenated line. Yolanda's network has thirteen members, and she perceives all but one to be similarly poor or worse off. She receives financial or material support from a friend and a neighbor (squares).

not give them and to whom they did not give requested support (informal support network; fourteen questions, including available financial and emotional support if none was received); and (3) whom they knew via the entity and now felt close to (third sector network; one question). Respondents could nominate as many people as they saw fit, and the same person could be nominated on multiple questions. Once a list of names was elicited, we asked about the attributes of each nominee, for example, the type of relationship (seventeen categories), emotional closeness, and perceived relative financial situation ("Would you say that the financial situation of [nominee's name] is much better, a little better, more or less the same, a

FIGURE 2
The Network of Asunción

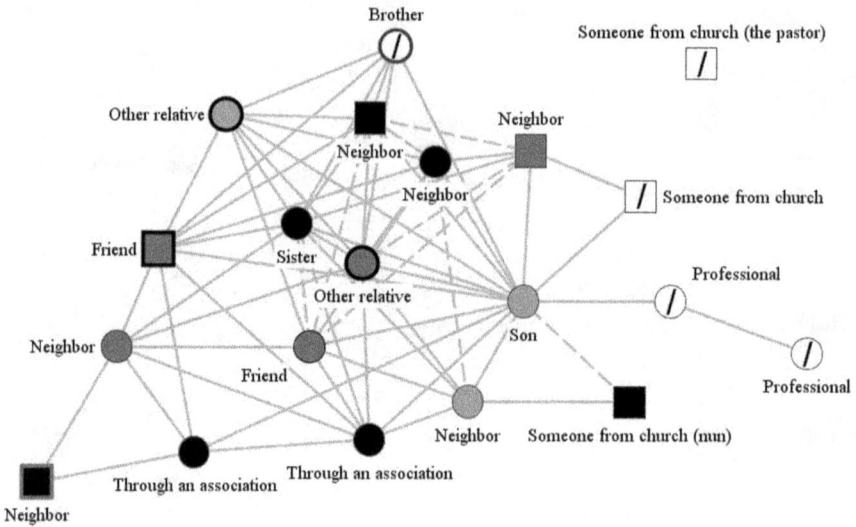

NOTE: See Figure 1 for key explanation. Asunción has a larger network (twenty members) than Yolanda, and she thinks most network members are better off (darkest nodes). The financial and material support she receives comes from neighbors, a friend, and churches where she begs for help.

little worse, or much worse than your own situation?"). Last, we asked respondents whether nominees had contact with one another, to visualize network structure. Figures 1 and 2 illustrate two such networks elicited with this method, using the software Visone (Brandes and Wagner 2004). The aggregated set of network data was first quantitatively analyzed, to generate descriptive statistics. For each case, the network visualization was also added to the transcription of the semistructured interview of the same respondent for the qualitative analysis (see above), following a triangulation approach (e.g., Creswell and Plano Clark 2007). On one hand, this mixed-methods approach allowed us to validate data about, for example, the support capacity of the networks or the presence of kin support. On the other hand, it allowed us to obtain a deeper understanding of networks by contrasting their structure (quantitative interview) with respondents' narratives about their meaning and mechanisms (qualitative interview).

Results

Economic circumstances and household practices

In the households of our sample set, poverty spells started for many reasons, chief among them unemployment, divorce, and chronic illness. Problems

TABLE 1
Descriptive Statistics of Network Size

Subnetwork	Mean Size	SD	Range (min.–max.)	Correlation with Position under Poverty Threshold[a]
Total network	14.5	5.9	3–34	0.35°
Proximity network	8.3	5.6	0–30	0.38°°
Support network	7.1	3.7	2–21	0.31°
Counseling	4.7	3.5	0–20	0.29
Practical support	5.0	3.8	0–19	0.28
Entity network	2.5	3.5	0–15	−0.11
Asked but not given	0.9	1.8	0–11	−0.09

Percentage of Sample Whose Support Is. . .[b]	Proximity (Companionship)			Counseling			Practical		
	Our Study	Toulouse[a]	NCCS	Our Study	Toulouse	NCCS	Our Study	Toulouse	NCCS
Inadequate	6	3	0	2	15	9	14	6	5
Marginal	16	11	1	8	20	10	31	19	15
Adequate	78	86	99	90	65	81	55	75	80

NOTE: The are forty-nine cases. Network size is the number of unique names elicited on sets of network questionnaire items, for the total network and for subnetworks. As people may have been nominated more than once, the subnetworks add up to more than the total. Statistics for the other studies with general populations using multiple name generators for support and companionship are given in Grossetti (2007): The Northern California Study of Fischer (1977) and the Toulouse study of Grossetti (2007).
a. For Pearson correlations, ° $p < .05$; °° $p < .01$.
b. Following Fischer and Grossetti, 0 or 1 network members is coded inadequate, 2 or 3 marginal, and 4+ adequate for proximity and practical support. For counseling, 0 is considered inadequate, 1 marginal, 2+ adequate.

accumulated in a snowball fashion: poverty led to depression and anxiety and increased the chances of eviction and divorce. As one respondent, Lourdes, said, "When money doesn't enter, love disappears through the window."

All households had already depleted whatever financial assets they once had, and a delay in welfare checks or an emergency could therefore cause serious problems. They had already sold things they did not need, including in three cases highly sentimental items such as wedding rings (while married) and first communion bracelets. Many visited charity organizations and civil associations to obtain material help, housing assistance, legal advice regarding pending evictions, and help with labor reinsertion. Other practices that households employed to make ends meet were stretching limited resources (buying minimally and secondhand, relying commonly on cheap foods such as legumes and pasta), not wasting any food (not even the tomato peels left after making gazpacho, as one respondent, Marisol, explained), not having household appliances such as washing machines repaired when they were broken unless a friend or relative could repair it, salvaging materials thrown away by others or gathering scrap metal, not attending social events, and subletting a room.

Often, respondents were deprived of even the most basic needs (food, shelter, heat, healthcare): having electricity or gas cut off; skipping meals to prioritize children and partners to the extent that eating caused feelings of guilt; and failing to pay mortgages, ultimately causing eviction (one respondent was living temporarily in a car). Moreover, some indebted themselves, even to buy food. Several respondents also resorted to illegal practices such as squatting; connecting illegally to water, electricity, or the Internet; evading metro fares, or taking up undeclared jobs (often small), all of which still proved insufficient to make ends meet and increased anxiety due to the risk of being caught. As this list shows, "careful household management" was completely insufficient to address needs. Let us therefore turn to the role of social networks.

Social foci and network size

The respondents elicited on average fifteen network members (see Table 1). If we exclude formal ties, such as social workers, the average is slightly lower ($M = 14.2$, $SD = 6.2$). Average network size is roughly similar to that observed in large samples of general populations that also used multiple name generator designs (cf. Fischer 1982; Grossetti 2007).[5]

Respondents felt close to or socialized with on average eight persons; exchanged support with seven; and had met three people at the entities they attended, with whom they now felt close. The support network and the socialization network only partially overlapped, which implies that not every person in the personal network is mobilized for support and that measures of network size based only on supportive ties would generate smaller networks. To improve comparison with the aforementioned studies of general populations, with different question wording and research contexts, we coded three types of network support as inadequate, marginal, or adequate following Fischer's (1982) coding scheme (see Table 1). Companionship and practical support (material, financial, and chores) in our sample were relatively more often marginal or inadequate than in general populations; whereas counseling (emotional support and job information) was more widespread among our respondents, perhaps due to the higher need for emotional support. Nevertheless, the majority of our respondents had adequate support according to these numerical criteria.

That being said, total network size varied considerably among respondents, with a minimum of three and a maximum of thirty-four network members. Moreover, poorer people in this restricted range tended to have smaller networks (see Table 1).

Many respondents recognized that they had lost contacts along the way. Problems that caused poverty spells cut them off from social foci:

I have also noticed that friendships, when I had my divorce, have put me aside. (Esther)

When you have a problem that you have a son with . . . with [drug use], people stay away. (Asunción; see Figure 2)

Moreover, economic resources, and sometimes depression, limited access to leisure activities.

> I don't do anything. I really liked to go and see *zarzuelas* [a Spanish genre of musical
> theater], for which they also charged 6 euros for the entrance, but I didn't go there
> anymore. Because to me those 6 [euros], plus 6, plus 6, well . . . I need them. Everything
> that I could stop doing, I have stopped doing. (Carmen)

Yet respondents also frequented new social environments, where they would
meet new people. Children were for example transferred from a private to a
public school, or from FC Barcelona to a less expensive, local soccer club.
Respondents also met people at the entities they attended for help (see Table
1). Probably because it had been started by others who had experienced eviction
and because of its reliance on the creation of horizontal ties, the association for
evicted people was particularly successful in creating ties among its members
compared to charity organizations (cf. Mazelis 2017). Members of this association had met on average 7.2 people at this organization whom they now felt relatively close to, compared to 2.9 for people who went to charity organizations. In
sum, some people disconnected from social foci, while others continued to
participate in organizations, or changed their participation in one organization
for another.

Income homophily and support capacity

As the previous section illustrated, some people stopped participating in
organizations that attracted people with a wider range of incomes and started to
frequent other organizations that had a more restricted income heterogeneity.
Additionally, a widening income gap between people led to loss of contact.
Respondents frequently felt that family, friends, and acquaintances avoided them
since their economic problems had started, or "fled" from them, as if they
brought "bad luck," even if they had never asked them for help. Many respondents alluded to this tendency:

> When you don't have a job and you don't have money, friends are a hello and goodbye
> and that's it. (Felipe)

> When I had money, they [relatives] sucked up to me a lot, and now that I don't have
> money . . . it's as if I don't exist. (Verónica)

In some cases, this may be *heterophobia* or *repulsion* of dissimilar people; for
others, friends or acquaintances may have distanced themselves to avoid being
asked for help in the future. Respondents too avoided more prosperous friends
who showed a lack of understanding for their situations. Miquel, for example,
resented his "spoiled" friends who were better off than him and dissociated himself from them.

A loss of contact due to widening income gaps, withdrawal from organizations
where more affluent individuals met, and other processes (e.g., intergenerational

TABLE 2
Perceived Homogeneity of Social Relationships

| Subnetwork | Percentage of Network Members Who Were Perceived to Be Financially. . . | | | | | |
	Much Worse Off	Worse Off	Same	Better Off	Much Better Off	M (SD)
Total network	4	7	15	42	32	3.9 (1.1)
Proximity network	5	5	11	44	36	4.0 (1.0)
Support network	3	5	13	41	37	4.1 (1.1)
Counseling	3	6	14	39	38	4.0 (1.1)
Practical support	3	3	14	39	41	4.1 (0.9)
Entity network	1	12	31	43	14	3.6 (0.9)

transmission of poverty) seem to restrict the economic heterogeneity of networks and, thus, their support capacity. Even so, respondents perceived that three-quarters of the elicited network members were a little or much better off than them (see Table 2), suggesting a certain support capacity, although "better off" does not necessarily mean "well off."

Again, interindividual variation was considerable: three respondents had zero network members whom they believed to be better off, while thirteen reported fifteen or more. Indeed, many respondents referred to the low support capacity of their networks:

> My whole environment is more or less like me. I only have one friend, who . . . has quite a lot, we grew up together, and he has quite a lot of money. (Ramón)

> Even if I ask them [friends], they will not be able to help me. Economically? They will not be able to help me. . . . My future is fucked up, but there are relatives and friends who are much more screwed than I am. (Yolanda; see Figure 1)

However, others perceived a higher support capacity:

> They all have jobs, they're well positioned, at least in my family. (Felipe)

> My social environment was not poor to say it in some way, it was medium-high, and I'd never have thought that this would happen. (Francesca)

Those with larger networks or a higher support capacity were aware of their benefits and maintained them with care:

> We've created a network of affected people, in which we've helped one another in any way. Eh . . . they've been evicted, they've gone into social housing and they have no furniture because the apartment is empty. With WhatsApp I have almost 800 high-level and low-level contacts. I need a bed of 1.35 [meters], it doesn't matter, secondhand. . . (Francesca)

They didn't think that I would go so far with the lawsuit and the papers. . . . Because they don't imagine what friendships I have, which I still have! Because I don't lose friendships. If not, how would I go to the General Prosecutor of Catalonia . . . how would I go? And without a lawyer, I alone. (Diego, a former entrepreneur)

The number of network members believed to be at least better off correlated, $r = .40$ ($p < .01$), as did the number believed to be much better off, $r = .50$ ($p < .01$), with household income (in terms of percentage of the median national income; see note 3). Thus, respondents with lower incomes had a lower support capacity. Whether support capacity translates into support depends among other factors on norms.

Norms regulating exchanges

Kin obligation. We now explore whether norms regulating exchanges in social networks hindered support mobilization among our respondents. Family was expected to be the first resort, unless the economic situation of family members was equal to or worse than respondents' own situation, or they had no contact:

How embarrassing, when you have parents, [and you have] to borrow money from a friend. (Ruth)

For many, the help of kin, particularly parents, siblings, in-laws, and adult off-spring was essential: these relatives provided them with shelter for short or long periods of time; structural, financial, and material help (e.g., giving them the car they don't use anymore, paying their phone costs or their child's school fees, offering a job in their enterprise); and food, and helped with bills and mobilized their contacts to obtain secondhand goods. Respondents described their help as "primordial" and "fundamental," and said, "I would have died without their help."

In many cases, however, family was unsupportive, even if they were economically able to help. Francesca, for example, was well off before she and her husband lost their jobs and, later, their house. She explained that her middle-/high-class family never helped them, for reasons she believed were pride or egoism.

Francesca: If my brother had lent me a little money, which he knew I would return when I'd find work, it would have saved me from ruining myself completely.
Interviewer: He never lent you any money?
Francesca: Never . . . never . . . ever.
Interviewer: Did you ask?
Francesca: Yes.

Furthermore, long-term help, particularly taking kin in, started with the best intentions but often ended in exhaustion and conflict due to violations of the norms of reciprocity, equity, and autonomy. This was a general problem among participants.

TABLE 3

Reciprocity of Received Support, Kin Support, and Homophily of Supportive Ties

	Received Support										Provided Support	
	Kin			Nonkin								
	% of Supportive Ties That Were Reciprocated with Support...			% of Supportive Ties That Were Reciprocated with Support...								
Type of Support	In Kind	Of Any Type	N Ties	In Kind	Of Any Type	N Ties	Total N Alters Ego to Receive Help	% of Total Supportive Ties That Are Kin	% of Total Supportive Ties That Are Perceived to Be Better Off		Total N Alters Ego to Give Help	% of Total Supported Ties That Are Perceived to Be Better Off
Emotional	33	50	58	49	56	117	175	33	76		169	69
Job information	0	71	7	6	59	49	36	12	73		30	40
Financial	10	53	30	3	62	29	75	51	88		37	51
Material	1	51	37	22	51	81	118	31	79		75	52
Chores	39	48	31	40	67	48	79	39	70		96	70

> And, well, when money does not enter the house, the problems begin, and a moment arrives when. . . . When you go to the fridge and grab a piece of bread it bothers them, when you take a shower it bothers them, and then it's a very toxic circle and . . . I was a year with them, and they threw me out. They threw me out. (Paco)

> Worse times . . . when my brothers threw me out of the house, when my mother died. . . . Yes, I lived in the house with my mother, in Barcelona, my mother got ill, I was the villain . . . and . . . they threw me out of the house. (Júlia)

Thus, while kin had important support functions of loyalty and care, chronic poverty gradually depleted these resources (cf. Desmond 2012) and jeopardized relationships.

Financial support from nonkin was normatively less expected. Ramón, talking about his childhood friend who had a much better job than he did despite having studied less, contemplated:

> But of course, it's your friend, it's not your . . . it's not your family. . . . You can't stretch that relationship that much.

Other respondents made similar comments:

> Mixing for example friends and money is not recommended. (Ruth)

> It's that friendships have no obligation. Neither do family members have an obligation, huh? (Celia)

In many situations, however, nonkin were also called upon. Table 3 shows that most people who provided support, including financial and material help, were nonkin, although the volume or frequency of help varied. Most of them were friends, with whom respondents exchanged secondhand clothes or furniture, food, help with repairing things, or child care. Some friends also lent them large sums of money or invited them to live in their houses. Celia's friend, for example, took her in for a low rent (€200 a month) and found her a job, whereas another friend paid for the repair of her car. Her family, in contrast, had never helped her.

To a lesser extent, neighbors, colleagues, church members, professionals, and other acquaintances played important roles in the day-to-day survival of the poor.

> In these six years, I've found people who worked in the town hall. People who've been affected [by the crisis] but who solved their case, and I haven't yet. And they've found work, and we went for a coffee and they said, "Here, 100 euros [Fran]," and they've helped me. . . . Clothes for me, shoes, my husband dressed in Levi's, secondhand, but Levi's. People who, look, who knew my daughter had to go on a school trip, which costed 180 euros, and they gave it to me. "[Fran], you'll give it back when you can." "[Fran], when you can, it means when you both work." (Francesca)

While some of these acquaintances were better off, others were in similar situations.

> The people who really helped me with some money at times when I needed it, well you're not going to believe it, but they were companions of the shelter. (Ruth)

Small gestures of help were not only instrumental, but also meaningful as an act of kindness. Carmen, an elderly widow and retired seamstress, buys cheese at a small grocery store in her neighborhood. The vendor often pretended that his prices were lower than others, although she was well aware that he did not charge her the full price. Other times, he whispered, "Take it" when she reached for her wallet, adding that she could pay him when she received her paycheck. With a smile, he added, "But don't push it, huh?" shaking off the awkwardness of the moment. Similar stories were told by others. Three months after Sara took up a new job in a hospital, her new colleagues had collected money to give her food. The school where Francesca's children went waived their tuition fees without saying anything. Thus, so-called weak ties complemented help that was expected to come primarily from kin.

Autonomy

The norm of autonomy ensures respect for the independence of the household unit and provides a counterbalance to that of obligation. Kin would feel obliged toward young people who transition to adulthood and toward the elderly, but other adults in the family were expected to be autonomous, even in parent-child relationships. This norm of autonomy was used by parents to justify the denial of support to adult children:

> My mother is retired. . . . My mother, instead of going to live in [another town], between us we could have rented a bigger apartment, and between the two of us we could pay for it. . . . But she has decided that she has already raised her children and that she isn't going to raise her grandchildren or anything. Since we left home, she half ignored it, you know? You're married and you're gone, it's your problem. (Marisol)

> If I have no money, she [mother] is the first one to [say] . . . "then don't go out" or "you should save more." Well . . . I think . . . I think she could have given me something to eat and not let me go to the community kitchen. . . . Come on, I have my son and I won't let him go to a community kitchen while I have money. (Cristian)

> I've asked my parents and they didn't give me because, sure, you're an adult, and well, and you must find out what life is about. (Ruth)

Sometimes, exemptions were made in the case of illness or the care of young children.

Conversely, if relatives helped on a sustained, nonreciprocal basis, they gained the right to interfere in the household's autonomy (cf. Portugal 2009). For example, Marisol's brother, a factory worker, helped her frequently, but he also questioned every decision she made.

> My brother . . . is also always harping on me and he brings me down. . . . I understand, what he must think, maybe my situation won't change. Truly with four children, little can change it. Then they start about the past. Why did you need to have that many children, why? They clearly don't realize that they're already there, that I can't do anything, I can't drown them. Then, when they light that little fire, yes, they go on and on about it.

Because kin are supposed to feel obliged, rejection by kin was particularly painful, to the extent that some people preferred not to ask for support. Tamara, a divorced mother of two, contemplated:

> But why was I so afraid that [mother] would tell me no [if asking for money]? Because I would have felt like an orphan. . . . So much so, I didn't take the risk.

Respondents, then, prioritized the continuation of kinship ties over possible assistance and maintained their autonomy. This is comparable to Smith's finding that unemployed African Americans were reluctant to mobilize their networks for support out of fear of rejection, a concept she named *defensive individualism* (S. Smith 2007; cf. Hansen 2004). In these cases, respondents tended to inform their relatives casually about their situation in the hope that they would offer help spontaneously. Sometimes they did, but often they did not.

Reciprocity

The norm of reciprocity was omnipresent in the narratives of the respondents. Calling on kin was by no means only associated with deferred, generalized reciprocity. Counterexpectations (monetary or not) were often in place. Felipe and his wife returned to live at his parents' home for over a year, and his father claimed rent:

> Even my father has come to complain why I didn't pay rent. [Simulating his response to his father:] "But don't you know my situation, ditched as I am? But you've let me come here and now you're going to claim me [rent], I'm working for you, I'm helping you, I'm cutting wood, so you have firewood for the whole winter . . . and this and that." That's why when that [conflict] happened with my brother and he told me to leave well I didn't think twice. (Felipe)

Moreover, although reciprocity with kin was sometimes generalized (e.g., Inés cared for her ill sister, and their elderly parents helped Inés financially), reciprocity with kin was mostly balanced. This is clearly different from Stack's (1974) and other early work, where reciprocity with kin was generalized and enforced on a community basis.

Another difference between our findings and Stack's (1974) work is the help that our participants received from nonkin. With them, reciprocity was typically balanced and short term. Respondents reciprocated material help to nonkin in both monetary and nonmonetary ways:

> Well, in addition, I do what I can: if I have to take care of some child, I do, you know? Oftentimes I bring many children here. . . . Of course, this rewards people. (Patricia)

> One day a friend for example needs that I take care of her child and another day she dyes my hair, if I'm cut off the light or whatever [someone] pays the bill and later on I compensate in another way. (Rosa)

Even Carmen gave back to the vendor of the grocery store, when he asked her to repair some clothes for him. She did it for free, although she charged others for it to make some money. "Love is paid with love," she said, "He does something for you, after that you can't be rude." By finding ways to reciprocate, supportive interactions could continue.

Financial help of nonkin was often in the form of a loan rather than a gift, regardless of how it was presented. It was tremendously helpful for managing income volatility (delayed pay checks, emergencies), but not a structural solution.

> What happens? That these people who've been helping me, one gave me 500, 400, 600, to the people who gave this money I told them, "Look, I don't guarantee you when I am going to return it, but I'm going to return it, I'll pay you back! But I don't know when." And it's no problem, but when I started working, the first payroll in February 2016 I started to give: 20, 20, 20, 20. My husband [said,] "For fuck's sake!" Noooo, they've helped us, I can't pay 100 to everyone, nor 50, but 20, 20, 20 . . . I have to start settling [debts]. (Francesca)

Table 3 confirms that most types of support were bilaterally reciprocated, in kind or (more frequently) with any type of support, while the tendency to reciprocate was approximately similar for kin and for nonkin.

Relational work

We expected that individuals would employ relational work to stimulate support mobilization. First, we explored whether respondents consciously created or "thickened" relationships to obtain support. Some romantic ties had an instrumental dimension. Livia, a single mother of four, most clearly verbalized this when talking about her childhood friend Sofía, who had reappeared in her life. Sofía was a successful businesswoman who had always had a crush on her. Although Livia did not identify as lesbian, she was "open to what might come," as Sofía could support her. She thought, "If she helps me and I can give her at some point the satisfaction of being with her and trying it out . . . no? I tried it out." Sofía gave Livia "unconditional help": a job, a home, a car. The relationship was highly conflicted but went on for years.

Instrumentalization was also mentioned by Sara, whose neighbor was as short on cash as Sara and her partner were. Deciding it was cheaper to combine their resources, they regularly cooked and dined together. However, when her neighbor's situation improved, she started to avoid Sara and her partner.

> Then you realize that really, when people don't have anything, they're friendly, they're nice, everything you want, but when they start to have [money] again, they become what they really were before. (Sara)

However, such mentions were rare and unlike Desmond's concept of disposable ties, none were characterized "by a short duration but high levels of propinquity and by low levels of trust but high levels of resource exchange" (Desmond

2012, 1329): Livia's relationship was long-lasting, and Sara and her neighbor only shared food on an equity basis. Only 11 of the 712 unique relationships (1.5 percent) had features of disposable ties: they were formed maximally two years ago, respondents felt close or very close to these people, they exchanged at least material or financial help, and ties were personal (e.g., not social workers). Yet even these eleven ties may be durable or exchange low volumes of help. Thus, most weak ties were not thickened for the purpose of support.

Second, respondents employed certain tactics during support mobilization to improve the likelihood of support. *Obfuscatory relational work* was primarily enacted by help providers, rather than by help seekers, at least in the narratives of the latter. Help providers obfuscated to avoid certain help requests (following nonreciprocation, or low-priority requests, such as lending money to pay the fees for an entrepreneurship course), by feigning not to have it, postponing help indefinitely, or by offering a different type of help than requested (cf. Wherry, Seefeldt, and Alvarez 2018). In contrast, help seekers mostly masked their economic conditions when trust was thin, to avoid stigmatization. Even small requests were carefully staged. For instance, Asunción did not have the money for detergent, and went in her nightdress to a neighbor:

> Well, I was going with . . . for not telling her that directly . . . a small [empty] jar of beans, of those made of glass, for cooked beans. A little jar, not too big, so she doesn't say that I come with a huge vessel. [Laughs about her strategy. Simulates the conversation:] "Oh, see if you've got a little bleach now girl, I just finished it, and at this moment, look you caught me in this robe, and to go shopping, well no. . . ." Well, she gave me a stingy dash [of detergent].

Rather than obfuscatory relational work, help seekers mostly enacted *elucidating relational work*, to signal their deservingness of help and justify their help request, considering the severity of the problem, their own efforts to deal with it, and their past contributions to others. First, they explained their genuine needs to others who they thought might be able to help. This could be challenging, as they perceived people with higher incomes to show little understanding, or even disbelief:

> He [brother] doesn't understand. He's never been in the situation himself, God forbid. (Marisol)

> In general, the people who could help you economically are people who don't understand your situation, or they don't agree with what you're doing or, sure, they hold the administration responsible and I can't blame them. (Ruth)

Some used dramaturgical tactics to stress their needs, like Diego, who sent his son to a debtor.

> It was because I sent my son, the youngest, and I said, let's see if [debtor] feels sorry and he gives us a thousand euros from what he owes us. And ooooh, when my son came back . . . he says, "Papa, I won't go there again." I said, "What did he say?" "That he'll give me money to go out, but that I shouldn't pay you anything." And that was the start of a fierce argument.

Respondents also stressed their own efforts to deal with the situation, to demonstrate that they did everything they could to avoid asking for help. Ramón, for example, had helped others, like his brothers-in-law, when they were poor. "But of course," he said,

"if they ask all the time, and you see that they don't . . . they don't do their best, they don't work. . . . But sure, if you see that it's a person who's doing his best, seeking, working, and the man doesn't make it, and he asks you [for help], well, I say give it to him, right? If you have it, of course. [But] [i]f you see it's a person who doesn't move things. . . .

He then turned to himself.

In my case that's not the case, because I don't stop. If I'm not doing one thing, I'm doing another. So, sure, if you ask people, they respond. They know you'll return it.

Furthermore, respondents frequently alluded to the past support provided to others, appealing for generalized delayed reciprocity. For example,

I don't like to say it in someone's face, but even so, you have conversations, [that] when I worked, I was the ATM of many people. (Rosa)

I'm helping a lot, I've helped their children a lot and with many things, but it seems they don't pay me in the same currency. (Celia)

In fact, the people who've helped me the most were the people who know what I've done for others. (Francesca)

Last, respondents brought up their trustworthiness as debtors, which benefited their moral self-representation and secured future help.

It's also true that I pay. It's also true that I return it. Even if the next month, well look . . . eat lentils, every day. (Dolores)

I'm a very good payer. . . . They'll never say "Alas, this woman." (Carmen)

For Carmen, the key to having a strong economic support network was knowing how to ask and returning favors and debts.

Conclusion

Previous academic literature has observed that people who struggle with poverty rely on dense support networks of family and close friends. Mediterranean welfare states, established in or before the 1970s, are also based on the premise of family solidarity. However, times have changed. The economic crisis, changing family structures, higher geographic mobility, and increasing individualism call into question the emergence of the lifelong, kin-based, geographically bounded, densely knit support networks reported in the past. Our in-depth investigation in urban households in poverty in Spain aims to reveal contemporary processes of social support mobilization and the limitations of support networks. We expected that people experiencing poverty would have smaller and resource-scarce support networks, which are regulated by norms that impede structural support mobilization in times of poverty. We also expected that respondents would enact relational work to improve support mobilization.

The results confirm earlier reported findings that family and friends give essential help in poverty, particularly for emergencies or short periods of time, but we also show that stopping the characterization there renders a portrait of network support that is far from complete. First, even with social support, many households hardly got by, as observed by their deprivation of even the most basic needs and their reliance on charity organizations and illegal practices for survival.

Second, by examining support mechanisms, we found that support mobilization transformed the network itself. Specifically, the norm of kin obligation raised expectations that put family relationships under pressure. On one hand, if family failed to give support to a member in need, by, for example, appealing to the norm of autonomy, this failure was experienced as a painful rejection, a lack of love, and damaged family ties. On the other, sustained family support often led to exhaustion and conflict, due to violations of the norms of reciprocity and autonomy. Thus, in chronic poverty, family social capital is gradually depleted (cf. Desmond 2012). Perhaps even more alarming than insufficient support is the observation that in the snowball of problems that quickly accumulate in poverty spells, families' rejection and long-lasting conflicts become additional sources of exclusion in an already highly fluid world formed by uncertain jobs, housing situations, economies, and marital ties. Particularly, considering the mental health problems that most respondents experienced (depression and anxiety), being cut off from or rejected by one's closest ties puts people even further at risk of poverty and at a further distance from solving their problems.

In this sense, having a well-to-do family was a double-edged sword. Its support could quickly get people back on their feet, avoiding further entrapment in poverty. However, affluent families could also display a lack of understanding for the situation, or even disbelief, and often turned a deaf ear to help requests. In contrast, low-income families tended to be more understanding and, simultaneously, exempted from help requests.

In contrast to earlier research, friends and even mere acquaintances also gave important help, either complementing family support or in its absence. While smaller material exchanges (e.g., children's clothes) among friends and acquaintances were frequent, larger sums of money and types of help were also exchanged. Maybe because ties were weaker, support of this kind was mostly bilateral and less subject to community sanctions. As nonkin are normatively not expected to help, such ties suffered less if they failed to provide support. However, even in the absence of support, nonkin relationships could deteriorate if the income gap increased. Furthermore, financial help needs to be paid back, even when no clear date is set for return, or return is not explicitly required. Thus, lending from friends and acquaintances helped to smooth household economies but was not a structural solution.

Notably, both the size and support capacity of networks were highly diverse in our sample. In contrast to an earlier classification into strong kin networks, disposable ties, and isolation (Desmond 2012, 1330), family support was not necessarily deeply embedded in networks, and acquaintances gave important help without the relationship eventually being disposed. Future research must investigate whether the greater complexity of support networks is replicated in other cultural settings and how it is related to income levels and other variables.

This study took place in Spain, which has the third highest unemployment rate in the OECD (OECD 2019a) and a Mediterranean welfare state system, which assumes that the family is the primary welfare provider. As our results show, this assumption is not only outdated and unsustainable, it damages individuals' most important social relationships, putting them at even higher risk of exclusion. Better national policies must be developed to protect people against poverty traps and mental health decline. Institutions for poverty alleviation could pay more attention to family relationships and optimize their institutional role as brokers in the formation of social capital (cf. Small and Gose, this volume). As our research and that of Mazelis (2017) show, grassroots associations that employ horizontal models of organization stimulate the creation of ties and empower people. Perhaps vertically organized institutions could learn lessons from these organizations and adopt practices that empower relational autonomy.

Notes

1. A mechanism is "a precise, abstract, and action-based explanation which shows how the occurring of triggering events regularly generates the type of outcome to be explained" (Hedström and Bearman 2009, 6). In this case, we explore how the networks of people in poverty generate a certain level of social support, by identifying the underlying micro-foundations (in this case, network mechanisms).

2. According to Portugal (2009), equity refers to individuals seeking parity in their relationships to people who occupy similar roles (e.g., giving birthday gifts of similar value to one's children) and differs from equality by granting justified exemptions from this rule. Our analysis does not provide sufficient information to study this.

3. "Survival Strategies in Poor Households: The Role of Formal and Informal Support Networks in Times of Economic Crisis" (2016–2020), funded by RecerCaixa (2015ACUP 00145). Principal Investigators: Miranda Lubbers and Hugo Valenzuela. All procedures contributing to this work comply with the ethical standards of the Helsinki Declaration of 1975, as revised in 2008. Ethical approval for data collection was obtained from the university's Institutional Review Board (ID 3327), the Ethics Committee on Animal and Human Experimentation (CEEAH) of the Universitat Autònoma de Barcelona. Data were anonymized and names replaced by pseudonyms.

4. The poverty threshold is determined at 60 percent of the median annual income per consumption unit (modified OECD scale) of the Spanish population. The income per consumption unit is obtained by dividing the total household income by the number of consumption units. The first adult in a household counts as 1 consumption unit; other adults or children over 14 count as 0.5 each, and minors under the age of 14 count as 0.3 each. The Spanish poverty threshold was 710 euros per consumption unit per month in 2017, corresponding to on average 800 U.S. dollars in the data collection year, 2017 (OECD 2019b).

5. Average network size is 12.4 (Fischer 1982) and 14.6 (Grossetti 2007), respectively.

References

Adler de Lomnitz, Larissa. 1977. *Networks and marginality: life in a Mexican shantytown*. New York, NY: Academic Press Inc.

Blau, Peter M. 1977. A macrosociological theory of social structure. *American Journal of Sociology* 83 (1): 26–54.

Böhnke, Petra, and Sebastian Link. 2017. Poverty and the dynamics of social networks: An analysis of German panel data. *European Sociological Review* 33 (4): 615–32.

Brandes, Ulrik, and Dorothea Wagner. 2004. Analysis and visualization of social networks. In *Graph drawing software*, eds. Michael Jünger and Petra Mutzel, 321⊠40. Berlin: Springer.

Byrne, Donn E. 1971. *The attraction paradigm*. New York, NY: Academic Press.

Campbell, Karen E., Peter V. Marsden, and Jeanne S. Hurlbert. 1986. Social resources and socioeconomic status. *Social Networks* 8 (1): 97–117.

Cresswell, John W., and Vicki L. Plano Clark. 2007. *Designing and conducting mixed methods research*. Thousand Oaks, CA: Sage Publications.

Curry, Oliver Scott, Daniel Austin Mullins, and Harvey Whitehouse. 2019. Is it good to cooperate? Testing the theory of morality-as-cooperation in 60 societies. *Current Anthropology* 60 (1): 47–69.

Desmond, Matthew. 2012. Disposable ties and the urban poor. *American Journal of Sociology* 117 (5): 1295–1335.

DiMaggio, Paul, and Filiz Garip. 2012. Network effects and social inequality. *Annual Review of Sociology* 38 (1): 93–118.

Domínguez, Silvia, and Celeste Watkins. 2003. Creating networks for survival and mobility: Social capital among African-American and Latin-American low-income mothers. *Social Problems* 50 (1): 111–35.

Edin, Kathryn, and Laura Lein. 1997. *Making ends meet: How single mothers survive welfare and low-wage work*. New York, NY: Russell Sage Foundation.

Feld, Scott L. 1981. The focused organization of social ties. *American Journal of Sociology* 86 (5): 1015–35.

Fischer, Claude S. 1982. *To dwell among friends: Personal networks in town and city*. Chicago, IL: University of Chicago Press.

Flaquer, Lluís. 2000. Family policy and welfare state in southern Europe. Working Paper 185, Institut de Ciències Polítiques i Socials, Barcelona. Available from https://www.icps.cat/archivos/WorkingPapers/WP_I_185.pdf?noga=1.

González de la Rocha, Mercedes. 2001. From the resources of poverty to the poverty of resources? *Latin American Perspectives* 28 (4): 72–100.

González de la Rocha, Mercedes. 2007. The construction of the myth of survival. *Development and Change* 38 (1): 45–66.

Grossetti, Michel. 2007. Are French networks different? *Social Networks* 29 (3): 391–404.

Hansen, Karen V. 2004. The asking rules of reciprocity in networks of care for children. *Qualitative Sociology* 27 (4): 421–37.

Harknett, Kristen S., and Carolina Sten Hartnett. 2011. Who lacks support and why? An examination of mothers' personal safety nets. *Journal of Marriage and Family* 73 (4): 861–75.

Hedström, Peter, and Peter Bearman. 2009. What is analytical sociology all about? An introductory essay. In *The Oxford handbook of analytical sociology*, eds. Peter Hedström, and Peter Bearman, 3–24. Oxford: Oxford University Press.

Hogan, Dennis P., David J. Eggebeen, and Clifford C. Clogg. 1993. The structure of intergenerational exchanges in American families. *American Journal of Sociology* 98 (6): 1428–58.

Jacobson, David. 1987. The cultural context of social support and support networks. *Medical Anthropology Quarterly* 1 (1): 42–67.

Komter, Aafke E. 1996. Reciprocity as a principle of exclusion: Gift giving in the Netherlands. *Sociology* 30 (2): 299–316. Available from https://doi.org/10.2307/42855683.

Lin, Nan. 2001. *Social capital: A theory of social structure and action*. Cambridge: Cambridge University Press.

Lubbers, Miranda J., Mario Luis Small, and Hugo Valenzuela García. 2020. Do networks help people manage poverty? Perspectives from the field. *The ANNALS of the American Academy of Political and Social Science* (this volume).

Lumino, Rosaria, Giancarlo Ragozini, Marijtje van Duijn, and Maria Prosperina Vitale. 2017. A mixed-methods approach for analysing social support and social anchorage of single mothers' personal networks. *Quality and Quantity* 51 (2): 779–97.

Marques, Eduardo Cesar. 2012. *Opportunities and deprivation in the urban south: Poverty, segregation and social networks in São Paulo*. Farnham: Ashgate Publishing.

Mauss, Marcel. 1923/1990. *The gift: The form and reason for exchange in archaic societies.* London: Routledge.

Mazelis, Joan M. 2017. *Surviving poverty: Creating sustainable ties among the poor.* New York, NY: NYU Press.

McCarty, Christopher, Miranda J. Lubbers, Raffaele Vacca, and José Luis Molina. 2019. *Conducting personal network research: A practical guide.* New York, NY: Guilford Press.

McPherson, Miller, Lynn Smith-Lovin, and James M. Cook. 2001. Birds of a feather: Homophily in social networks. *Annual Review of Sociology* 27:415–44.

Menjívar, Cecilia. 2000. *Fragmented ties: Salvadoran immigrant networks in America.* Berkeley, CA: University of California Press.

Nelson, Margaret K. 2000. Single mothers and social support: The commitment to, and retreat from, reciprocity. *Qualitative Sociology* 23 (3): 291–317.

OECD. 2019a. Labour: Labour market statistics. Main Economic Indicators (Database). Available from https://doi.org/https://doi.org/10.1787/data-00046-en.

OECD. 2019b. PPPs and exchange rates. OECD National Accounts Statistics (Database). Available from https://doi.org/https://doi.org/10.1787/data-00004-en.

Offer, Shira. 2012. The burden of reciprocity: Processes of exclusion and withdrawal from personal networks among low-income families. *Current Sociology* 60 (6): 788–805.

Portugal, Sílvia. 2009. What makes social networks move? An analysis of norms and ties. *RCCS Annual Review,* no. 1. Available from https://doi.org/10.4000/rccsar.150.

Roschelle, A. R. 1997. *No more kin: Exploring race, class, and gender in family networks.* Thousand Oaks, CA: Sage Publications.

Rossman, Gabriel. 2014. Obfuscatory relational work and disreputable exchange. *Sociological Theory* 32 (1): 43–63.

Sahlins, Marshall. 1972. *Stone age economics.* New York, NY: de Gruyter.

Skvoretz, John. 2013. Diversity, integration, and social ties: Attraction versus repulsion as drivers of intra- and intergroup relations. *American Journal of Sociology* 119 (2): 486–517.

Small, Mario Luis. 2009. *Unanticipated gains: Origins of network inequality in everyday life.* Oxford: Oxford University Press.

Small, Mario L., and Leah Gose. 2020. How do low-income people form survival networks? The role of routine organizations as brokers. *The ANNALS of the American Academy of Political and Social Science* (this volume).

Smith, Edward Bishop, Tanya Menon, and Leigh Thompson. 2012. Status differences in the cognitive activation of social networks. *Organization Science* 23 (1): 67–82.

Smith, Sandra Susan. 2007. *Lone pursuit: Distrust and defensive individualism among the black poor.* New York, NY: Russell Sage Foundation.

Stack, Carole B. 1974. *All our kin: Strategies for survival in a black community.* New York, NY: Harper & Row.

Thoits, Peggy A. 2010. Stress and health: Major findings and policy implications. *Journal of Health and Social Behavior* 51:S41–53.

Van Eijk, Gwen. 2010. Does living in a poor neighbourhood result in network poverty? A study on local networks, locality-based relationships and neighbourhood settings. *Journal of Housing and the Built Environment* 25 (4): 467–80.

Wherry, Frederick F., Kristin S. Seefeldt, and Anthony S. Alvarez. 2018. To lend or not to lend to friends and kin: Awkwardness, obfuscation, and negative reciprocity. *Social Forces* 98 (2): 753–93.

Wimmer, Andreas, and Kevin Lewis. 2010. Beyond and below racial homophily: Documented on Facebook. *American Journal of Sociology* 116 (2): 583–642.

Wrzus, Cornelia, Martha Hänel, Jenny Wagner, and Franz J. Neyer. 2013. Social network changes and life events across the life span: A meta-analysis. *Psychological Bulletin* 139 (1): 53–80.

Zelizer, Viviana A. 2005. *The purchase of intimacy.* Princeton, NJ: Princeton University Press.

Zelizer, Viviana A. 2012. How I became a relational economic sociologist and what does that mean? *Politics and Society* 40 (2): 145–74.

How Do Low-Income People Form Survival Networks? Routine Organizations as Brokers

While supportive social ties help to buffer against the consequences of poverty, few researchers have examined how people form such ties. New ties are often formed in routine organizations such as businesses, churches, and childcare centers, which, beyond being places to work, shop, or receive services, are institutionally governed spaces of social interaction. Based on the notion of *organizational brokerage*, we introduce a perspective that specifies when routine organizations contribute to tie formation and use it to reexamine data from existing qualitative studies of such organizations among the poor. We argue that successful brokerage will depend on the degree to which an organization's institutional norms render interaction among participants frequent, long-lasting, focused on others, and centered on joint tasks; and that the ensuing networks may differ from other supportive ties in the sense of belonging they may cultivate, the form of generalized exchange they may engender, and the organizational connections they may create.

Keywords: social networks; brokerage; network formation; routine organizations; poverty; social support

By
MARIO L. SMALL
and
LEAH E. GOSE

A large literature has shown that social networks are essential for the ability of low-income populations to buffer against the consequences of poverty (Stack 1974; Nelson 2000; Domínguez and Watkins 2003; Small 2009; Raudenbush 2016; Desmond 2012). In fact, the literature is so large that one could be forgiven for believing that being poor somehow provides automatic access to a network of supportive social ties (Nelson 2000; see Smith 2007). However, many low-income people do not have such a network (Campbell, Marsden,

Mario L. Small is the Grafstein Family Professor of Sociology at Harvard University and is an expert on poverty, inequality, ego networks, and field methods; his most recent book is Someone to Talk To: How Networks Matter in Practice *(Oxford University Press 2017).*

Correspondence: mariosmall@fas.harvard.edu

DOI: 10.1177/0002716220915431

and Hurlbert 1986). In fact, survey-based studies have found that poorer people living in high-poverty neighborhoods have smaller nonkin networks and are more likely to be isolated than those living in low-poverty areas (see Small 2007; van Eijk 2010; Burdick-Will 2018; Soller et al. 2018; see also Offer 2012). How, then, do low-income people form networks of support?

We examine the role of the organizations in which people interact with others on a routine basis as part of daily life: organizations such as workplaces, churches, childcare centers, schools, soup kitchens, gyms, bars, neighborhood restaurants, community centers, and other establishments (Oldenburg 1989; Small 2009; also Hsung, Lin, and Breiger 2009; Mollenhorst, Völker, and Flap 2008; Mazelis 2017; Klinenberg 2018). Though routine organizations are arguably the primary means through which low-income—and other—populations form ties outside the family, there are few systematic theories about how this process works; about why people form new ties in some contexts but not others; or about how, if at all, the ensuing relations differ from family or other ties in their supportiveness (but see Small 2009). We develop a theory of how people, regardless of their income, form social ties in such organizations; probe its applicability based on a reading of published U.S. field studies in the literature on the poor; propose at least four factors that distinguish routine organizations in which people are likely to form ties from those in which they are not; and identify several ways organizationally brokered ties may differ from other supportive ties.

Our Study

Our study is motivated by substantive, theoretical, and policy concerns. The substantive motivation is the arguably rising importance of nonfamily support networks. Support networks are valuable to individuals at all points in the income distribution. Yet the last two decades have heightened the need for low-income families in the United States to secure social, economic, and practical resources from their networks. Over this period, cash assistance has decreased for low-income mothers of young children, part of an ongoing restructuring of the U.S. welfare state (Moffitt 2015, 742–43). The Personal Responsibility and Work Opportunity Reconciliation Act (PRWORA) of 1996 dramatically reduced welfare rolls and made the poorest nonelderly families increasingly have to fend for themselves. Subsequent studies of how people avoid homelessness, material hardship, and other difficulties repeatedly found that social networks, especially family networks, were important (Domínguez and Watkins 2003; Watkins-Hayes 2013; Harvey 2018; see also Newman and Massengill 2006). Yet such conditions

Leah E. Gose is a doctoral student in sociology at Harvard University studying community organizations and social service provision.

NOTE: We thank Miranda Lubbers, Hugo Valenzuela, and the anonymous reviewers for comments and criticisms that have improved this article. We acknowledge the generous support of Harvard University's Faculty of Arts and Sciences; its Business School; and its Project on Race, Class, and Cumulative Adversity, at the Hutchins Center.

have strained many family networks; for example, many low-income parents have been forced to move in with adult relatives (Harvey 2018). As cash assistance has subsided and employment has become more unstable, people increasingly turn to their networks for support. Yet the strain on family has become substantial, heightening the importance of forming nonfamily ties.

The theoretical motivation of our study is the need for clearer theories of how organizational processes play a role in both urban poverty and social inequality (Marwell 2007; Small 2009; Wacquant 2009; Sampson 2012; Avent-Holt and Tomaskovic-Devey 2019). While research on urban poverty has traditionally focused on either the individual or the neighborhood, researchers have recently rediscovered the role of organizations in many aspects of the urban condition, including how concentrated poverty affects life chances; how people decide where to live and work; and how information, goods, and other resources are distributed across networks (Marwell 2007; Allard 2009, 2017; Small 2009; Sampson 2012; Allard and Small 2013; see Galaskiewicz and Marsden 1978; Warren 1978). A similar recognition is evident among students of social inequality, who have argued that organizations are central to differences in resource access, to the development of status distinctions, and to the functioning of relational inequities (Tilly 1998; Small 2009; Avent-Holt and Tomaskovic-Devey 2019). Organizations are equally central to the formation of social ties among urban poor populations, and the processes through which they operate remain undertheorized and poorly understood.

The policy motivation is the need for clear guidance for practitioners and legislators who seek to intervene at the level of the network. Though U.S. policymakers have frequently invoked the importance of social networks and social capital to the survival of low-income families, they remain uncertain on how to incentivize or otherwise help people to build those connections (see, e.g., Sommer et al. 2017). After all, just asking people to make more friends is not an effective strategy. Furthermore, such ideas can come close to "blaming the victims" (Ryan 1976, xiii), given that conditions that often result from structural factors may seem to result from inadequate networking. Organizations such as childcare centers and community centers can be effective places to intervene, provided one knows how to do so. Yet the research has produced precious few models for how practitioners would intervene in local organizations to make them more effective places to build such ties.

In what follows, we address these needs by examining when routine organizations help low-income people to form new social ties, identifying the mechanisms through which it happens, and documenting the operation of these mechanisms based on an extensive literature review of U.S.-based case studies of routine organizations frequented by low-income families. We build on network theories about the importance of brokers as conduits between previously unconnected actors and suggest that the process of meeting others in routine organizations results from *organizational brokerage* (cf. Small 2006). Organizations, not just individuals, can connect people to others.

We argue that routine organizations can broker social connections via multiple types of mechanisms, which include those driven by actors and those driven by institutional practices. We focus primarily on one kind of institution-driven mechanism—the impact on social interaction among participants—and argue that successful brokerage will depend on the extent to which institutional norms render interaction frequent, long-lasting, focused on others, or centered on joint tasks. We suggest that the ensuing networks may differ in important ways from other supportive ties. We conclude by outlining a set of issues that remain unanswered.

A Perspective on Tie Formation

Previous work

The literature on how actors form ties to others is vast, diverse, and multifaceted[1] (e.g., see Lazarsfeld and Merton 1954; Newcomb 1961; Verbrugge 1977; Feld 1981; McPherson, Smith-Lovin, and Cook 2001; Rivera, Soderstrom, and Uzzi 2010). We cannot review it all. For our purposes, the most relevant body of work has taken the individual as the unit of analysis and conceived of tie formation as the result of two separate processes, "meeting" and "mating," or coming into contact with others and then deciding to associate (Verbrugge 1977). The literature has isolated the meeting process to examine the factors that affect the *opportunities for social interaction*. As Blau and Schwartz (1997) put it, "Rates of social association depend on opportunities for social contact. . . . [T]he extent of contact opportunities governs the probability of associations of people, not merely of casual acquaintances but even of intimate relations, like those of lovers" (p. 29; see also Blau 1977, 90; Marsden 1990, 397; Gans 1961). For example, researchers have examined at length how organizations and other "foci" bring unconnected people into contact (Feld 1982; Small 2009). The literature has isolated a second process to examine the factors affecting *the decision to form a tie*. As Marsden (1990) put it, from this perspective, "variation in network composition [is] the result of differing levels of individual preference for associates of particular kinds" (p. 397).

Dividing the process into the opportunities to come into contact and the decisions to associate given that contact is powerful and useful. But it has an important limitation. When applied to our current context, what factors affect the probability that a person will patronize, say, a barbershop (providing a chance to meet), and then separately the process through which they decide to associate (choosing to mate)? The problem with this perspective is the assumption that once people come into contact with others, it is merely up to them. For example, many people go to barbershops and connect with no one; that outcome, from this perspective, would have to be a function of their low self-efficacy, extraversion, motivation, friendliness, or general inclination to make friends. Such an account is implausible, since equally motivated or efficacious people can patronize different barbershops and differ in the rate at which they interact with others, depending on the barbershops' environments. In fact, Small (2009) has reported such differences among equally motivated parents who patronize different childcare centers, with some expanding their networks meaningfully and others not doing so. As we document below, the conditions of the organization can dramatically affect the degree of network formation among people who have already had the opportunity to come into contact. Presuming that the second, postmeeting part of the formation process depends only on individual decisions is an undersocialized understanding of human actors (Wrong 1961). In sum, the distinction between contact and choice, or between the opportunity to interact and the decision to befriend, elides the important mediating roles that organizations can play even after the "meeting" process has taken place.

A different perspective

We propose a theory that begins where the "meeting" process ends. Rather than presuming that, once contact has been established, only the decisions of the individual matter, we assume that the postcontact process is shaped by the organizations in which contact took place. We take for granted that agency matters, that some people are more efficacious than others, and that highly efficacious people will, except in extremely inhospitable contexts, essentially introduce themselves to others (see Emirbayer and Goodwin 1994; Emirbayer and Mische 1998). Even among such actors, organizations can make the process easier or more difficult, so the mediating role of organization must be understood.

A mediator is a broker, and our model builds on brokerage theory. A broker is traditionally defined as the link between two unconnected actors (Simmel 1950, 1955; Gould and Fernandez 1989; Burt 1995, 2005). As Stovel and Shaw (2012, 141) write in a recent review, "Brokerage [is] the process of connecting actors in systems of social, economic, or political relations in order to facilitate access to valued resources." While literature has examined brokers as *tertius gaudens* (Simmel 1950; Marsden 1982; Burt 1995), people who gain advantage as a result of their position, we instead explore brokers as *tertius iungens*, those who, because of their location, bring others together (see Obstfeld 2005). Our model of how brokers join others relies on three core assumptions: that brokerage is a process, that the process is organizational, and that the organizational effect is multifaceted.

Brokerage is a process. We assume that brokerage is a process. The majority of research on brokerage in network analysis has focused on the structure of relations that give brokers their advantage or opportunity to connect others. In contrast, Obstfeldt, Borgatti, and David (2014) argued persuasively that brokerage is not merely a structure but also a process. Brokers must do things to connect people, and the things they do can be important. In fact, focusing only on structural conditions may miss that the things a broker does to connect two people may be more important than whether those people had never met before or only had a passing acquaintance (and were, thus, not technically unconnected). Conversely, the things a potential broker fails to do may result in a missed opportunity, regardless of how well positioned in a structure the broker is. As the authors argue, brokerage theory must take into account "the social behavior of brokering" (Obstfeldt, Borgatti, and David 2014, 139). Consistent with this prior research, we focus not on formal structure but on the process through which brokerage happens.

The process is organizational. We assume that brokerage may be affected not merely by individuals but also by organizations. We define a routine organization as a space of interaction where a set of actors, guided by institutional norms and understandings, orient their activities and practices loosely toward a global purpose (see Powell and DiMaggio 1991; Scott 1995; Small 2009). Routine organizations include workplaces, restaurants, barbershops, childcare centers, grocery stores, bodegas, churches, botanicals, gyms, community centers, neighborhood clinics, coffee shops, bars, and so on. Though routine organizations vary in scope, mission, profit status, funding source, orientation, and many other conditions, they all constitute a space where actors interact around institutionally shaped norms and understandings.[2]

Our view that organizations can operate as brokers differs in important ways from the existing research. To date, researchers have understood the role of organizations as brokers in one of two ways. One, they have conceived the organization as an *actor* whose behavior is analogous to that of an individual. For example, an organization, not just an individual, might be said to gain from its brokerage position, thus having greater power to set prices (see, e.g., Marsden 1982; Stovel, Golub, and Milgrom 2011; Stovel and Shaw 2012). From this perspective, the organization and the individual are two instances of the same general class, and analogous processes occur in each subclass. Two, researchers have conceived the organization as a *community*, equivalent to any entity comprising members, including groups, parties, associations, affiliations, or even identities. For example, any community might be said to affect how a broker performs a role depending on whether the broker is a member (and thus, say, a "representative") or not (and thus, say, a "liaison") (see Gould and Fernandez 1989). From this perspective, organizations are analogous to any membership entity that might affect whether a broker is an insider or an outsider—a broker who is Christian is a member of the community of Christians vis-à-vis any non-Christian, a Democrat broker is a member of the community of Democrats vis-à-vis Republicans, and so on.

In contrast, we assume that organizations are analogous to neither individuals nor communities. Though routine organizations range widely in type and orientation, all constitute a space of interaction, which cannot be said of individuals or all other kinds of communities. As a result, some forms of brokerage are distinct to organizations.

The organizational effect is multifaceted. We assume that organizational brokerage may occur through not one but multiple types of mechanisms. An organization is a space of interaction, a set of actors, and a constellation of practices, all shaped by institutional norms and understandings. Indeed, the difficulty in developing a clean conceptual model of how they shape networks is that people can create ties as a result of multiple processes. There are multiple ways an individual who enters a space, who interacts with actors, or who responds to norms or understandings may come to meet others whose resources prove useful to their survival.

Actor-Driven Brokerage

One way to systematize these various processes of interaction is to focus on the entity doing the brokerage. Sometimes, it is just a person, and the process is a straightforward application of brokerage theory. Any time an individual interacts with an acquaintance in an organization, that acquaintance may introduce the individual to others. In that case, the acquaintance would be acting as *tertius iungens*, precisely as described by previous researchers, merely in the confines of an organization. Just as in traditional brokerage (which we will call "type A"), the process is being driven by an *actor* who is a member of the organization. For our purposes, an organizational member may be a manager, employee, client, patron, or volunteer of the organization—since the act of brokerage may be perpetrated by anyone in the organization.[3]

This actor-driven brokerage process can take at least two different forms, depending on whether the broker is connecting the individual to another member or to a nonmember of the organization (see Figure 1, panels A, B, and C). For example, a church pastor may connect a parishioner to a pastor at a sister church (type B) or to another parishioner in the same church (type C).

Both of these types of brokerage have been documented in research on routine organizations in urban contexts. Desmond's (2012) fieldwork in Milwaukee uncovered that low-income people made connections in "welfare offices, food pantries, job centers, Alcoholics Anonymous clubs, methadone clinics, even the waiting areas of eviction court" (p. 1313). One of Desmond's cases illustrated vividly the type-B organizational brokerage seen in Figure 1: Scott and Mike met while attending a Cocaine Anonymous meeting. Mike introduced Scott to Pito, a contact of Mike's outside of the support group, who then introduced Scott to David. After Scott was evicted, he ended up rooming with David (p. 1312).

Researchers have also documented the type of simple brokerage in which individuals introduce unconnected actors in the same organization (type C). This type of brokerage is particularly evident in schools, as Lukasiewicz and her coauthors (2019) found after studying social capital among low-income parents in New York City. One parent served as the president of the Parent Teacher Association (PTA) and often brokered relations between parents and between parents and staff. She explained that her role was especially important for parents who did not speak English: "They could come to me and I will speak for [them]. So it has helped, it has changed the school. . . . And we have done a lot of events for the school, for the kids, that wasn't going on for a couple years" (p. 287).

In both cases, the process is just conventional brokerage; nevertheless, it is rightly thought of as organizational, because in the absence of the organization, the brokerage would not have happened—Scott would not have met Pito, and

FIGURE 1
A Model of Organizational Brokerage

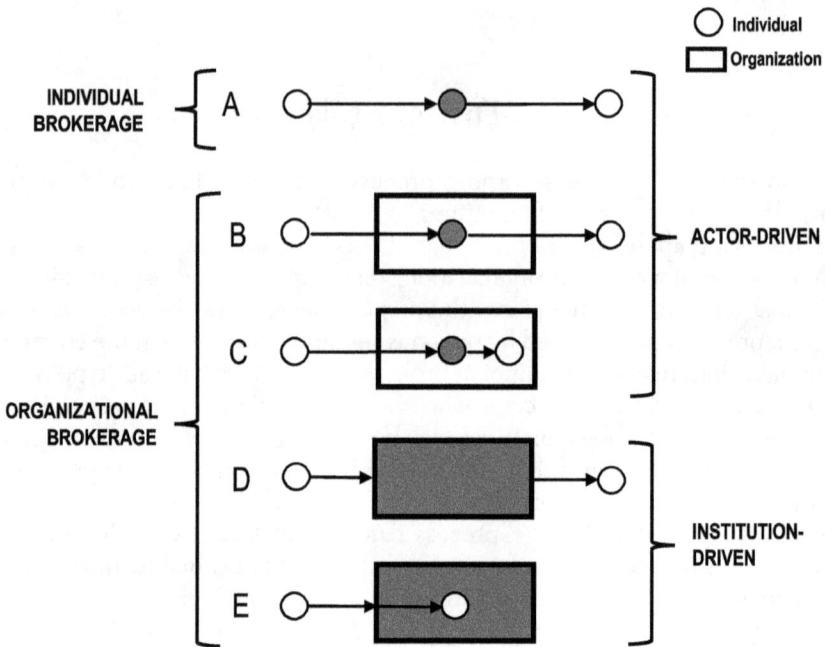

the non-English-speaking parents would not have communicated with others. The organization placed Mike and the PTA president in a position to connect others.[4]

Institution-Driven Brokerage

Organizational brokerage may be driven not only by actors but also by the organization itself. An organization can structure the formation of ties among its members in a large number of ways, including its rules of membership or participation, its physical layout, and its institutional norms or understandings of social interaction (see Small and Adler 2019). We focus on the latter, on routine organizations' institutional practices. Practices may be "institutional" in the normative sense—via formal rules or informal norms that encourage or discourage forms of behavior; or in the cognitive sense—via understandings of the self or others that are produced by the organization (Small 2009; see Scott 2003). An organization may encourage practices through which members meet people in different contexts (see Figure 1, panel D), as when clinics send health workers on mobile outreach operations to serve families in low-income neighborhoods. Or an organization may have rules of social interaction that encourage people to meet other members (see Figure 1, panel E), as when schools expect parents to collaborate on fundraising activities. In such cases, no individual is actually doing the brokering.

Researchers have also documented cases of low-income individuals meeting others through organizations despite that no actor is introducing one actor to another. In such circumstances, the institutional practices of the organization have been key. The first of these, type D in Figure 1, has been reported in different forms. In his Boston study of twenty-nine religious organizations in low-income neighborhoods, McRoberts (2003) found that the churches "are not just places where people meet to worship"; instead, they also acted as "interactive social spaces and as architects of vertical and horizontal networks," helping congregants form connections within and between churches (p. 127).

An examination of type-E brokerage

The bulk of our discussion, however, is on type-E processes. We examine how institutional norms shape four aspects of social interaction among members of an organization: how repeated it is (frequency), how long-lasting it is (duration), how focused it is on others (outward orientation), and how centered it is on the accomplishment of joint tasks (collaboration). These factors can dramatically affect whether a routine organization will successfully broker connections.

Frequency. Repeated interaction is the foundation of friendship formation (Homans 1961; Lazarsfeld and Merton 1954). Such interactions can lead to the discovery of similarities and the subsequent operation of other mechanisms such as homophily (McPherson, Smith-Lovin, and Cook 2001). Local routine organizations shape the support networks of low-income families to the extent that they allow, encourage, or require repeated visits that serve as opportunities for relationships to form between individuals (Small 2009).

Research on churches has often documented this relationship, given the repeated nature of church participation. Ellison and George (1994) examined the relationship between church participation and network size based on North Carolina survey data ($n = 2,956$). They found that respondents who reported attending church "several times a week" had, on average, 2.25 more nonkin ties than those who "never" did; and the more they attended, the more nonkin ties they had (p. 56; see also Taylor and Chatters 1988). In her fieldwork in a mixed-class African American neighborhood in Chicago, Pattillo (2013) found that many young people developed strong bonds to others through weekly choir rehearsals at a local Catholic church (see also Marwell 2007).

Likewise, the daily requirements surrounding childcare make for multiple opportunities in which parents and childcare providers can interact (see Small 2009; Reid, Martin, and Brooks-Gunn 2017). Small found that "practices such as constrained pickup and drop-off times and monthly meetings with teachers facilitated frequent interactions," which contributed to tie formation (2009, 103). Researchers have also documented the formation of other kinds of ties that provided social support. For example, Rolfe and Armstrong (2010) examined communication with early childhood professionals among mothers at their child's daycare center and found that thirty-eight of the forty surveyed mothers reported speaking in person with their early childcare providers at least three times a week. Most of them perceived the early childhood professionals to be a "source of social support"; furthermore, the frequency of interaction "determined how much support mothers considered they received" (pp. 62, 60; see also Hughes 1985).

Research on community centers has documented this idea as well, given that such centers often support programs that require participants to meet regularly. Colistra and colleagues conducted a case study with fourteen program participants and found strong evidence of this process shaping tie formation and trust (Colistra, Schmalz, and Glover 2017; Colistra, Bixler, and Schmalz 2019). As one parent whose child attended the after-school program explained, the daughter "became close" to the other participants because she was "seeing them every day" (Colistra, Bixler, and Schmalz 2019, 10; see also van Eijk 2010).

Another context in which researchers have found this relationship is hair salons and beauty salons, given the routine nature of interactions in the space (see Furman 1997; Harris-Lacewell 2004; Shabbazz 2016). Exploring the social relationships formed in a black barbershop on Chicago's South Side, Harris-Lacewell (2004) found that major social connections were forged through frequent and extensive conversations in the shop—"authentic everyday talk" (p. 201)—which, notably, extended beyond class lines.

Soller at al. (2018) interviewed 178 recently resettled refugees in a large southwestern city to understand their community attachment and social networks. The authors asked respondents about the number of times they visited specific "grocery stores, restaurants, and places of worship in the last thirty days" in the community (p. 337). Refugees who engaged more at local stores and organizations had a more robust local network. The authors concluded that "members of ethnic communities who share interactional settings with other members when engaging in their routine activities are more strongly attached to other members and have enhanced access to resources that are embedded within their communities" (p. 340).

Duration. A second factor that plays a role in brokerage is the presence of institutional norms, which allow people to spend extended periods in the company of others. The passage of time contributes to sociability (Simmel 1950), the possibility of conversation with no instrumental purpose other than the conversation itself, a process through which strangers become acquaintances, and acquaintances friends. Research on "third places," the bars, pubs, beer gardens, and other establishments where people can socialize at length without being mindful of the clock, has often made this point (Oldenburg 1989,17).

Research on neighborhood restaurants has confirmed this idea. Duneier's (1992) study of a neighborhood cafeteria on Chicago's South Side illustrated the extensive community that can form when clients can patronize an eating establishment for long periods. The cheap prices and lack of expectation for patrons to depart upon payment encouraged many to stay for hours and interact with one another throughout the day. Over months of observation, Duneier found that the men of Slim's Table passed time at Valois by "participating in the same rhythm of various routinized episodes that yield both companionship and solitude" over the many hours and days regulars spent there (p. 34). In fact, the "ties binding members of the larger collectivity [at Valois] have developed over decades" (p. 5).

Research on neighborhood bars suggests the same (e.g., May 2001; Anderson 1978). Anderson's (1978) study of a neighborhood bar and liquor store on the South Side of Chicago examined the social interactions that emerged among regulars, who spent hours at a time at the bar. The relations formed were so significant that the author termed them, following Cooley (1909), an extended primary group, and described them as possessing a "we" feeling (Anderson 1978, 33) in which the group provided "supportive social ties for its own" (Anderson 1978, 180).

In the community center Colistra and colleagues studied, seniors met for four hours during each programming session. The results were as expected. As Barbara explained, "I think it is really the program what brings us all together, when we join in and do things together as a group, and that connects us you know" (Colistra, Bixler, and Schmalz 2019, 10).

We note that in this and other forms, routine organizations may differ widely not only across types but also within them. For example, contrary to the one Duneier (1992) studied, most restaurants in the United States do not permit patrons to linger for hours after eating, lest it cut into the businesses' often slim profit margins. The difference across entities of the same kind is part of why we focus not on organizations as "types" but on the mechanisms through which they shape interaction.

Outward focus. In a series of important papers, Feld (1981, 1982, 1984) proposed that social ties were formed when people interacted around a common focus of activity. This "focused interaction" could happen in multiple ways and across many kinds of foci. In an organization, the institutional norms or understandings may encourage interaction to be less or more focused in nature. The interaction may be focused in at least two ways, as we describe in this section and the following one.

The first is the extent to which the activity of any given member is oriented toward others, rather than themselves. Orienting one's activities toward others contributes to tie formation through several processes. It naturally encourages social interaction; it helps people to identify common values (Lazarsfeld and Merton 1954); and it facilitates their ability to discover similarity or homophily in background (McPherson, Smith-Lovin, and Cook 2001). These conditions, in turn, help actors to find points of cognitive empathy, the ability to understand another's predicament from their perspective, which builds trust (Small 2017). An organization's institutional norms may encourage this kind of outward focus, particularly as a result of purposeful group engagement.

Researchers have documented such practices among organizations patronized by low-income populations, including churches, community centers, and service agencies. Based on ethnographic fieldwork in Brooklyn, Marwell (2007) found that a major church managed to develop especially strong relations among congregants through its *fraternidades*—communal living groups centered on spiritual practice and religious connection through prayer, reflection, community service, and chores. Members of the *fraternidades* were expected to participate in *revisión de vida* sessions, intimate group gatherings where participants shared personal stories with one another and reflected on their "daily lives" (p. 193). Watkins-Hayes (2013) interviewed eighty-two HIV-positive women who attended weekly group meetings at an AIDS service organization. As part of the meetings, participants were expected to share their experiences and listen constructively as others described theirs, encouraging each to focus on the others. The shared experiences produced a natural environment for network formation, emotional support, and advice (p. 91). As a participant explained, "I'm just outreaching for anyone because I've been there and I know sources. . . . I don't mind plugging nobody in because we're all in this together" (p. 92; see also Watkins-Hayes 2019).

Community centers can have a similar effect, as many of their programs require participating in collective sessions. Bess and Doykos (2014) studied a "cradle-to-college" program for parents and caregivers in an East Nashville community center (p. 272). Participants were required to attend multiple kinds of activities, including those during which family shared personal or community news with the others. The authors found that the majority of program graduates had formed new relationships to other participants (p. 275). Similar kinds of programs are often run either at or by schools. Shoji et al. (2014) interviewed parents and ran focus groups with participants in one such program aimed at "empowering" parents and increasing their involvement at the children's school (p. 602). The parents met weekly for eight weeks and were expected to participate in group discussions, where they shared aspects of their predicament. Supportive social ties were formed, as expected. Activities of this kind are particularly common among organizations with a service orientation.

Joint tasks. A second way the activities in an organization may be focused is the extent to which people collaborate to perform concrete tasks. Research in social psychology has uncovered that positive affect and trust may increase when strangers collaborate on a joint project (Lawler 2001). To work successfully with others, people must represent their best selves, adopt a collaborative attitude, and communicate. To the extent institutional norms require collaborations among members to meet organizational needs or objectives, they will encourage the formation of social ties (Small 2009).

Research among low-income populations has also uncovered this relation. Several studies have focused on childcare centers, which often expect parents to work on activities to meet collective ends. In a study based on survey and ethnographic research from childcare centers, Small (2009) found many centers expected parents to collaborate with one another to accomplish major tasks. Parents may be expected to help organize fieldtrips; to plan special events, such as Mother's Day celebrations; to arrange spring cleanings of playgrounds; or to put together fundraising activities to meet annual targets. These activities consistently contributed to the formation of social ties. Reid, Martin, and Brooks-Gunn (2017) found something similar based on interviews with parents associated with childcare centers in New York City. They found that when parents engaged in center activities such as open houses and conferences, their interactions with one another and with center staff increased, promoting the exchange of information and emotional support (p. 148).

What Resources Do These Ties Provide?

One might imagine that the ties low-income individuals form in such organizational contexts are somehow less valuable than those formed otherwise, that the formal settings in which they were forged perhaps lack the intimacy needed for truly dependable relations. The evidence is not consistent about this. In fact, organizationally brokered ties are not only useful in the ways other ties are; they are valuable in ways distinctive to *organizationally embedded* ties. We briefly identify three conventional resources formed through organizational brokerage and three different kinds of resources that derive from the organizational nature of the ties.

Emotional support

Organizationally brokered ties have been documented to provide emotional support. Klinenberg's (2018) survey- and interview-based study of libraries and other local organizations found these establishments useful in "buffering isolation and loneliness" (p. 34). Denise, a young mother who frequented her local library, explained that she found a lot of support from other mothers and babysitters. "You just kind of start chatting . . . and it's amazing, but you wind up having these really personal, really intense conversations" (p. 35). Using interview and observational data at a youth-centered community technology center, Clark (2005) found cases of bridging social capital, in that activities at the center, like decorating a Christmas tree, brought together participants from different neighborhoods (p. 437). The center offered youth participants a space in which to talk openly and freely about issues at school or home with one another, particularly because of the openness of the space. Participants talked about issues such as sex education, how to deal with bullies, and family life. Using nationally representative data, Small (2009) found that mothers who enrolled their children in childcare centers and formed ties were substantially less likely to experience depression than those who enrolled but did not form ties or than those who did not enroll, after accounting for prior depression.

Information

Organizationally brokered ties are also good sources of information. Colistra, Schmalz, and Glover (2017) examined social relationships and well-being at a county-owned community center through interviews and focus groups with fourteen adults who frequently visited the center. The authors found that social relationships supported well-being through the "exchange of resources, services, and information" (p. 42). For example, Brenda sought legal assistance from other community center members who worked as lawyers: "We have lawyers in pro-grams and things here so I get to reach out to them and pose my little question to them and they will guide me and let me know how to work things out with whatever the problem might be, especially my house. But, you know, I've met a lot of people who have helped me since I have been here, and especially in the legal field" (p. 42; see also Delgado 1996, 1997, 1998; Delgado and Santiago [1998] on shops; Johnson 2010; Lopez, Caspe, and Simpson 2017; Khoir et al. 2017; Klinenberg [2018] on libraries).

Services and material goods

These ties have also been sources of more concrete forms of support, includ-ing services and material goods. In the community organization studied by Shoji and colleagues (2014), parents expressed the value of the new social ties in terms related explicitly to the services they offered. One parent explained, "When my baby was born, I couldn't go on Fridays because of my baby boy, and I could tell one of them [the other parents in the program], 'Can you pick up my daughter? Can you bring her home?' You know what I mean? And if I hadn't met them, it would have been more trouble" (p. 607; see also Lukasiewicz et al. 2019). In her study of a social services assistance and advocacy group in Philadelphia, Mazelis (2017) found repeated evidence of resource exchange. One member, James, explained, "People always been helping me since like I got involved with [the organization]. I done met different people in different relationships that allowed me to be able to function, me and my [immediate] family. From transportation stuff to money stuff to food stuff, to you name it, people that helped me over the last seven years" (p. 155).

Generalized exchange

Some resources derive from the organizational context in which the ties are created. One such resource, which results because ties can take collective form, is the security that derives from generalized exchange. We cannot do justice to the vast literature on the topic here, but we note that researchers have defined *generalized exchange* as a system in which the receipt of goods or services may be reciprocated by someone other than the receiver (Malinowski 1922/2014; Blau 1964/1986; Molm, Takahaski, and Peterson 2000). When ties are formed in a group context, and particularly when they stem from collective activities, their relationships may naturally evolve into this kind of system.

In the community center studied by Colistra, Schmalz, and Glover (2017), participants often described such systems. Linda explained, "like when I needed food, transportation . . . and you know, [other members] don't just direct me, they will help me themselves, they will give me something, or 'here [participant's name] take this home'" (Colistra, Schmalz, and Glover 2017). Similar systems can emerge even in places that might not seem "community-focused," such as bars. Anderson (1978) reported such relations in the bar that he studied, where extended socialization over drinks helped the regulars to feel "themselves among equals, especially in relation to wider society" (p. 29). When Herman, one of the more prominent regulars, was showing up infrequently and run down because his wife had fallen ill, other regulars asked their wives to pack food for him or otherwise brought extra "grub" from their restaurant jobs for him (p. 181).

Mazelis (2017) reported a similar process based on interviews and fieldwork in a Philadelphia organization that helps low-income families obtain housing and social services. To maintain membership and receive aid, the group required members to volunteer their time at the local office, in assisting others, or at rallies. Such expectations ultimately encouraged generalized reciprocity. One member, Cate, learned to navigate the welfare system and reported increased self-esteem: "[being a member] feels like you're secured. People are securing you. . . . Like before it's like I felt doors was locked. When I feel that people's helping me, doors are opening" (p. 128). To fulfill the expectations for giving back, Cate lets "new members stay with her, travels with the group, goes on food distributions, and brings in other members" (p. 128).

A sense of belonging

The collective nature of much of tie formation can also create, at times, a sense of belonging to a group larger than oneself. In May's work (2001), people found their engagement with others at a neighborhood bar to contribute positively to their self-worth. May concluded that the "exclusionary" nature of the tavern created an "environment where a regular clientele affirms its own racial or ethnic identity" (p. 172). According to May, for some clients the experience of conversation was akin to visiting a therapist, as the bar was a safe space where patrons could "claim positive identities for themselves" (p. 163).

Researchers have made similar claims about barbershops (Shabazz 2016). Men who frequented the barbershop Shabazz observed over a summer found social opportunities to learn "about black history, developing skills in argumentation and debate, and male bonding," building a sense of group identity (2016, 310). Rock, a frequent customer, explained, "I used to take my son with me all the time so he could soak the knowledge. You can't get that love anywhere else" (2016, 306). The engagements within the barbershop give clients, particularly those who are younger, a space in which to develop ideas and arguments and to learn more about their history and their own identities.

Access to other organizations

Finally, some of the ties formed are not merely to other people (as in B and D) but to other organizations. In Colistra, Bixler, and Schmalz's (2019) aforementioned study, the community center "collaborated with other community centers to deliver programs, thus connecting people from different neighborhoods" (p. 11). Center-user Barbara explained, "We get invited to different centers to join them for different functions they have and two or three times out of the year, and then we invite other centers here to interact to join in with us" (p. 11). These connections to centers, churches, or other entities provided their own resources and opportunities to combat isolation. Another user explained, "We have a choir of seniors and they get invited to [local church], and they have been to [the community center] to sing," and there are "some people who stay very closely contacted and connected with seniors in other programs" (p. 11). McRoberts's (2003) study of Boston-area churches found multiple organizational ties between one church and other community organizations. One church "heavily involved" their congregants in outreach work (p. 118), which included "a night patrol aimed at establishing contact with youth in the street, a number of educational programs for young people and their parents, and the Four Corners Planning Committee" (p. 126).

Conclusion

We have developed a perspective on tie formation in which organizations are conceived as brokers and their institutional practices as the mechanisms through which brokerage occurs. We have applied this perspective to understand and document tie formation particularly among U.S. low-income families. We have argued that successful brokerage will depend on the degree to which institutional norms render social interaction frequent, long-lasting, outwardly focused, and centered on joint tasks; and that the ensuing networks may differ in important ways from other supportive ties.

We take our article to be a starting point; many questions remain unanswered. Three of them are particularly important. One question relates to the role of agency, preferences, and decision-making in how people respond to institutional conditions. While we have focused on how institutional conditions shape behavior, people are agents in their network formation process, and whether they ultimately create a tie depends on their decision to do so (Emirbayer and Goodwin 1994; Emirbayer and Mische 1998). For example, people will likely seek those who resemble them demographically (Lazarsfeld and Merton 1954; McPherson, Smith-Lovin, and Cook 2001; Wimmer and Lewis 2010). In addition, the friendship formation process is dynamic in ways likely to matter. For example, people will differ in how much they invest in relations they have begun to form, thereby affecting whether fragile new ties become strong or dissipate. Similarly, they may or may not decide to sustain a relation once the initial brokerage provided by the organization has taken place. The interactions between agency and context remain a fruitful area for new work.

A second set of questions involves the factors motivating organizations to serve as brokers. As we discussed, the motivations, interests, and benefits to brokers have concerned researchers for many years (Burt 1995; Stovel and Shaw 2012). The organizational dimension does not eliminate those concerns; it merely complicates them. The process through which the routine organizations shaped tie formation in the cases we discuss did not necessarily derive from an intention to form connections among patrons or members; in fact, in most cases, they derived from other organizational imperatives (Small 2009). The variations in intentionality and objectives, and the unintended consequences that ensue, deserve substantial attention. This set of issues is vast and represents a particularly rich space for new research.

A final set of questions involves variation in the types of organizational member-ship that individual actors may have. Our theoretical perspective identifies three kinds of actors: the focal one, the broker, and the person connected by the broker to the focal actor. In strict theoretical terms, any of them may be organizational members, and such membership may take any form: client, patron, manager, employee, volunteer, and so on, as long as the form involves interaction in a space with other members. Because of length constraints we have been forced to ignore the consequences of this heterogeneity. And because of the article's focus on low-income populations, and the cases the literature has chosen to explore, we have primarily documented scenarios where the focal actor and the connected person are both usually a client. This focus has left many questions unanswered. Indeed, panels B, C, D, and E in Figure 1 are all affected by these conditions. Even in those circumstances where the focal actor is a client, whether the connected person is a client versus an employee carries vastly different implications for how the broker-age process will ensue, for how likely the relation is to be maintained, and for what kind of social support resources are available through it. In this respect, our appli-cation has only scratched the surface of the questions needing examination.

We believe that these and other questions can help to inform an agenda in which research on poor populations focuses not only on the individual or the neighborhood but also on the organization. This agenda also provides a clearer path for practitioners and policy-makers. The effort to stimulate network forma-tion among low-income populations has reason to work through local organiza-tions. The particular mechanisms that we have identified provide a potential starting point.

Notes

1. The literature is even larger when we include studies of network formation and evolution (e.g., Hallinan 1978; Snijders, Van de Bunt, and Steglich 2010; Butts et al. 2012). We adopt an egocentric per-spective wherein the individual is the unit of analysis (Perry, Pescosolido, and Borgatti 2018; McCarty et al. 2019). We note that sociocentric perspectives can be particularly useful in the study of organizational tie formation, and researchers have proposed ideas consistent with ours (Frank, Muller, and Mueller 2013).

2. The role of space is far more multifaceted than we can cover in these pages, since the configuration of the physical space may itself affect network formation. For more on this topic, see Small and Adler (2019).

3. Naturally, different kinds of members may have different motivations to act as brokers. Given space constraints, that examination will await future work.

4. In fact, the organization may have shaped the extent to which Mike and the PTA president could operate as brokers. We discuss the role of institutional practices in the next section.

References

Allard, Scott W. 2009. *Out of reach: Place, poverty, and the new American welfare state*. New Haven, CT: Yale University Press.

Allard, Scott W. 2017. *Places in need: The changing geography of poverty*. New York, NY: Russell Sage Foundation.

Allard, Scott W., and Mario L. Small. 2013. Reconsidering the urban disadvantaged: The role of systems, institutions, and organizations. *The ANNALS of the American Academy of Political and Social Science* 647 (1): 6–20.

Anderson, Elijah. 1978. *A place on the corner*. Chicago, IL: University of Chicago Press.

Avent-Holt, Dustin, and Donald Tomaskovic-Devey. 2019. Organizations as the building blocks of social inequalities. *Sociology Compass* 13 (2): e12655.

Bess, Kimberly D., and Bernadette Doykos. 2014. Tied together: Building relational well-being and reducing social isolation through place-based parent education. *Journal of Community Psychology* 42 (3): 268–84.

Blau, Peter M. 1964/1986. *Exchange and power in social life*. New Brunswick, NJ: Transaction Publishers.

Blau, Peter M. 1977. *Inequality and heterogeneity: A primitive theory of social structure*. New York, NY: Free Press.

Blau, Peter M., and Joseph Schwartz. 1997. *Crosscutting social circles: Testing a macrostructural theory of intergroup relations*. New Brunswick, NJ: Transaction Publishers.

Burdick-Will, Julia. 2018. School location, social ties, and perceived neighborhood boundaries. *City & Community* 17 (2): 418–37.

Burt, Ronald. 1995. *Structural holes: The social structure of competition*. Cambridge, MA: Harvard University Press.

Burt, Ronald S. 2005. *Brokerage and closure: An introduction to social capital*. Clarendon Lectures in Management Studies Series. Oxford: Oxford University Press.

Butts, Carter T., Ryan M. Acton, John R. Hipp, and Nicholas N. Nagle. 2012. Geographical variability and network structure. *Social Networks* 34 (1): 82–100.

Campbell, Karen E., Peter V. Marsden, and Jeanne S. Hurlbert. 1986. Social resources and socioeconomic status. *Social Networks* 8 (1): 97–117.

Clark, Kevin. 2005. Serving underserved communities with instructional technologies: Giving them what they need, not what you want. *Urban Education* 40 (4): 430–45.

Colista, Craig, Robert Bixler, and Dorothy Schmalz. 2019. Exploring factors that contribute to relationship building in a community center. *Journal of Leisure Research* 50 (1): 1–17.

Colista, Craig Michael, Dart Schmalz, and Troy Glover. 2017. The meaning of relationship building in the context of the community center and its implications. *Journal of Park and Recreation Administration; Urbana* 35 (2). doi:10.18666/JPRA-2017-V35-I2-7448.

Cooley, Charles Horton. 1909. The significance of communication. In *Social organization*, 61–65. New York, NY: Charles Scribner's Sons.

Delgado, Melvin. 1996. Puerto Rican food establishments as social service organizations. *Journal of Community Practice* 3 (2): 57–77.

Delgado, Melvin. 1997. Role of Latina-owned beauty parlors in a Latino community. *Social Work* 42 (5): 445–53.

Delgado, Melvin. 1998. Latina-owned businesses: Community resources for the prevention field. *Journal of Primary Prevention* 18 (4): 447–60.

Delgado, Melvin, and Jorge Santiago. 1998. HIV/AIDS in a Puerto Rican/Dominican community: A collaborative project with a botanical shop. *Social Work* 43 (2): 183–86.

Desmond, Matthew. 2012. Disposable ties and the urban poor. *American Journal of Sociology* 117 (5): 1295–1335.

Domínguez, Silvia, and Celeste Watkins. 2003. Creating networks for survival and mobility: Social capital among African-American and Latin-American low-income mothers. *Social Problems* 50 (1): 111–35.

Duneier, Mitchell. 1992. *Slim's Table: Race, respectability, and masculinity*. Chicago, IL: University of Chicago Press.

Ellison, Christopher G., and Linda K. George. 1994. Religious involvement, social ties, and social support in a southeastern community. *Journal for the Scientific Study of Religion* 33 (1): 46–61.

Emirbayer, Mustafa, and Jeff Goodwin. 1994. Network analysis, culture, and agency. *American Journal of Sociology* 99:1411–54.

Emirbayer, Mustafa, and Ann Mische. 1998. What is agency? *American Journal of Sociology* 103 (4): 962–1023.

Feld, Scott L. 1981. The focused organization of social ties. *American Journal of Sociology* 86 (5): 1015–35.

Feld, Scott L. 1982. Social structural determinants of similarity among associates. *American Sociological Review* 47 (6): 797–801.

Feld, Scott F. 1984. The structured use of personal associates. *Social Forces* 62 (3): 640–52.

Frank, Kenneth A., Chandra Muller, and Anna S. Mueller. 2013. The embeddedness of adolescent friendship nominations: The formation of social capital in emergent network structures. *American Journal of Sociology* 119 (1): 216–53.

Furman, Frida Kerner. 1997. *Facing the mirror: Older women and beauty shop culture*. New York, NY: Routledge.

Galaskiewicz, Joseph, and Peter V. Marsden. 1978. Interorganizational resource networks: Formal patterns of overlap. *Social Science Research* 7 (2): 89–107.

Gans, Herbert J. 1961. Planning and social life: Friendship and neighbor relations in suburban communities. *Journal of the American Institute of Planners* 27 (2): 134–40.

Gould, Roger, and Roberto Fernandez. 1989. Structures of mediation: A formal approach to brokerage in transaction networks. *Sociological Methodology* 19:89–126.

Hallinan, Maureen T. 1978. The process of friendship formation. *Social Networks* 1 (2): 193–210.

Harris-Lacewell, Melissa. 2004. *Barbershops, Bibles, and BET - Everyday talk and black political thought*. Princeton, NJ: Princeton University Press.

Harvey, Hope. 2018. Economic exchange and relational work within doubled-up households. Paper presented at the annual meeting of the Society for the Study of Social Problems (SSSP), 10 August–12 August 2018, Philadelphia, PA.

Homans, George Caspar. 1961. *Social behavior: Its elementary forms*. New York, NY: Harcourt, Brace, and World.

Hsung, Ray-May, Nan Lin, and Ronald L. Breiger. 2009. *Contexts of social capital: Social networks in markets, communities, and families*. New York, NY: Routledge.

Hughes, Robert. 1985. The informal help-giving of home and center childcare providers. *Family Relations* 34 (3): 359–66.

Johnson, Catherine A. 2010. Do public libraries contribute to social capital? A preliminary investigation into the relationship. *Library & Information Science Research* 32 (2): 147–55.

Khoir, Safirotu, Jia Tina Du, Robert M. Davison, and Andy Koronios. 2017. Contributing to social capital: An investigation of Asian immigrants' use of public library services. *Library & Information Science Research* 39 (1): 34–45.

Klinenberg, Eric. 2018. *Palaces for the people: How social infrastructure can help fight inequality, polarization, and the decline of civic life*. 1st ed. New York, NY: Crown.

Lawler, Edward J. 2001. An affect theory of social exchange. *American Journal of Sociology* 107:321–52.

Lazarsfeld, Paul F., and Robert K. Merton. 1954. Friendship as social process: A substantive and methodological analysis. In *Freedom and control in modern society*, eds. Morroe Berger, Theodore Abel, and Charles Page, 18–66. New York, NY: Van Nostrand.

Lopez, Elena M., Margaret Caspe, and Christina Simpson. 2017. Engaging families in public libraries. *Public Library Quarterly* 36 (4): 318–33.

Lukasiewicz, Karolina, Ozge Sensoy Bahar, Samira Ali, Priya Gopalan, Gary Parker, Robert Hawkins, Mary McKay, and Robert Walker. 2019. Getting by in New York City: Bonding, bridging and linking capital in poverty-impacted neighborhoods. *City & Community* 18 (1): 280–301.

Malinowski, Bronislaw. 1922/2014. *Argonauts of the western Pacific*. New York, NY: Routledge.

Marsden, Peter V. 1982. Brokerage behavior in restricted exchange networks. *Social Structure and Network Analysis* 7 (4): 341–410.

Marsden, Peter V. 1990. Network diversity, substructures and opportunities for contact. In *Structures of power and constraint: Papers in honor of Peter M. Blau*, eds Craig Calhoun, Marshall W. Meyer, and W. Richard Scott, 397–410. New York, NY Cambridge University Press.

Marwell, Nicole P. 2007. *Bargaining for Brooklyn: Community organizations in the entrepreneurial city*. Chicago, IL: University of Chicago Press.

May, Reuben A. Buford. 2001. *Talking at Trena's: Everyday conversations at an African American tavern*. New York, NY: New York University Press.

Mazelis, Joan Maya. 2017. *Surviving poverty: Creating sustainable ties among the poor*. New York, NY: New York University Press.

McCarty, Christopher, Miranda J. Lubbers, Raffaele Vacca, and José Luis Molina. 2019. *Conducting personal network research: A practical guide*. New York, NY: Guilford Publications.

McPherson, Miller, Lynn Smith-Lovin, and James M. Cook. 2001. Birds of a feather: Homophily in social networks. *Annual Review of Sociology* 27 (1): 415–44.

McRoberts, Omar M. 2003. *Streets of glory: Church and community in a black urban neighborhood*. Chicago, IL: University of Chicago.

Moffitt, Robert A. 2015. The deserving poor, the family, and the U.S. welfare system. *Demography* 52 (3): 729–49.

Mollenhorst, Gerald, Beate Völker, and Henk Flap. 2008. Social contexts and personal relationships: The effect of meeting opportunities on similarity for relationships of different strength. *Social Networks* 30 (1): 60–68.

Molm, Linda D., Nobuyuki Takahashi, and Gretchen Peterson. 2000. Risk and trust in social exchange: An experiment of a classical proposition. *American Journal of Sociology* 105 (5): 1396–1427.

Nelson, Margaret K. 2000. Single mothers and social support: The commitment to, and retreat from, reciprocity. *Qualitative Sociology* 23 (3): 291–317.

Newcomb, Theodore M. 1961. *The acquaintance process*. New York, NY: Holt, Reinhart, and Winston.

Newman, Katherine S., and Rebekah Peeples Massengill. 2006. The texture of hardship: Qualitative sociology of poverty, 1995–2005. *Annual Review of Sociology* 32:423–46.

Obstfeld, David. 2005. Social networks, the Tertius Iungens orientation, and involvement in innovation. *Administrative Science Quarterly* 50 (1): 100–130.

Obstfeld, David, Stephen P. Borgatti, and Jason Davis. 2014. Brokerage as a process: Decoupling third party action from social network structure. In *Contemporary perspectives on organizational social networks*, vol. 40, 135–59. Bradford, UK: Emerald Group Publishing Limited.

Offer, Shira. 2012. The burden of reciprocity: Processes of exclusion and withdrawal from personal networks among low-income families. *Current Sociology* 60 (6): 788–805.

Oldenburg, Ray. 1989. *The great good place: Cafés, coffee shops, community centers, beauty parlors, general stores, bars, hangouts, and how they get you through the day*. 1st ed. New York, NY: Paragon House.

Pattillo, Mary E. 2013. *Black picket fences: Privilege and peril among the black middle class*. 2nd ed. Chicago, IL: University of Chicago Press.

Perry, Brea L., Bernice A. Pescosolido, and Stephen P. Borgatti. 2018. *Egocentric network analysis: Foundations, methods, and models*, vol. 44. New York, NY: Cambridge University Press.

Powell, Walter W., and Paul J. DiMaggio, eds. 1991. *The new institutionalism in organizational analysis*. Chicago, IL: University of Chicago Press.

Raudenbush, Danielle. 2016. "I stay by myself": Social support, distrust, and selective solidarity among the urban poor. *Sociological Forum* 31 (4): 1018–39.

Reid, Jeanne L., Anne Martin, and Jeanne Brooks-Gunn. 2017. Low-income parents' adult interactions at childcare centres. *Early Child Development and Care* 187 (1): 138–51.

Rivera, Mark T., Sara B. Soderstrom, and Brian Uzzi. 2010. Dynamics of dyads in social networks: Assortative, relational, and proximity mechanisms. *Annual Review of Sociology* 36 (1): 91–115.

Rolfe, Sharne A., and Kirsten J. Armstrong. 2010. Early childhood professionals as a source of social support: The role of parent-professional communication. *Australasian Journal of Early Childhood* 35 (3): 60–67.

Ryan, William. 1976. *Blaming the victim*. Rev. updated ed. New York, NY: Vintage Books.

Sampson, Robert J. 2012. *Great American city: Chicago and the enduring neighborhood effect*. Chicago, IL: University of Chicago Press.

Scott, W. Richard. 1995. *Institutions and organizations*. Thousand Oaks, CA: Sage Publications.

Scott, W. Richard. 2003. *Organizations: Rational, natural, and open systems*. Upper Saddle River, NJ: Prentice Hall.

Shabazz, David L. 2016. Barbershops as cultural forums for African American males. *Journal of Black Studies* 47 (4): 295–312.

Shoji, Megan N., Anna R. Haskins, David E. Rangel, and Kia N. Sorensen. 2014. The emergence of social capital in low-income Latino elementary schools. *Early Childhood Research Quarterly* 29 (4): 600–613.

Simmel, Georg. 1950. *The sociology of Georg Simmel*. Trans. K. H. Wolff. Glencoe, IL: Free Press.

Simmel, Georg. 1955. The web of group affiliations. In *Conflict and the web of group affiliations*, 125–95. New York, NY: Free Press.

Small, Mario Luis. 2006. Neighborhood institutions as resource brokers: Childcare centers, interorganizational ties, and resource access among the poor. *Social Problems* 53 (2): 274–92.

Small, Mario Luis. 2007. Racial differences in networks: Do neighborhood conditions matter? *Social Science Quarterly* 88 (2): 320–43.

Small, Mario Luis. 2009. *Unanticipated gains: Origins of network inequality in everyday life.* New York, NY: Oxford University Press.

Small, Mario Luis. 2017. *Someone to talk to.* New York, NY: Oxford University Press.

Small, Mario Luis, and Laura Adler. 2019. The role of space in the formation of social ties. *Annual Review of Sociology* 45:111–32.

Smith, Sandra Susan. 2007. *Lone pursuit: Distrust and defensive individualism among the black poor.* New York, NY: Russell Sage Foundation.

Snijders, Tom A. B., Gerhard G. Van de Bunt, and Christian E. G. Steglich. 2010. Introduction to stochastic actor-based models for network dynamics. *Social Networks* 32 (1): 44–60.

Soller, Brian, Jessica R. Goodkind, R. Neil Greene, Christopher R. Browning, and Cece Shantzek. 2018. Ecological networks and community attachment and support among recently resettled refugees. *American Journal of Community Psychology* 61 (3–4): 332–43.

Sommer, Teresa Eckrich, Terri J. Sabol, P. Lindsay Chase-Lansdale, Mario Small, Henry Wilde, Sean Brown, and Zong Yang Huang. 2017. Promoting parents' social capital to increase children's attendance in Head Start: Evidence from an experimental intervention. *Journal of Research on Educational Effectiveness* 10 (4): 732–66.

Stack, Carol B. 1974. *All our kin: Strategies for survival in a black community.* New York, NY: Harper & Row.

Stovel, Katherine, Benjamin Golub, and Eva M. Meyersson Milgrom. 2011. Stabilizing brokerage. *Proceedings of the National Academy of Sciences* 108 (suppl. 4): 21326–32.

Stovel, Katherine, and Lynette Shaw. 2012. Brokerage. *Annual Review of Sociology* 38 (1): 139–58.

Taylor, Robert Joseph, and Linda M. Chatters. 1988. Church members as a source of informal social support. *Review of Religious Research* 30 (2): 193–203.

Tilly, Charles. 1998. *Durable inequality.* Berkeley, CA: University of California Press.

van Eijk, Gwen. 2010. Does living in a poor neighbourhood result in network poverty? A study on local networks, locality-based relationships and neighbourhood settings. *Journal of Housing and the Built Environment* 25 (4): 467–80.

Verbrugge, Lois M. 1977. The structure of adult friendship choices. *Social Forces* 56 (2): 576–97.

Wacquant, Loïc. 2009. *Punishing the poor: The neoliberal government of social insecurity.* Durham, NC: Duke University Press.

Warren, Roland Leslie. 1978. *The community in America.* 3rd ed. Chicago, IL: Rand McNally.

Watkins-Hayes, Celeste. 2013. The micro dynamics of support seeking: The social and economic utility of institutional ties for HIV-positive women. *The ANNALS of the American Academy of Political and Social Science* 647 (1): 83–101.

Watkins-Hayes, Celeste. 2019. *Remaking a life: How women living with HIV/AIDS confront inequality.* Berkeley, CA: University of California Press.

Wimmer, Andreas, and Kevin Lewis. 2010. Beyond and below racial homophily: ERG models of a friendship network documented on Facebook. *American Journal of Sociology* 116 (2): 583–642.

Wrong, Dennis H. 1961. The oversocialized conception of man in modern sociology. *American Sociological Review* 26 (2): 183–193.

"My Crying Is Not a Cry by Itself": Building Sustainable Social Ties through a Poor People's Organization

Research has highlighted that social ties help poor people to survive, but has also shown that nonkin ties often only last a short time. In this article, I argue that organizations that serve the needs of poor people can help to create more sustainable supportive ties among them. Drawing on participant observation and ethnographic interviews with twenty-five members of the Kensington Welfare Rights Union (KWRU) in Philadelphia—an organization of, by, and for poor people—I found that supportive ties among members of KWRU can last years or even decades. I show how this organization enabled poor people to create and maintain supportive ties. KWRU provided people living in desperate poverty space for frequent interaction, connection, and cooperation. The organization supported a sense of kinship among members, and group leaders often helped to mend rifts between members. While KWRU is distinctive, other organizations that serve the needs of poor people could use this model to be more responsive to the needs of those in poverty.

Keywords: social ties; poverty; social support; survival strategies; sustainable ties

By
JOAN MAYA MAZELIS

Social scientists have long documented the importance and utility of social ties (Domínguez and Watkins 2003; Edin and Lein 1997; Granovetter 1973, 1974/1995; Mazelis 2015, 2017; Seccombe 1999; Stack 1974). A

Joan Maya Mazelis is an associate professor of sociology in the Department of Sociology, Anthropology and Criminal Justice at Rutgers University–Camden, and an affiliated scholar at Rutgers–Camden's Center for Urban Research and Education. She is the author of Surviving Poverty: Creating Sustainable Ties among the Poor *(NYU Press 2017).*

NOTE: This study was made possible by a National Science Foundation Doctoral Dissertation Improvement Grant Award, a School of Arts and Sciences Dissertation Fellowship Award at the University of Pennsylvania, two Otto and Gertrude K. Pollak Summer Research Fellowships from the Department of Sociology at the University of Pennsylvania, and a National Science Foundation RU FAIR ADVANCE award at Rutgers University.

Correspondence: mazelis@camden.rutgers.edu

DOI: 10.1177/0002716220918165

range of studies indicate that the poor in particular rely on such ties to further employment opportunities (Newman 1999; Smith 2005, 2007) and as a means of survival (Edin and Lein 1996, 1997; Harknett 2006; Hansen 2004; Nelson 2000). Since the Personal Responsibility and Work Opportunity Reconciliation Act of 1996, commonly known as welfare reform, the U.S. public safety net has become increasingly threadbare. Social service organizations provide support to poor people (Domínguez and Watkins 2003), but they cannot meet all needs. As a result, private safety nets of social ties—typically kin ties—have become ever more crucial for the poor (Edin and Lein 1997; Harknett 2006; Mazelis 2017; Stack 1974). Those without kin to depend on sometimes develop fleeting ties with new acquaintances that can further the instability of their lives (Desmond 2012). This article argues that an organization that serves the needs of poor people can create conditions in which they can build highly supportive ties with nonkin that last for the long term and provide deep support for those in dire need.

This article focuses on the Kensington Welfare Rights Union (KWRU), a grassroots anti-poverty organization in Philadelphia, Pennsylvania. In KWRU, people who were poor enough that most had experienced homelessness built *sustainable ties* through membership in this distinctive organization of, by, and for poor people. I use the term "sustainable ties" for these nonkin ties because they lasted at least a year and sometimes lasted decades. The term suggests greater durability than "disposable ties" (Desmond 2012); disposable ties dissolve in weeks or months, despite strong sentiment and mutual support. This article focuses on the research question: How did this distinctive organization enable poor people to develop and maintain supportive nonkin social ties?

Since its founding by poor women in 1991, KWRU has drawn membership from throughout Philadelphia. Dedicated to raising awareness of the perspectives and experiences of poor people, it has held regular demonstrations making a case for poverty alleviation and destigmatization over the years. Its ultimate goal is to end poverty nationwide, but it has supported members' day-to-day survival as well: distributing free food, providing temporary housing, and addressing other urgent issues. I found that in lieu of membership dues, it expected members to participate in rallies, volunteer at the office, and help other members however they could. As this article describes, the *sustainable ties* it has created and maintained have provided deep and broad support to extremely poor members. The resilience of sustainable ties gives such ties particular power in the lives of people with few advantages.

Background

Supportive social ties among poor people

Research on social support among poor people has demonstrated that social networks provide significant benefits (Domínguez and Watkins 2003; Edin and Lein 1997; Mazelis 2015, 2017; Mazelis and Mykyta 2011; Newman 1999; Stack

1974). Carol Stack documented "a cooperative lifestyle built upon exchange and reciprocity" among kin and fictive kin that provided deep support (1974, 125). Stack's study participants relied on the social networks she described, as well as the social support they provided, to cope with the daily challenges of poverty (see also Edin and Lein 1997; Seccombe 1999).

The literature shows that kin and fictive kin provide different kinds of assistance, ranging from free meals to child care to financial support to employment referrals. Sharing benefits from the federal Supplemental Nutrition Assistance Program (SNAP; commonly called food stamps) is common in part because in some jurisdictions recipients may receive their stamps at different times of the month, and some may be running short just as others have received them (see, for example, Henly, Danziger, and Offer 2005). As Kristen Harknett noted, "social networks play an important role in providing financial and in-kind support to poor families" (2006, 174; see also Domínguez and Watkins 2003; Edin and Lein 1996, 1997). Margaret Nelson showed that shared economic circumstances support such networks, stating that "the assurance that those who live in similar circumstances will understand, and be sympathetic about, one's circumstances," fuels supportive ties even more than kinship terminology does (2005, 69; see also Nelson 2000). At the same time, the networks to which poor people have access tend to have meager resources, so immense need may quickly drain those resources (Edin 2001).

When traditional social ties are lacking

The work demonstrating social support among the poor is compelling, yet researchers have found that support is not universally available in poor communities (Levine 2013; Offer 2012a, 2012b; Putnam 2000; Roschelle 1997; Sampson 2012; Small 2009b; Smith 2007; Stack 1974). Many researchers have documented the limits of kin networks for the poor, who must seek employment referrals, material assistance, or emotional help elsewhere, due to kin's reluctance or inability to help (Desmond 2012; Harknett 2006; Henly 2002; Henly, Danziger, and Offer 2005; McDonald and Armstrong 2001; Offer 2010, 2012b; Smith 2005, 2007). Harknett (2006) demonstrated, using a large survey dataset, that those without support from family were less likely to be employed, earned less money, and had greater dependence on public assistance. As Shira Offer stated: "The most vulnerable and disadvantaged mothers, those in greatest need for support, are the least likely to have it available from their networks" (2012a, 120; see also Offer 2010).

The difficulties of the poor do not somehow dissipate when there are no kin available to provide assistance. As Matthew Desmond stated, getting by without kin support is "next to impossible" for the poor (2012, 1298). The "brittle and fleeting" "disposable" ties he documented between recently evicted individuals helped poor people to move forward from one day to the next. But they contrasted sharply with the ones Stack documented because their short duration "bred instability and fostered misgivings" (pp. 1296–97). Conflict frequently destroyed the ties that Desmond's participants had relied upon.

Deindustrialization and the increase of concentrated poverty have left those in poor neighborhoods with few social ties, which exacerbates high levels of unemployment and poverty (Portes 1998; Putnam 2000; Wilson 1987). The spatial concentration of poverty has created disadvantaged environments that became progressively isolated socially and economically (Anderson 1990; Massey and Denton 1993; Offer 2012a; Wilson 1987, 2001). In structurally isolated neighborhoods, poor people also isolate themselves from peers while trying to become upwardly mobile (Mazelis 2017; Portes 1998), an aspiration they are unlikely to realize (see, for example, Fader 2013). In addition, a strongly held individualistic ideology, general distrust of others, perceptions that other poor people are dangerous, pervasive poverty stigma, and fear of obligations to others also lead poor people to prefer to avoid social ties (Mazelis 2017).

Mutual support and strong ties require trust, and trust can be in short supply in poor communities (Fader 2013; Furstenberg 2001; Levine 2013; Seccombe 1999; Smith 2007). Kathryn Edin and Maria Kefalas described trust among their poor study participants as "astonishingly low," noting that most had no close friends, and many distrusted close kin (2005, 34). As Levine stated, "The desperation that powerlessness creates means that everyone must be out for him- or herself at times" (2013, 40–41).

The role of organizations in social ties

Neighborhood institutions can provide a mechanism for tie creation, brokering both social ties to occasion friendship and organizational ties to help clients gather resources (Small 2009b; see also Marwell 2007; Marwell and McQuarrie 2013; Offer 2010, 2012a; Small and Allard 2013; Watkins-Hayes 2013). Mario Luis Small documented that organizations can foster trust between people, and thereby "perform much of the 'work' required to sustain strong friendships" (2009b, 87). In Small's research, childcare centers "generate multiple opportunities and inducements for parents to interact" (2009b, 51). The childcare centers he studied create a focus in the purest sense, a separate point of attention that orients the actions of the parties. And therein lies the advantage and disadvantage of this type of relation: a place to interact and institutionally set times for the parties to do so sustains the relationship without requiring much effort from the parties to maintain it (2009b, 106).

Small identified the importance of repeated interaction through such practices as monthly parents' association meetings and school trips. Respondents supported one another through information relevant to parenting and through occasional child care assistance. Some of these people became friends and stayed in touch as their children aged out of the childcare centers, and some considered each other family; whether the ties would last more than a few years was beyond the scope of the study. Other studies of ties formed through organizations do not address duration either (Marwell 2007; Marwell and McQuarrie 2013; Watkins-Hayes 2013).

Small asserted that people trust each other more as they encounter each other more; he also said that "centers represent a kind of safe space" in which to build trust (2009b, 184). Other studies have also shown that organizations can help to facilitate trust and foster relationships among members or clients (Marwell 2007; Marwell and McQuarrie 2013; Small 2009b; Watkins-Hayes 2013). Small's research did not focus on poor people, but Desmond wrote that for poor people, institutions that serve those with urgent needs were often sites of disposable tie formation, including "welfare offices, food pantries, job centers, Alcoholics Anonymous clubs, methadone clinics, even the waiting areas of eviction court" (2012, 1313). Similarly, AIDS service organizations (Watkins-Hayes 2013) and community-based organizations (Marwell 2007) have supported deep and meaningful ties among poor people. While tie formation among poor people likely resembles tie building among any other group in many respects, these environments and the emotional and financial vulnerability of the people in them may put pressure on ties—a pressure not present when wealthier people build ties. Greater dependence on them for basic needs may also strain ties, especially among people with few resources (Edin 2001).

While it is possible that organizations offer mechanisms to support the maintenance of ties in the face of stressors that might lead to their dissolution, the literature has focused on tie formation rather than maintenance. Desmond's (2012) research suggests that such maintenance could be vital, given the disruption and increased instability he attributed to the dissolution of ties between poor people.

Methods

I conducted participant observation and in-depth, semi-structured interviews with fifty low-income individuals in Philadelphia, including twenty-five interviews with members of KWRU, selected nonrandomly (see below). At the time of the research, KWRU could offer temporary shelter in Takeover Houses and Human Rights Houses—the former being an extra-legal response to lack of housing, using abandoned buildings; and the latter being homes they rented with foundation funding. Members sometimes received cash assistance from welfare and housing vouchers from the city because of KWRU protests. Sometimes referred to as "Section 8," the official name of the housing voucher program is the Housing Choice Voucher Program. It is a federal program administered at the local level that pays approved rental amounts above 30 percent of a family's income. Under the time limits on cash assistance created by welfare reform, KWRU members were living on a patched-together system of various forms of aid, including SNAP, medical assistance or low-cost clinic care, occasional grants to pay utility bills, and food banks.

During my research, there was no official count of membership or formal procedure involved in becoming a KWRU member. Generally, members had gotten help from the group, came to a protest, or volunteered to help out at the office and kept coming back, thereby maintaining the connection over time. There also was no formal process for designating leaders; people willing to take on more responsibility and spend more of their time on organizational activities became leaders. They typically led member meetings and chants at protests. Members referred new individuals to them for questions, and they often served as informal spokespersons to the press.

In late 2003 when my research with KWRU began, members and activists had a busy daily schedule, and the office on North 5th Street was often abuzz with activity, providing practical assistance to members and walk-ins and planning protests. Interviews concluded in mid-2006, but I reconnected with the group in 2012. By that time, many of the activists had reoriented much of their energy to political and national concerns, investing time and resources in the Poor People's Economic Human Rights Campaign (PPEHRC), an umbrella organization encompassing dozens of groups and spearheaded by KWRU leaders, with which the group had effectively merged. As of 2019, PPEHRC continues to maintain a local office where they assist people who call or walk in needing assistance, although they now lack foundation funding to provide Human Rights Houses.

During my research, I spent a few days each week at the KWRU office over a period of several months, meeting people, building trust and rapport, and requesting interviews. No one turned me down. Most involved members came to know me by face and name; they began referring me to other members. All interviews took place in locations of participants' choosing: fifteen in participants' homes, one on the telephone due to the participant's health limitations, five participants at the KWRU office, one at my office, and three organization leaders I interviewed on the go—at restaurants, in their cars, or other locations. For eleven participants, we finished our conversations in one visit. Nine interviews took two visits each, and five interviews we completed in three or more visits. Interviews ranged from two to seven hours. All names used are pseudonyms chosen by participants, and oral consent was obtained from all participants. I audio recorded all interviews with participant permission.

Questions centered on participants' life histories, including occupational, educational, and welfare experience; their views on welfare and on work; their opinions about what should be done about poverty; their self-images and experiences with stigma; their perceptions of both the working and the nonworking poor and how they think other poor people see these groups; what they think other poor people's views on welfare and poverty are; what kind of help they receive; what kind of help they give to others; and their experiences in KWRU. The existence of ties and sustainable ties emerged from the data in an inductive coding process relying on grounded theory.

The qualitative research this study used was well-suited to the research questions, due to the focus on the feelings, meanings, and experiences of participants (Berg and Lune 2012; Strauss and Corbin 1998). As Small stated, "The strengths of qualitative work come from understanding *how* and *why*, not understanding *how many*. . ." (2008, 170; emphasis in original). Rather than aiming to present a representative account of social ties among the poor, this study describes the range of experiences among members of an antipoverty organization.

At the time of interview, participants ranged in age from 21 to 59 years old; 23 were women and 2 were men; 9 were African American, 8 were white, and 8

were Latina. The majority of participants were women due to the larger research
project's aims.[1] While I sought racial and ethnic balance in the study sample, in
part to reflect KWRU membership, I did not select participants as a means to
achieve representativeness. Rather, I recruited a varied sample to maximize variability across the range of potential participants and responses. The study provides theoretical insights but not generalizable findings (see Small 2008 and
2009a for relevant discussions). In-depth interviews, which allowed themes to
emerge inductively, also yielded theoretical saturation (Small 2009a): each participant provided insights, and participant observation and interviews revealed
the range of different experiences, eventually producing only affirmation of previously recorded information. Therefore, participants' statements reported below
do not represent frequencies of particular responses, as the meaning lies in the
range of variability.

Findings

KWRU membership supplied crucial support for extremely poor members, both
because members shared their scarce resources and because the organization
helped them to find resources. Sustainable ties were a part of that crucial support, and KWRU offered physical spaces and opportunities to encourage members to form ties, providing a context in which members built trust. The
organizational embeddedness of these social ties enabled not only their formation but also their strength and durability. KWRU members signaled the supportive nature of their ties through understanding them as similar to kin ties.
KWRU helped members to maintain these ties, furthering their sustainability, by
helping to smooth conflicts that arose and by relying on reciprocity within the
group to keep people connected. Yet KWRU ties did not work for all members.
In addition to the people who never came to my attention because their involvement with the organization was fleeting, I interviewed three individuals who
received substantial support for a period but who were no longer significantly
connected to the organization at the conclusion of the research.

Broad and deep support for those falling without a net

KWRU members' description of their circumstances reflected the continued
disintegration of the public safety net, coupled with a lack of family on whom to
rely, that created an urgent need for social support. Twenty-three out of the
twenty-five KWRU members who participated in this study had experienced
homelessness, yet most were unable to rely on family at even the most desperate
times. Only seven participants had received housing assistance from family members at any time in their adult lives, and only one was doing so at the time of the
interview—Stefanie, who was paying rent to her parents and purchasing food for
herself and her children, although she was poor enough to qualify for SNAP
benefits. Rosa's cousin not only did not take her and her daughter in when they

were living on the streets, but asked her to pay for water if they bathed at the cousin's house. Pauline was homeless when she came to KWRU, because, she said, her family had "turned their backs on" her. Colleen was in foster care as a child and was homeless in her teen years. Her biological parents struggled with drug addiction throughout her childhood and had not been a source of support in her adulthood either.

With no other private safety net to speak of, members often came to KWRU in times of desperate need, such as when they faced homelessness. They reported learning about KWRU in a variety of ways: from family members who were already involved, acquaintances, or neighbors; seeing a sign or a poster; walking past the office, a protest, or members distributing food to hungry people in their neighborhoods; or seeing local news coverage of the organization. Participants often held distrustful and stigmatized views of their neighborhoods and about poor people generally. Only desperation led them to overcome, reluctantly, their resistance to connecting with other poor people. Yet they built trusting, supportive relationships with others within the organization. KWRU filled a vacuum, providing a safety net for people without reliable kin ties. These ties provided support that was both broad and deep.

Most housing support came directly from the organization, including help securing a housing voucher and space in temporary KWRU housing. Other kinds of help—such as with navigating welfare programs, health care, and utilities; with money, transportation, and child care; finding information about schools and legal services; and obtaining clothes, food, furniture, and other material items—were often member-to-member. Amanda, a member of KWRU who had maintained her tie with the organization since the early 1990s, described the types of member-to-member support at KWRU, suggesting the wide range of support, which included "anything, you know, from the car breaks down every other day kind of thing to help with food, help with keeping a utility on if it's gonna be shut off . . . every possible thing." Members who had received help getting a housing voucher from the organization often allowed new, homeless members to stay with them temporarily; in one case a member provided housing for the adolescent niece of another member, who was homeless due to parental abuse.

Members frequently cooked for each other, and some might get their only complete and balanced meals on a given day from each other in this way. I was present when Paloma served a meal that was completely sugar-free because a member with diabetes was present—a vital form of support given he did not always have enough money for food. Sharing food was normalized in the organization; CC told me she and Shy, who she met at a KWRU house, "share everything," including food.

KWRU was a source of peer emotional support as well. KWRU provided the warmth and caring members often lacked from friends and family members. When Becky's son had legal trouble, members of KWRU came to court with her to support her. Amanda listed ten members of KWRU she had authorized to pick up her child at school. Three of the four people Colleen listed as those who gave her emotional support regularly are people she met through KWRU. She told me, "I view KWRU as a safe place for me . . . to be just who I am."

KWRU members relied on each other for frequent and urgent support that addressed fundamental needs. Jessie and Cate met through KWRU. As Jessie described, she had recently brought a big trash bag full of freshly washed, wet clothes to Cate's house. "She dries them for me, she folds them for me and puts them back in the bags and I just picked them up. So that's the relationship that I have with [Cate]." KWRU is the social glue that facilitated Jessie and Cate's tie, and this kind of relationship, lasting for several years, was not atypical between KWRU members. Jessie and Cate were living in extreme poverty. Like most of the other members of KWRU, they have experienced homelessness, and Jessie, like many members, had young children. Lacking a clothes dryer, as Jessie did, was not unusual. Few members had cars, although public transportation was thin in their neighborhoods. Members often could not be sure of three meals a day. The creation of social ties was a major way KWRU addressed their problems.

Creating ties: Making opportunities through shared spaces

KWRU actively sought to create opportunities for members to develop ties with one another. Walter, a group leader, told me that KWRU deliberately put people "in relation to others" so that they felt acknowledged, cared for, and "know that they're not crying alone." For him, a key reason to be active in KWRU was the value in "being out there and realizing that my crying is not a cry by itself. There's other people crying too. And by putting myself in relationship to other people, I gather strength. . . . There's no way that we can exist without each other." This active encouragement of relationships was part of KWRU's strategy for increasing membership, and it created a climate in which people established trusting, supportive ties with one another that lasted for years.

Walter described a straight line between building ties and KWRU's position that poverty reflects unjust structural factors rather than personal failings. However, even for the many KWRU members I interviewed who did not fully embrace KWRU's ideological position, the sense of shared experience had an impact and supported the building of ties. Shy emphasized the importance of shared experiences with Valerie. She met Valerie through KWRU and they lived in the same Human Rights House. She attributed their closeness to that shared experience and sense of shared struggle to survive, that they became close "because we needed each other . . . in order to survive."

Shared time in close quarters provided the physical opportunity for members who shared housing to develop ties. Members shared food as well as SNAP benefits. Jessie told me that if she ran out of food, another KWRU member "would give me her food stamps or some of her food stamps and I would go and buy some stuff, and then when I got mine I would give them back to her." And when Jessie had to leave early in the morning to bring her son to school, she would leave her daughters sleeping in the KWRU house, having asked Rebecca and Naomi, who were living in the same house, to keep an eye on them until she got back. Volunteering in the office, walking picket lines outside the Office of Emergency Shelter and Services, and staging sit-ins at the mayor's office in city hall put KWRU members in the same spaces and allowed them to talk and get to know each other. Time together occasioned conversations about shared difficulties, allowing people to see their commonalities and begin to forge bonds.

Maintaining ties through a sense of kinship

Beyond creating ties, a sense of kinship helped to maintain ties among members. Pauline noted that when KWRU helped her when she was homeless and had lost her welfare benefits, "they treated me like a family, like I was part of their little family." Rebecca was living rent-free in a KWRU Human Rights House when she told me KWRU had "done more for us than my family has ever done." Becky, a member for nearly 10 years, told me, "If anything goes wrong in my life, it's KWRU. To me they have become my family." These members' use of kinship terms acknowledged that the help they received, in times of desperation, was deeper than people typically receive outside the context of family, and this encouraged them to treat KWRU ties as essentially permanent. For example, Jessie described Cate as like a mother to her, and said that Cate and her adult son Max "welcomed me right in like if I was family. Right off. No one else ever did that for me, not even family. . . . So for some stranger to do that to me made me feel that, you know, I have lots of love for them." Jessie later asked Cate and Max to be her daughters' godparents.

The language of kinship was common among those loosely designated as group leaders, including James, Walter, and Paloma, who modeled this understanding for others. James said he saw members "as like my brothers and sisters all the way around the board." Walter met a homeless youth through his work with KWRU, and ended up taking him into his home; he came to see this young man as his son. While this kind of all-but-legal adoption was unusual, having a group leader take this step probably had an impact throughout the organization, demonstrating to members the value of close ties in KWRU. Paloma set a tone that other members frequently echoed when she said: "They're family. Hell, fuck friends. You can choose your friends; you can't choose your family. They're family."

Paloma's statement pointed out a difference between the ties members built in KWRU and the nonkin ties other researchers have found: they did not rely in the same way on a sense of personal compatibility and mutual affinity. While participants chose to be members of the organization, they came looking for help in times of desperation, not for personal connection, and they did not choose one another specifically. The ties they built were less likely to dissolve in the face of rifts than tenuous ties that new acquaintances form based on affinity typically are. Of course, mutual fondness strengthened ties between KWRU members who liked one another: just as in a family, personal compatibility affected the way support worked. But some members felt inexorably connected to each other by KWRU, regardless of how much they liked each other. This provided a sustainability that mutual affinity simply could not have.

Maintaining ties through healing conflict and smoothing rifts

KWRU's role in healing conflict between members was even more distinctive and also helped to maintain ties. Cate and Paloma had a conflict over child care during my research, but both remained KWRU activists and colleagues, working together and speaking of each other with admiration and respect. When I reconnected with the organization in 2014, Cate was caring for Paloma's children during a meeting. Similarly, CC and Shy shared resources for a period, but remained friendly even when CC pulled back from the arrangement.

When conflicts did drive members apart, KWRU served as a bridge to replacement ties because the rift with another member did not end KWRU's support. This applied even if the conflict was between a newer or less-involved member and someone firmly enmeshed in the group. Rosa lived with Paloma for a period, but they had a falling out. Rather than ejecting Rosa from the organization, KWRU provided Rosa space in a KWRU Takeover House. Pauline and Shy had personal issues with James, but they continued to receive help from the organization. While leadership in KWRU is quite informal, Paloma or James could certainly have acted to complicate Rosa's, Pauline's, or Shy's relationship to the organization. Paloma and James were generous, but more importantly, they deeply respected the KWRU norm that personal rifts should not threaten group cohesion.

KWRU leadership had identified ties between members as crucial to the organization's effectiveness, recognizing that many poor people lack social ties. As Walter told me, "You show me a poor person, I'll show you a person who's isolated . . . [but] increasingly people have no other recourse but to rely on each other." He explained, "There's no way that we can exist without each other." Because of this, highly involved members sometimes directly intervened in rifts, the way an elder in an extended family might. Pauline's conflict with James, which related to his brother who was also active in the group, led KWRU's founder to pull them aside. She said she was going away on a trip soon and, according to Pauline, "she didn't want no problems or nothing while she was going away, so [James and I] talked. . . . We got straightened out."

Maintaining ties through generalized reciprocity

While reciprocity's role in the organization is beyond the scope of this article and I have explored it elsewhere (Mazelis 2015, 2017), it was KWRU's major currency, as reciprocating to the organization for help substituted for membership dues. For the most part, members paid these dues by attending rallies and volunteering at the office. While these activities created space and opportunity for members to form relationships with one another, they were also part of a system of reciprocity that spilled over to members, creating generalized reciprocity within the organization in which members paid forward the help they received by helping other members who had not directly helped them. Members gave to the organization not only because the organization would benefit them but also because other members would aid them too, and they supported each other in part because the organization had supported them. This built trust, significantly supporting the maintenance of ties.

KWRU needed to support ties between members so that reciprocity functioned smoothly and the organization would have resources, which were in short supply as members paid no dues and KWRU had no paid staff. The organization needed to encourage ties between members so that they would help one another, because a significant amount of the support it provided was member-to-member. This led to generalized reciprocity, which rewarded members for giving to other members. CC volunteered at the office, helping other members, in the hope that when the organization received housing vouchers to distribute to members, she would get one. When Paloma cooked for other members, it was not that she believed they would cook for her in the future, nor that some other KWRU member would help her with food necessarily. She helped other members in part out of gratitude for the housing voucher she secured with KWRU's help in the past. She also had a general expectation—frequently met—that other members would be generous with her in the future. This system of generalized reciprocity stretched extremely thin resources such that many could benefit.

Membership in KWRU provided real value through the organization and its members, through access to resources and as a resource broker. Generalized reciprocity allowed members to give help to each other more freely, trusting members of the group as a collective and removing some of the emotional complications that often accompanies reciprocity between individuals. There was a downside of this, however, as KWRU protected this generalized reciprocity by exacting consequences for members who did not fulfill reciprocity expectations, as described in the next section.

The limits of social ties through KWRU

I found that most members of KWRU felt positively about the ties they built in KWRU—about their involvement and connections with other members of the group. Paloma described the help she'd gotten through these ties as "enormous . . . from a plate of food to a house." Thinking about this support, she said, "I think I'm fortunate, like I'm one of those rare few people who can truly say that my life hasn't been easy, but I've been blessed. . . . I've been truly blessed."

Yet a few members left the organization or were effectively forced out because of negative feelings about reciprocity. Rebecca and Naomi, residents of the same KWRU house, were forced out of it at the same time. I watched this situation unfold during my research; both women failed to comply with the organization's reciprocity norms, which were key to building sustainable ties. In only requiring members to give their time, KWRU made it possible for even the desperately poor to conform to its norms. Nonetheless, even time was a thin resource for members.

Another reason Naomi and Rebecca had not fulfilled reciprocity norms is that they found doing so frustrating. Naomi told me, "as much as they want us to come [to the office], they really don't be having anything for us to do down there." While volunteering at the KWRU office aided in the building of social ties, I observed people with little to do there. Rebecca walked to the office to volunteer on a bitterly cold day and found it locked and empty (I also went to the office more than once for a pre-scheduled appointment and found the same thing). While I cannot say with certainty that Rebecca and Naomi were forced out because they failed to meet reciprocity obligations, it appeared so, as reciprocity was key to KWRU's functioning. The ongoing support that Rosa, Pauline, and Shy received despite conflicts with highly involved members suggests that the organization was reluctant to expel people. Rebecca's and Naomi's loss of ties represent how the organization's greatest strength—the ability to build lasting ties between people whose lives are deeply unstable—sometimes became a weakness. Yet this weakness was not pervasive. Jessie had built ties with Rebecca and Naomi, which dissolved when Rebecca and Naomi were effectively forced out. Nevertheless, Jessie retained her tie to the organization because she fully recognized its value in helping her obtain crucial resources and emotional support.

Helen did not recognize KWRU's value in the same way that Jessie did. Unlike Rebecca and Naomi, she *chose* to leave. But she had sustainable ties once: she was a member of KWRU for five years, and she acknowledged that the group's efforts prevented her from losing her heat one winter. She still spoke with affection for KWRU's founder. However, Helen had pulled back, deciding KWRU membership was a poor investment because it was unlikely to help her achieve upward mobility. Ultimately, she said that her involvement made her:

> think about doing everything on my own because that's the only way it's gonna get done. That's the way I feel. I even told them that . . .why would I want to work with people that's gonna keep me down there instead of putting me up where I want to be? . . . There's people out there that really wants to get homes and stuff, and they act like they can help 'em, but they really can't. . . . It looks like it doesn't go anywhere.

Yet Helen's standard of living was among the worst I observed. She was working intermittently at one of the Philadelphia stadiums, but her work schedule was inconsistent and her income unpredictable. She was not receiving cash assistance, and she and her common-law husband had several children. Their home was literally falling apart; the sink was detached and hanging by a thread from the bathroom wall with no running water. It seemed likely that KWRU could have helped Helen improve her living conditions.

Becky's view of KWRU and what the organization had given her contrasted with Helen's, demonstrating the strength of what KWRU could provide and summarizing the more common view of ties built through the organization:

> [KWRU] became my life. They gave me everything, everything back. . . . A person feels as though you don't know where to turn and you're backed up against the wall and you have nothing and you have children to take care of and your health is not that great and along comes an organization that says, "Look I will teach you step by step how to get your life situated."

Becky had already been a member for many years when I interviewed her. Her experience of long-lasting ties within the group was not unusual, and she was one of several participants who were still members of the group in 2014 when I attended a PPEHRC meeting. At that meeting, I saw several participants interacting with the same warmth and familiarity I had observed years before, some of them enjoying supportive relationships they had built in KWRU and sustained for more than 20 years. Such support does not typically come from social ties outside of family members and is evidence of the value and the exceptional distinctiveness of the sustainable ties that KWRU provides.

Discussion

KWRU bolstered and strengthened otherwise thin and fragile bonds between people who started off as strangers. Poor individuals developed ties to the group, and through the group to other individuals, and the organization strengthened a tenuous strand between them through its emphasis on kinship, healing rifts, and generalized reciprocity. This combination created social ties in which KWRU was embedded as an organization, making the ties better able to bear the heavy burdens they faced, more likely to withstand swift winds of crisis, and therefore more likely to be sustainable. KWRU fostered trusting ties between people, but it *also* provided a means for ties to work even before individuals knew enough to trust each other, secure in the knowledge that they would retain the tie to the organization even if the person with whom they had begun to build a tie left KWRU.

For many study participants, KWRU ties were deep, trusting, and long-lasting, which is unusual outside of kinship. While they lack the permanence of kin ties, these ties frequently lasted for years, even decades. This sustainability distinguishes them from the ties that Desmond (2012) documented and therefore protected KWRU members from many of the downsides of disposable ties. Although Desmond's findings include housing support in the form of doubling up with new acquaintances, he noted that because the ties that prompted these exchanges of support did not last long, they were a source of instability instead of security. Disposable ties may in fact be an indispensable resource for the poor, but *sustainable ties* can provide many of the same benefits with fewer of the drawbacks. Like disposable ties, but unlike those Small (2009b) documented among parents who met through childcare centers, the ties discussed in this article were between very poor people who shared crucial resources.

The organizational embeddedness of these ties demonstrates that KWRU provided a means for people to trust each other. Levine found that people decided if they could trust others "based on direct interactions themselves, similar past experiences, or the experiences of others they knew" (2013, 40). Small (2009b) found that childcare centers alleviated this need by serving as a broker for ties, and KWRU provided similar support by vouching for people, but for a uniformly poor population. KWRU ties were a great source of support and stability for those members who remained a part of the organization for extended periods.

Of course, my sampling method steered me toward people with ties to others in the group, as in many cases people referred me to one another. And the organization was so unusual—a multiracial activist organization, of, by, and for poor people that provides social services but was unquestionably not a social service agency—that findings reported here are not generalizable. But the existence of sustainable ties within the organization is notable. The organization's distinctiveness is precisely what allows us to understand how powerful its strategies were, and to speculate that if more conventional social service organizations adopted these strategies, they might be able to build sustainable ties as well, including across lines of race and ethnicity. As noted above, my participants were mostly women due to the larger research project's aims, but the organization included many men as well. I did not find gender or race and ethnicity to be deciding factors in the creation or maintenance of ties in this study.

Social service organizations could both offer direct support and encourage ties, fostering trust among people who normally would not trust each other, and in doing so allow clients to build social ties that last for years. The first mechanism that fostered the sustainability of KWRU ties, a sense of kinship, might not be a natural part of most social service organizations without the kind of grassroots leadership that created KWRU. Yet over time and with the trust that organizations could build among clientele, a sense of kinship might arise.

The second mechanism that aided in the sustainability of ties in KWRU was smoothing conflicts and healing rifts between members. Social service organizations could smooth rifts between individuals, increasing the sustainability of ties. Past research suggests the importance and rarity of this mechanism, as no one plays this role when peers forge social ties in most circumstances, and conflict was a major reason for tie dissolution in Desmond's research (2012). Small's (2009b) child care centers, like KWRU, offered a bridge to replacement ties, but did not specifically soothe conflicts; Small did not describe rifts as serious as the ones between Rosa and Paloma or Pauline and James, or their consequences. Yet social service organizations might have even more authority to heal rifts than KWRU's informal leadership had. Much as it did within KWRU, this mechanism would maintain social ties as well as help to form them.

Creating generalized reciprocity among members was the third mechanism that helped to foster sustainability of KWRU ties. Social service organizations might also be able to improve on KWRU's approach to generalized reciprocity, such that clients like Rebecca, Naomi, and Helen would be more likely to sustain ties. By creating generalized reciprocity, much as KWRU did, organizations could eliminate some of the emotional complications of reciprocity that often characterize relationships between individuals, making it possible for clients to share as a group the benefits as well as the burdens of support. The fact that clients would be able to rely on the organization itself, instead of only on other individual clients for help, would take pressure off the ties between them so that they could invest in a relationship knowing it would strengthen their connection to the organization even if the individual tie were to dissolve. This is one of the benefits of generalized reciprocity that includes an organization: the organization offers help, and people give back to the group. The model also encourages them to give to others, expecting a return in some form from someone in the group, instead of a balanced reciprocal relationship between two individuals. KWRU members recognized that KWRU would repay the help they gave to the organization and to other members, even if the person they had helped never offered them direct assistance or left the group, or they had a conflict with another member.

The reciprocity expectation created a vulnerability in KWRU's system, one that social service organizations might be able to address. The objections Helen, Rebecca, and Naomi expressed toward KWRU's reciprocity norms suggest that the KWRU model might work for more people if the organization had reliable funding and could better organize and scale back its requirements of members. For example, a social service organization with a few more resources could ensure that when members came to volunteer, the office was always open and the organization ready to put them to work.

KWRU's leaders in part framed the organization's fostering of relationships between members as a way to build the organization and its power. But most members talked more about emotional and practical benefits. The common experience of poverty, coupled with spending time together through that shared struggle, had the profound ability to create feelings of warmth, camaraderie, and love. Helen's case suggests that forsaking sustainable ties did not improve circumstances. Mutual experiences of suffering were a starting point, but when people lived together and began to depend on one another for practical and emotional needs, a deeper bond could develop, as it did for Cate and Jessie and for Shy and Valerie.

Dissolution of sustainable ties for Naomi, Rebecca, and Helen does not negate their existence for others or their distinctiveness from the ties other research has found. Being linked to a member who left the group did not mean losing the benefits of that social bond. The person who stayed still had a connection to the organization. Individuals could be replaced, with KWRU as the mediator and voucher for new individuals, and their embeddedness in the organization enabled ties that were strong and often very long-lasting. More often, members stayed and their shared membership helped to sustain their ties. Thus, members generally did not build ties with others who then left; rather, they knew if someone were to leave, it did not mean developing the tie had been a waste of time and energy because the group provided a sense of continuity.

Poor people have very little individually, and they tend to be very isolated. KWRU members shared many of the attributes that isolate most poor people. Their ability to build sustainable ties through KWRU shows that social isolation is not a natural and inevitable consequence of poverty in the twenty-first century; KWRU did not even need very many resources to create ties between strangers. KWRU members built an organization with wider possibilities than most people who share their circumstances can find. By providing a return on investment that offered emotional and practical benefits, they encouraged people to invest their meager resources in the organization and in one another.

KWRU/PPEHRC is a distinctive organization. At least in its current form, it serves a tiny number of poor people in America. But its ability to support sustainable ties suggests that the problems past research has identified in creating such ties among the poor are solvable, and other organizations that serve poor people might benefit by using the KWRU model. Social service agencies, for example, could provide a literal space for new friendship, as KWRU provided at its office, its rallies, and its houses. They could create generalized reciprocity and find ways to heal rifts. My findings show that such efforts would likely provide sustained practical benefits as well as meaningful emotional support.

Poor people in the United States lack many of the things that one of the richest countries in the world should be able to supply, including safe, decent, stable housing; quality affordable child care; reliable healthcare; and a living wage. The enormous benefits of sustainable supportive ties should be added to the list of what is attainable, if only we made the investment.

Note

1. The larger research project began as a study about stigma and social connection among poor people post-U.S. welfare reform. It compared the KWRU sample with twenty-five similarly poor women who were not members of KWRU. Adult recipients of welfare (cash assistance) have mostly been women because the program is designed to aid poor children, and mothers are more likely than fathers to be custodial parents. Social service programs at which I recruited the non-KWRU members also mostly served women. This research led to a book, *Surviving poverty: Creating sustainable ties among the poor* (NYU Press 2017).

References

Anderson, Elijah. 1990. *Streetwise: Race, class, and change in an urban community*. Chicago, IL: University of Chicago Press.

Berg, Bruce L., and Howard Lune. 2012. *Qualitative research methods for the social sciences*, 8th ed. Essex, England: Pearson.

Desmond, Matthew. 2012. Disposable ties and the urban poor. *American Journal of Sociology* 117 (5): 1295–1335.

Domínguez, Silvia, and Celeste Watkins. 2003. Creating networks for survival and mobility: Social capital among African American and Latin American low-income mothers. *Social Problems* 50 (1): 111–35.

Edin, Kathryn. 2001. More than money: The role of assets in the survival strategies and material well-being of the poor. In *Assets for the poor: The benefits of spreading asset ownership*, eds. Thomas M. Shapiro and Edward N. Wolff, 206–31. New York, NY: Russell Sage Foundation.

Edin, Kathryn, and Maria Kefalas. 2005. *Promises I can keep: Why poor women put motherhood before marriage*. Berkeley, CA: University of California Press.

Edin, Kathryn, and Laura Lein. 1996. Work, welfare, and single mothers' economic survival strategies. *American Sociological Review* 62 (2): 253–66.

Edin, Kathryn, and Laura Lein. 1997. *Making ends meet: How single mothers survive welfare and low-wage work*. New York, NY: Russell Sage Foundation.

Fader, Jamie J. 2013. *Falling back: Incarceration and transitions to adulthood among urban youth*. New Brunswick, NJ: Rutgers University Press.

Furstenberg, Frank F., Jr. 2001. The fading dream: Prospects for marriage in the inner city. In *Problem of the century: Racial stratification in the United States*, eds. Elijah Anderson and Douglas S. Massey, 224–46. New York, NY: Russell Sage Foundation.

Granovetter, Mark. 1973. The strength of weak ties. *American Journal of Sociology* 78 (6): 1360–1380.

Granovetter, Mark. 1974/1995. *Getting a job: A study of contacts and careers*. Chicago, IL: University of Chicago Press.

Hansen, Karen V. 2004. The asking rules of reciprocity in networks of care for children. *Qualitative Sociology* 27 (4): 421–37.

Harknett, Kristen. 2006. The relationship between private safety nets and economic outcomes among single mothers. *Journal of Marriage and Family* 68 (1): 172–91.

Henly, Julia R. 2002. Informal support networks and the maintenance of low-wage jobs. In *Laboring below the line: The new ethnography of poverty, low-wage work, and survival in the global economy*, ed. Frank Munger, 179–203. New York, NY: Russell Sage Foundation.

Henly, Julia R., Sandra K. Danziger, and Shira Offer. 2005. The contribution of social support to the material well-being of low-income families. *Journal of Marriage and Family* 67 (1): 122–40.

Levine, Judith. 2013. *Ain't no trust: How bosses, boyfriends, and bureaucrats fail low-income mothers and why it matters*. Berkeley, CA: University of California Press.

Marwell, Nicole P. 2007. *Bargaining for Brooklyn: Community organizations in the entrepreneurial city*. Chicago, IL: University of Chicago Press.

Marwell, Nicole P., and Michael McQuarrie. 2013. People, place, and system: Organizations and the renewal of urban social theory. *The ANNALS of the American Academy of Political and Social Science* 647 (1): 126–43.

Massey, Douglas S., and Nancy A. Denton. 1993. *American Apartheid: Segregation and the making of the underclass*. Cambridge, MA: Harvard University Press.

Mazelis, Joan Maya. 2015. *I got to try to give back*: How reciprocity norms in a poor people's organization influence members' social capital. *Journal of Poverty* 19 (1): 109–31.

Mazelis, Joan Maya. 2017. *Surviving poverty: Creating sustainable ties among the poor*. New York, NY: NYU Press.

Mazelis, Joan Maya, and Laryssa Mykyta. 2011. Relationship status and activated kin support: The role of need and norms. *Journal of Marriage and Family* 73 (2): 430–45.

McDonald, Katrina Bell, and Elizabeth M. Armstrong. 2001. De-romanticizing black intergenerational support: The questionable expectations of welfare reform. *Journal of Marriage and Family* 63 (1): 213–23.

Nelson, Margaret K. 2000. Single mothers and social support: The commitment to, and retreat from, reciprocity. *Qualitative Sociology* 23 (3): 291–317.

Nelson, Margaret K. 2005. *The social economy of single motherhood: Raising children in rural America*. New York, NY: Routledge.

Newman, Katherine S. 1999. *No shame in my game: The working poor in the inner city*. New York, NY: Vintage Books.

Offer, Shira. 2010. Agency-based support: A "last-resort" strategy for low-income families? *Social Science Quarterly* 91 (1): 284–300.

Offer, Shira. 2012a. Barriers to social support among low-income mothers. *International Journal of Sociology and Social Policy* 32 (3): 120–33.

Offer, Shira. 2012b. The burden of reciprocity: Processes of exclusion and withdrawal from personal networks among low-income families. *Current Sociology* 60 (6): 788–805.

Portes, Alejandro. 1998. Social capital: Its origins and applications in modern Sociology. *Annual Review of Sociology* 24:1–24.

Putnam, Robert D. 2000. *Bowling alone: The collapse and revival of American community*. New York, NY: Simon and Schuster.

Roschelle, Anne R. 1997. *No more kin: Exploring race, class, and gender in family networks*. Thousand Oaks, CA: SAGE Publications.

Sampson, Robert J. 2012. *Great American city: Chicago and the enduring neighborhood effect*. Chicago, IL: University of Chicago Press.

Seccombe, Karen. 1999. *So you think I drive a Cadillac? Welfare recipients' perspectives on the system and its reform*. Boston, MA: Allyn and Bacon.

Small, Mario Luis. 2008. Lost in translation: How not to make qualitative research more scientific. In *Workshop on interdisciplinary standards for systematic qualitative research*, eds. Michèle Lamont and Patricia White, 165–71. Washington, DC: National Science Foundation.

Small, Mario Luis. 2009a. "How many cases do I need?" On science and the logic of case selection in field based research. *Ethnography* 10 (1): 5–38.

Small, Mario Luis. 2009b. *Unanticipated gains: Origins of network inequality in everyday life*. New York, NY: Oxford University Press.

Small, Mario Luis, and Scott W. Allard. 2013. Reconsidering the urban disadvantaged: The role of systems, institutions, and organizations. *The ANNALS of the American Academy of Political and Social Science* 647 (1): 6–20.

Smith, Sandra Susan. 2005. "Don't put my name on it": Social capital activation and job-finding assistance among the Black urban poor. *American Journal of Sociology* 111 (1): 1–57.

Smith, Sandra Susan. 2007. *Lone pursuit: Distrust and defensive individualism among the black poor*. New York, NY: Russell Sage Foundation.

Stack, Carol B. 1974. *All our kin: Strategies for survival in a black community*. New York, NY: Harper & Row.

Strauss, Anselm, and Juliet Corbin. 1998. *Basics of qualitative research: Techniques and procedures for developing grounded theory*, 2nd ed. Thousand Oaks, CA: SAGE Publications.

Watkins-Hayes, Celeste. 2013. The micro dynamics of support seeking: The social and economic utility of institutional ties for HIV-positive women. *The ANNALS of the American Academy of Political and Social Science* 647 (1): 83–101.

Wilson, William Julius. 1987. *The truly disadvantaged: The inner city, the underclass, and public policy*. Chicago, IL: University of Chicago Press.

Wilson, William Julius. 2001. Jobless poverty: A new form of social dislocation in the inner-city ghetto. In *Social stratification: Class, race, and gender in sociological perspective*, 2nd ed., ed. David B. Grusky, 651–60. Boulder, CO: Westview Press.

Holiday Clubs as Community Organizations

Holiday clubs—publicly or privately operated organizations that provide child care services and healthy food to disadvantaged children in the United Kingdom (UK) when schools are not in session—are increasing in number. We know a good deal about the effectiveness of the clubs in terms of nutrition-related outcomes, but little is known about the anti-poverty resources these holiday clubs may provide. The possibility that club funding may be centralized through the national government requires a better understanding of holiday club resources. This study describes the range of resources that holiday clubs deliver and reports on how these resources are acquired and brokered by club staff and volunteers. We use data from seventeen clubs operating in disadvantaged communities in North East England during the summer of 2017, and find that clubs deliver an assortment of anti-poverty resources that are often tied to staff (personal and professional) networks.

Keywords: holiday hunger; food poverty; food security; UK food policy

By
PAUL B. STRETESKY,
MARGARET ANNE
DEFEYTER,
MICHAEL A. LONG,
ZEIBEDA SATTAR,
and
EILISH CRILLEY

Many UK families with school-age children face "holiday hunger" because they lack adequate levels of healthy and nutritious food during the school holidays (Defeyter, Graham, and Prince 2015; Garthwaite 2016; Graham et al. 2018; Graham et al. 2016). Low-paid work, high levels of unemployment, and inadequate social benefits have intensified holiday

Paul B. Stretesky is associate director of the Healthy Living Lab and professor of social sciences at Northumbria University Newcastle. He has authored six books and more than 100 articles and book chapters on inequality and social justice. He currently lectures on research methods and statistics.

Margaret Anne Defeyter is director of the Healthy Living Lab and professor of psychology at Northumbria University Newcastle. She has authored more than ninety articles and book chapters on school feeding and physical activity programs.

Correspondence: paul.stretesky@northumbria.ac.uk

DOI: 10.1177/0002716220917657

hunger and led local governments, charities, and religious organizations to establish holiday clubs to help families feed children during the summer school holiday (Mann et al. 2018). While summer programs for disadvantaged youth have existed in the UK for some time, holiday clubs are a relatively new type of organization. These clubs are similar to Summer Food Service Program sites funded by the United States Department of Agriculture that guide regulations concerning staff, operating times, nutritional requirements, and meal preparation. In the UK, holiday clubs are managed locally, rather than centrally as is the case in the United States, making summer food provision for children more uncoordinated and less uniformly prescriptive (Nord and Romig 2006).

Because holiday clubs are primarily associated with food provision, nearly all of the existing research in this area focuses on food-related outcomes and policy (Caplan 2016; Defeyter, Graham, and Prince 2015; Graham et al. 2016; Lambie-Mumford and Sims 2018; Long et al. 2018; Machin 2016; Purdam, Garratt, and Esmail 2016). Current studies of holiday clubs provide interesting insights into food insecurity, food poverty, and food justice, but not into general anti-poverty services that the clubs may provide.

The UK's national government is currently considering the funding of holiday clubs (i.e., by the Department for Education), and a move toward central funding will likely drive important key performance indicators that the clubs must meet. Given that extant research has not investigated the possibility that clubs provide general anti-poverty services not related to food, changes in funding may end up causing significant disruptions. The aim of this study is to expand our understanding of holiday clubs by (1) describing the different resources that holiday clubs provide and (2) examining whether and how club staff and volunteers acquire and broker resources.

We draw upon Mario Small's investigation of U.S. childcare centers to situate our study of holiday clubs (2009; see also Small 2006; Small, Jacobs, and Massengill 2008). We are aware of no existing studies that look at holiday clubs from this unique perspective, and we organize the remainder of our analyses into four sections. The first section draws on Small's (2009) theoretical approach to

Michael A. Long is an associate professor of sociology at Oklahoma State University. He has published four books and more than seventy journal articles and book chapters in the areas of food insecurity and environmental degradation.

Zeibeda Sattar (Zeb) is a senior research assistant in the Healthy Living Lab. She has extensive experience in mixed methods research and currently lectures on undergraduate and postgraduate public health modules.

Eilish Crilley is a PhD student at The Northumbria University Newcastle and part of the Healthy Living Lab. She has previous experience evaluating holiday feeding programs.

NOTE: An earlier version of this article was presented at the Autonomous University of Barcelona (Spain), February 7–8, 2019, in the "Who Cares? Workshop." We would like to thank Professors Miranda Lubbers and Hugo Valenzuela García for inviting us to participate in that workshop and for their encouragement and support during the revision of our manuscript. We would also like to acknowledge the anonymous reviewers who provided insightful comments and suggestions. This research was funded by Children North East and the North East Child Poverty Trust.

frame the organization, network, and neighborhood effects literatures. That review covers basic concepts and ideas about the potential role of clubs as heterogeneous organizations (i.e., organizations that provide a number of different community resources) that improve the well-being of residents in disadvantaged communities. In the second section we describe the study's data sources and analytical methods. Third, we present qualitative findings detailing how club staff and volunteers help to provide and broker a variety of resources for families with school age children. Finally, we conclude by suggesting that any national attempts to direct the composition of club resources must be carefully considered.

Theoretical Perspective

The ability of the poor to access resources is critical to their well-being (Amato and Zuo 1992; Bradshaw 2016; Bratt 2002; Nordenmark and Strandh 1999; Olson 1999; Sampson 2003; Stiehm 2000). However, poor individuals and residents in disadvantaged communities have fewer interactions with organizations that promote well-being than do more affluent individuals and residents in wealthier communities (Jencks and Mayer 1990; Wilson 2011, 2012). While the traditional literature on the relationship among neighborhoods, poverty, and community organizations is important to understanding well-being, it is not without limitations. Over the past decade, contemporary research on the potentially complex relationship between neighborhood effects and organizations has developed. This new line of work provides important additional theoretical specification about the impact of neighborhoods on organizations. For instance, Small and colleagues have shown that access to organizational resources depends on more than just the levels of neighborhood poverty, but also on other organizations within and outside of the neighborhood (Small 2006; Small and McDermott 2006; Small, Jacobs, and Massengill 2008; Small 2009).

Small (2006) has pointed out that local organizations in poor communities may, despite levels of poverty, improve community well-being because they can act as institutional resource brokers under the right set of circumstances (Small, Jacobs, and Massengill 2008). Small (2006, 277) defines institutional resource brokers as "those organizations that transfer resources to individuals." We rely on Small's (2006, 277–78) assumptions that institutional resource brokers (1) are networked with other neighborhood institutions; (2) reflect a variety of interests of staff, volunteers, and clients; (3) experience a variety of pressures, such as those from clients, the community, local government, political figures, and funders; and (4) are "a site of social interaction."

Small's arguments concerning resource brokers and neighborhood effects are situated within the organizational ecology literature (Carroll and Hannan 2004; DiMaggio and Powell 1983), which directs attention to an existing organizational population as a way of better understanding organizational forms (i.e., what organizations look like), as well as the poverty adaptation literature that demonstrates how the poor can, in particular circumstances, build and rely upon social ties and support networks to attenuate problems created by living in poverty (Belle 1983; González de la Rocha 1994; Mazelis 2017; Stack 1975; Valenzuela-García et al. 2014). Following Small's (2009) research, we propose that holiday clubs, because of their links to other organizations, provide a variety of important and diverse resources, including material goods, services, and information within impoverished North East England communities. We also believe that these clubs employ staff and volunteers who aid in brokering resources within disadvantaged neighborhoods. Similar to Small's (2006) argument that organizational resources in poor neighborhoods must respond to community needs, we too argue that holiday clubs should reflect the interests of parents, children, volunteers, and staff.

Data and Methods

Rates of childhood poverty are increasing across the UK; in 2019 approximately 34 percent of all children are believed to live in poverty (Social Metrics Commission 2019, 5). North East England has one of the highest poverty rates (37 percent), second only to London (Social Metrics Commission 2019, 44). While the central government has generally downplayed the extent of childhood poverty (see Bullman 2019), many nongovernmental organizations and local governments have been working toward poverty reduction. Holiday clubs have been a local approach to poverty reduction, and club efforts are often uncoordinated and sometimes even criticized as ineffective and too embedded in neoliberal solutions (Simpson, Lumsden, and Clark 2015; see also Craig and Dowler 1997). Nevertheless, it is within this general tension of scales and ideologies that holiday clubs have emerged (Mann et al. 2018).

The current study is based on data collected during an evaluation of holiday clubs in North East England. In particular, the Children North East Charity was awarded funding from the Big Lottery to provide financial support to four holiday club providers that operate seventeen clubs in disadvantaged communities across the North East during summer 2017. Club providers were required to use funding to bolster holiday club provision. Monies were spent on club resources, including food provision. This provision was monitored by an evaluation to ensure it met basic nutritional requirements set out by Children North East. Children North East also coordinated networking and norming events (i.e., meetings with all club operators and staff to ensure consistent delivery) and encouraged providers to share resources across clubs. While other holiday clubs operated in North East England, our research only examined those clubs whose providers were funded by the Children North East Charity.

Our research team's evaluation included both qualitative and quantitative methods to understand the experiences of staff, volunteers, caregivers, and children. Thirty-five paid staff, 29 volunteers, 77 parents, and 220 children (in 17 focus groups) were interviewed for the evaluation. This research is based on the qualitative data from that evaluation and uses the interviews with stakeholders to better understand the resources that clubs provide and the role that staff and volunteers play in brokering resources.

Children who attended clubs generally came from the disadvantaged neighborhoods where clubs were located, and the recruitment strategy focused on all children from all economic backgrounds within those neighborhoods by emphasizing physical activities and trips to fun places alongside food preparation and provision. There was no mandatory requirement that clubs only allow free school meal children to attend. This strategy of inclusion was purposeful because providers and the funder believed it would attenuate the holiday club stigma (e.g., that clubs were only for the very poor). In addition, the funder named and advertised the project as a "Day Out, Not a Handout" because it was suggested by previous holiday club attendees. While this title was debated among the providers, the name makes clear that a holiday club stigma does exist. Despite recruitment efforts to reach out to all children through social media and school flyers, children from low-income households were often still identified as candidates for holiday clubs by school staff so that they could be directly recruited to the clubs by staff and volunteers. In this sense, low-income children had little choice about whether they would attend a holiday club, especially when it was their sole source of food during the summer. This "deserving" recruitment was often emphasized by staff because they saw clubs as places where they could provide food and aid to those most in need. Sometimes this approach caused problems and resentment. Local parents were reported to have complained when clubs enrolled children from non-club neighborhoods if their child was informed that the club was full.

Holiday club staff and volunteers were recruited by core staff who were employed permanently in community centers and/or nonprofits that operated year-round but were responsible for running holiday clubs. All clubs relied on local networks, including schools, places of worship, and community centers to recruit and employ additional staff and volunteers. Many holiday club staff and volunteers were employed at other organizations during the school year. For example, our sample of sixty-four staff and volunteers included more than a dozen teachers, nurses, and social workers. In addition, many staff and volunteers were parents of children attending clubs or retirees who were residents in the local community. Most recruitment occurred by word of mouth, and parents sometimes became club volunteers after attending clubs with their children. As we suggest in our findings, staff and volunteers sometimes brought their personal and professional networks to the club and could use them to help acquire and broker resources.

Given the relatively short duration that holiday clubs operate, our interviews took place when clubs opened in July 2017 and continued for six weeks until August 2017, when the clubs closed for the summer. Additional details about the seventeen clubs are presented in Table 1.

Children North East required clubs to operate for at least four weeks during the summer and be open a minimum of four days per week for at least four hours per day. All of the clubs were free to attend and those who attended were between 4 and 14 years old. UK clubs appear to serve younger children (i.e.,

TABLE 1
Description of Holiday Clubs (2017)

Club Number	Hours of Operation	Number Weeks Open	Club Venue	Median Number of Children Attending Club Session	Age of Attendees	On-Site Cooking	Median Number of Staff/Volunteers Attending Club Session	Index of Deprivation in Club Neighborhood (b)
1	10 to 2pm	5	Community Centre	24	5 to 12	Yes	5/1	Top 10%
2	9am to 4pm(a)	4	Community Centre	7	7 to 14	Yes	3/5	Top 40%
3	8:30am to 2:30pm(a)	4	School	4	11 to 12	Yes	5/0	Top 10%
4	10am to 2pm	6	School	9	4 to 10	Yes	2/0 (b)	Top 10%
5	9am to 1pm(a)	4	Community Centre	20	5 to 12	Yes	2/3	Top 20%
6	10am to 2pm(a)	4	Community Centre	24	5 to 11	Yes	6/3	Top 10%
7	10am to 2pm	4	Community Centre	8	7 to 11	No	3/1	Top 60%
8	10am to 2pm	4	Community Centre	17	7 to 12	No	3/1	Top 70%
9	9am to 3:30pm(a)	5	Community Centre	26	6 to 13	Yes	4/2	Top 10%
10	10am to 3pm	6	Community Centre	12	4 to 11	Yes	3/0 (b)	Top 10%
11	1pm to 5pm	5	Community Centre	9	9 to 12	Yes	3/0	Top 10%
12	10am to 2pm(a)	5	Community Centre	10	7 to 12	Yes	2/3	Top 50%
13	10am to 2pm	4	Community Centre	24	7 to 10	Yes	2/3	Top 30%
14	9am to 5pm(a)	4	Community Centre	21	5 to 11	No	2/0(b)	Top 10%
15	9am to 5pm(a)	4	Community Centre	19	4 to 12	Yes	2/0(b)	Top 10%
16	9am to 5pm(a)	4	Community Centre	23	5 to 12	No	2/2(b)	Top 10%
17	9am to 5pm(a)	4	School	9	5 to 8	No	4/0(b)	Top 20%

(a) Hours were not consistent.
(b) Parents of younger children attended clubs to help supervise and are not included in counts of volunteers.
(c) The Index of Deprivation combines economic, social, and housing indicators into a single score for each neighborhood. Scores represent the decile of deprivation among all UK neighborhoods.
(n = 17)

those 14 years old and younger) when compared to other countries. For example, the U.S. Summer Food Service Program caters to youth up to 18 years old. These differences might relate to cultural expectations about who should be eligible for food aid in a neoliberal system. In the UK, youth are viewed as self-reliant at a younger age and many begin working apprenticeships at 16; the same age at which most U.S. youth are still attending high school. Thus, the fact that UK children attending clubs tend to be younger than children in other countries might reflect cultural differences concerning the age at which individuals are viewed as responsible for providing for themselves.

Holiday clubs operated in schools, church halls, and community centers and were staffed by volunteers and seasonal employees, some of which had backgrounds as teachers, youth workers, social workers, sports coaches, and cooks. Most clubs had been open in the previous summer and operated by obtaining funding and spaces from charities and other organizations. Two clubs, opened by the same charity, were in their first year of operation. While clubs were distinctive, a quantitative evaluation found few differences in nutritional uptake among children, meaning that in the case of food provision club structures mattered little (see Defeyter et al. 2018).

We obtained ethics approval from their university to interview all participants, including children, parents, staff, and volunteers (Northumbria Reference Number 879). All interviews were voluntary and confidential. As Table 1 suggests, 10 of the 17 clubs are located in the top 10 percent of the most deprived communities in England in 2015 as ranked by income, employment, education, health, crime, housing, and living environment (Payne and Abel 2012).

A semistructured interview schedule comprising open-ended questions invited caregivers, children, employees, and volunteers to talk freely about their experiences in holiday clubs. Interviews were conducted by two of the authors and took place at the holiday clubs during normal hours of operation. All interviews were recorded, transcribed, and loaded into NVIVO so that the key resources that clubs provided could be readily identified. Themes representing similar resources that emerged from those data were then given initial codes to identify their content and were finally grouped according to the key type of resource that emerged (i.e., material goods, services, and information). This inductive approach was focused on identifying important resources as well as staff and volunteer networks (Auerbach and Silverstein 2003).

Findings

Consistent with the idea that holiday clubs provide for a variety of needs, children, caregivers, parents, volunteers, and staff reported their experiences with various material goods, services, and information. Table 2 provides a summary of these resources. We organize our analysis by looking at the most frequently mentioned resources in each category, noting the networks used to broker those resources when relevant.

TABLE 2
Resources Provided by Holiday Clubs

Club Resource	Examples
Material Goods	
Breakfast, lunch, & snacks	Fruit, vegetables, grains, smoothies, pizza, pasta salad, rice dishes
Entertainment equipment	Video game console, sports equipment, pool & foosball tables
Services	
Childcare activities like sports, arts/ crafts & games	Cricket, football, fencing, drama, painting, clothing design, bug hunts, board games, water balloons, yoga, woodworking, painting, boat building
Help with disabilities	Access to events, help with transportation, increasing access to activities
Transportation & admission	Museums, movies, beaches, golf, parks, sporting events, and camping
Social networks	Physical spaces, activities, and people to meet.
Information	
Traditional education	Language (French/German), environmental science, energy & society, astronomy, horticulture, world foods
Cooking & nutrition	Cooking, NHS nutrition visits, healthy shopping, food hygiene
Physical education & well-being	Cardio exercise, yoga, therapy, meditation
Safety	Police safety talks, first aid
Finances, budgeting & employment	Banking, employability checks, budgeting

Material goods

As one staff member put it, "To run a holiday club you need food." Staff and volunteers' explanations about sourcing and preparing food varied. In particular, staff and volunteers in some clubs were able to draw on personal and organizational networks to source and prepare food for their clubs. For instance, a staff member at one club was able to broker an arrangement between his/her club and a national charitable organization to provide the club with free and/or reduced cost food that would have otherwise gone to waste ("I get the food from FareShare that they do in conjunction with Tesco"). Staff and volunteers also relied on existing relationships with other people and organizations to help recruit additional staff and volunteers who could prepare the types of healthy meals that the club's funder required. For instance, a volunteer at one club recruited a professional chef to help prepare meals, noting "Our food is brought in freshly each day. . .we have a chef who does it." A staff member at another club told us that someone working in his/her club was able to convince a cook employed at a local college to volunteer at the holiday club: "The club cook is from a local college and is also a tutor. He has been fantastic in feeding children healthy meals which they have eaten the majority of them."

In most cases, however, holiday club staff and volunteers did not have the networks to source free or discounted food or acquire free food preparation at their clubs. In such instances, staff and volunteers relied on club budgets to purchase food for children (e.g., "We bought it from Costco and stored it here in the fridge," or "We just go to a local supermarket like Aldi or Tesco"). Some clubs even resorted to paying private providers to prepare and deliver lunches ("It was the provider who planned [and brought] the meals for us"). These clubs then brokered food provision for children and parents by connecting resources at local catering companies and supermarkets with their clubs. However, there was more financial pressure on these particular clubs as they required significant funding to acquire and prepare food. Staff and volunteers in these clubs often said that their club's biggest challenge was to "see where we could source the money" to continue to pay for food provision. This point was driven home by one volunteer who indicated that "without funding there would be nothing on."

Staff and volunteers in nearly every club emphasized that their food provision was subject to oversight based on national school food standards that were checked by the funder (Children North East) to ensure it met nutrition requirements. As one volunteer explained:

> Our meals go through the Food Standards Agency to ensure that it is up to standard and that the menus are how they should be. We have all been given [by Children North East] guidelines on portion sizes that our children should be given.

Club staff and volunteers reported that serving healthy food was important, as children might not get these foods at home. Staff and volunteers talked about providing healthy snack options like "fruit salad with melon, watermelon, strawberries, blueberries and grapes" that were too expensive for many parents and caregivers to purchase regularly. Children in several clubs reported taking extra food home so they could eat again later (e.g., "I took my bowl of fruit home, it was massive!"). Food was a hot topic of conversation with children:

> We get breakfast every morning except on Thursday because we go at 1 [pm] and we get dinner straight away. . . We get cereal, toast and bread and for drinks we get water, milk or juice. . .I love it!

Parents and caregivers also said club food provision was critical and helped them to manage the household budget:

> They get their meals. So, knowing that they have had their lunch is one less meal that we have to find. That's why we come for the Tuesday evening meals, because it is cheap to feed the kids.

One single mother explained that meals provided by holiday clubs allowed her to have access to food and alleviated fears that her children would be taken away because they were malnourished: "I lost my job. In order to keep the children, I was skipping meals regularly so that they were fed. So, sometimes just eating what they left of their meals." Finally, some holiday clubs were able to provide additional help to families simply because of their physical proximity to other local organizations. In such cases, volunteers and staff could provide parents with information about where they could get additional food for their households. For example, one volunteer noted that her club doubled as a food pantry:

> In this building we have the pantry for 52 weeks of the year. We have been able to tell club parents that if they put in £5 a week then they can choose £10 worth of food. So, whereas food parcels from food banks are just given to them, at this project they can actually choose what food they have. I think a lot of people find that very helpful.

In short, similar to Small's (2009) study of childcare centers that finds staff and volunteer networks matter because they increase well-being, we find evidence that a few clubs leveraged staff and volunteer networks to feed children (Galaskiewicz, Bielefeld, and Dowell 2006). Thus, in at least a few instances, staff and volunteer networks helped to lower food costs and ease the financial pressure associated with providing food to children during the summer months.

While food was the major material good that clubs provided, some clubs also purchased, or were gifted, popular entertainment equipment for children to use free of charge at the club. For example, one staff member recalled, "My son is an ex-PE teacher and he had given me some equipment which I brought to the coach [at the club] and that was used for a variety of games." Equipment often provided children with access to forms of entertainment that they would not have access to during the summertime or in their households. As one child noted, "I wouldn't be playing pool because I don't have a pool table and I wouldn't be playing on the football table or having like a Wii [video game equipment] room all to myself."

While all equipment remained at the holiday clubs, children often reported that they had daily access to these resources. Moreover, several children noted that entertainment equipment that they did not have access to at home gave them similar experiences to their middle-class peers.

Services

All holiday clubs provided childcare services in some form, and staff and volunteers in four of the seventeen clubs said that their clubs provided specialized care for children with disabilities. Parents and other caregivers felt that without holiday clubs, their children were more susceptible to crime, deviance, and anti-social behavior. That is, clubs gave kids "something to keep them busy." For children, summer boredom was a frequent topic of conversation with the interviewers. Children reported that on days they were not at a club they were "sitting around bored" and "stuck in the house [with] nowhere to go . . . like being in jail." Children said clubs reduced boredom, providing them physical activities like archery or surfing and entertainment like arts and crafts. In some cases, club leaders worked together to employ specialized staff who they could share across their organizations. These shared staff traveled from club to club to provide specialized activities such as football lessons (see also Guo and Acar 2005). The networks among clubs, then, allowed those clubs to employ staff jointly to leverage resources to provide additional services for children during the summer. For many staff and volunteers, clubs were similar to childcare facilities. These staff and volunteers often said that holiday clubs provided an important service to families who could not afford to send their children to standard childcare centers (e.g. "It is £2 for four hours [to attend holiday club] and some places charge up to £50 for an hour"). One challenge associated with childcare is bringing on properly trained staff and volunteers to provide childcare services. Clubs relied on staff with training they obtained through other organizations and settings: "I am a qualified nursery nurse and I am also a qualified youth worker and a qualified social worker, and I have done all the safeguarding children and everything you need to work with children. I have first aid [training]."

Staff and volunteers with less experience and training were often paired with experienced staff and volunteers to ensure that children's needs could be met (see also Brass et al. 2004). This practice of matching experienced and inexperienced staff provided an informal training mechanism for staff and volunteers. For instance, one staff member noted, "So long as there are [experienced] members of staff then those other [inexperienced] volunteers and staff are fine to come and join in."

Some staff and volunteers suggested that clubs were a more relaxed version of school rather than a childcare center. One staff member and school teacher explained:

> [I like] being in that positive role model, but in a relaxed format rather than being stuck in front of 30 kids and having that sort of behavior and discipline. We still have problems, but it is a more relaxed social format. We are dressed in more casual clothes. So, it's just the normal things that a teacher would do.

Children and parents were concerned about safety during the summertime—a finding consistent with literature on childcare centers in disadvantaged neighborhoods (García and White 2006; Kling, Liebman, and Katz 2005). In particular, one child recalled a "scary" experience. She described, "This man was just sitting there being really inappropriate. So, we ran to my mam's house and told my mam's boyfriend. He took us to a different park, but the inappropriate man was there." Most children suggested that they were closely monitored by caregivers when they were not at club and many were "not allowed to go out," and some younger children told researchers they "must stay on the grass" in front of their home.

While parents and other caregivers often pointed out that childcare services were equally important to food because it allowed them to work and carry out other tasks, club staff indicated that they believed feeding children (i.e., providing the material resources to children and their families) was the most important function of clubs. These staff often sought out ways to identify children in need, often suggesting that clubs partner with schools to identify children who were the most economically disadvantaged: "It was my idea to actually get schools to pinpoint parents who would benefit from holiday club. I didn't want parents who were only going to use it just for childcare." Thus, while there was a clear sense by parents, staff, volunteers, and children that material goods such as food were important, staff and volunteers often ranked services such as childcare as less important than parents, while children viewed childcare as something that kept them from being bored at home.

Several parents also came to rely on club staff and volunteers for disability support. One parent pointed out that she was apprehensive about leaving her son at a club but discovered that the staff had the knowledge and resources to look after him. Another noted, "My middle son has autism and I need to separate the children over the holidays. I am the only adult who can supervise, and it is very difficult and expensive to take children out." That parent reported that the holiday club volunteer recognized her son's autism immediately and she then knew her son would be treated well. Several club volunteers reported having experience working with autistic children in their schools.

Providing disability and health services was sometimes possible because staff were affiliated with other organizations in the community. For instance, a few staff and volunteers reported that they were employed as social workers. Another volunteer said, "I am training to be a social worker and I was able to help with confidential information. I have dealt with it before." Parent volunteers also pointed out that clubs often had adequate disability support. One mother noted, "My youngest one has disabilities; she is able to come on the trips with the club. She enjoys it and it gets her out because she never ever goes anywhere." Clubs also provided disability services to parents and other caregivers. One grandmother of a club attendee explained:

> I have a wheelchair and I cannot wheel it myself, so obviously I need someone to push me. . . . There was always someone [at the club] to push me. [Staff member] at the club she said she would push me. You know that was lovely. Just being able to get out and about.

In sum, disability services were largely based on staff and volunteer skills developed in the school setting and were often described as important to parents, staff, volunteers, and caregivers.

Clubs also provided a space to promote friendship networks for children and parents (see also Van Eijk 2010). In this sense, holiday clubs broker friendships among children and parents that may have important implications for creating relationships that can help residents to adapt to poverty during times of crisis (Stack 1975). Friendship brokering often took on special meaning for newer community residents who found themselves without any attachments to community organizations when school was not in session or for those parents who were new to the community (Min 1992). For instance, children told the researchers that they had made new friends (e.g., "I have made friends with a girl and she plays with me every time I come, and she is just really nice"). For some children, the holiday club was the only source of interaction with peers during the summer since geographic isolation in disadvantaged neighborhoods is a common challenge for disadvantaged residents. In one case when a researcher asked a child whether she had seen her school friends she replied, "No, they all live far away from me."

Holiday club staff and volunteers often said that their "clubs provide a chance for the parents to come and join in something free." Likewise, parents and other caregivers told researchers that they made friends at the club (e.g., "I have met loads of different people," or "You get to meet people and can do some of the activities that you would never do at home"). The structure of the holiday club promoted friendship networks among parents and caregivers. In particular, most clubs provided important places and times for parental social interactions. Clubs achieved this when staff and volunteers invited parents and caregivers to the club so that they could eat with their children and visit with other parents and caregivers. Parents at several clubs were also able to accompany children on field trips where they could interact with other parents. In addition, several holiday clubs required parents with younger children to attend the club with their child. Parents and caregivers often explained that the holiday club helped them to form meaningful relationships with their peers while their children were engaged in club activities with other children. As one parent described, "I have talked to a few of the mums, we don't normally talk a lot through the school term. I have got to know a couple of the mums now from holiday club. So, it has been quite good."

Communication with other parents whose children attended the club also helped to build a sense of community and belonging. As one parent explained, "I feel accepted in the community now. Do you know what I mean? I haven't up until this last 12 months." These friendship connections may also help parents to adapt to busy and complicated lives. As one mother reported, she spent all day with her new friend she met through a club and who "has given lifts to my kids." In short, the clubs served an important service function in the community by strengthening friendship networks and increasing resilience and well-being on the part of parents and other caregivers.

Finally, clubs also provided children, and sometimes families, with transportation costs and entry fees to cultural institutions and recreational spaces. Cultural and recreational experiences improve well-being and bring children and families into contact with people outside of the community. These experiences are also characterized as an important human right (Babey, Brown, and Hastert 2005; Chatterjee and Noble 2016; Moore 1998). One child said that the club took her out of her neighborhood to play "crazy golf and [visit] the museum for free." Children often told researchers that they could not afford to go to fun places during the summer without the club:

> I would not come here because my mam, she has to pay the bills, and it takes her a lot of money and she has to use the money that she has got. So, that is why I like to come here because we get to go on the trips and my mam doesn't have enough money to take us all to the places.

Overall, most children mentioned the trips to fun places as often as they mentioned food. And many children reported that they wished they could take trips every day. Staff and volunteers also often emphasized that planning and funding trips to parks, museums, and entertainment establishments was important for the well-being of children: "Some of these children come from very disadvantaged backgrounds, so [day trips] are a new experience for them. . . . They get trips to the beach and all of these cool places that they have never been before. So, it is a good experience for them."

Holiday clubs provided critical access to cultural events, recreational spaces, and entertainment for children and their families. This service was mentioned by all interviewees as a positive aspect of clubs. When staff or volunteers in a club had connections that could help to realize a trip, they said they used those connections. For instance, one volunteer recalled how a friend of the club leader helped to arrange and pay for a camping trip for the entire club: "One of the ladies that [the club leader] knows came in at Easter and they were going camping. That lady just found out about the club and provided the food [and organized the club] camping trip and it was quite a nice thing to be part of." In most instances, however, the money provided by the funder typically allowed clubs to carry out this service function.

Information

Clubs provided information about food and nutrition, physical activity, and other more formal classroom-based educational topics to children and parents. Clubs also served as more traditional resource brokers by providing information about other community organizations and services in times of crises. While clubs provided education about food differently, they all had a food education component that staff reported was important for well-being (Colatruglio and Slater 2014; Rozin 2005; Utter et al. 2016). For instance, one club's staff taught children how to grow their own vegetables:

> We were planting onions, so they learnt how to plant onions and how to cut herbs correctly. They harvested some beans and made a meal with the different beans. We have been trying to introduce them to food in a slightly different way. We made homemade ketchup and things, so it is really teaching them to cook from scratch and a little bit of life skill. Just teaching them to do stuff in the kitchen so they can understand a little bit more about how you can make basic food taste good.

Some clubs focused on world foods, food culture, food identification, and even food sales (e.g., in a child-run community café). Education about nutrition was mentioned by all volunteers and staff. The majority of clubs that were able to prepare food in buildings emphasized that they taught children skills by including them in the process (e.g., "It is always the children cooking as well"). Unfortunately, those clubs that did not have the staff or facilities to prepare their own food were at a disadvantage when it came to teaching children food preparation skills.

Several staff and volunteers said they taught children how to purchase food at local shops and grocery stores. These staff taught children how to shop in stores, save money, and make good nutritional choices. For instance, one club gave children a fixed amount of money and a list of grocery items to teach them how to shop for nutritious meals within a budget:

> We have taken the kids to a couple of trips to Tesco if we have needed veg[etables] and stuff. We gave them a shopping list and they would go and get it and we gave them the money to pay for it. They have some proper responsibilities, which has been really good.

Children also learned transferable skills from staff, such as how to prepare meals at home; many staff worked in school kitchens, restaurants, or local colleges during the school term. One volunteer said, "They never quite know what they are cooking until they get here. Like when we made the pizza, they liked making the dough, getting their hands in the dough, and they liked actually being in charge of cooking something in a pan."

Children told the researchers that the club expanded their diets and motivated them to prepare meals at home (e.g., "We eat lots of different things, and we like it, and we like making our own food for healthy cooking"). Parents and children said that their new cooking abilities influence household dynamics (Fiese and Schwartz 2008). One staff member explained that "the kids get to try some different foods from around the world which they probably normally wouldn't have tried and tested." An eleven-year-old boy at the same club later explained that learning about world foods (i.e., increasing his cultural competencies [see Utter et al. 2016]) in a holiday club with his sibling has made him more motivated to cook at home: "Food Nation inspired us to like to cook a lot more. We never used to cook. We always used to get our dad to cook for us." This change in motivation to prepare meals at home was also emphasized by parents who said that they relied less on takeaway meals since the children attended holiday clubs: "They want to do more cooking now. I thought they would never go in the kitchen. It was always left to me. But now they are coming home and saying, 'I have cooked this, can we do it at home?'"

Finally, staff and volunteers were often approached by parents and caregivers for information about sourcing food when they were still struggling to feed their children. One volunteer explained, "We have had people that have come in such desperate situations that they just haven't got the money. There is a food bank very close to here that we can [also] refer people to." When these situations arose, club staff and volunteers reported knowing about local resources to help link parents and caregivers to other food service organizations in the local communities.

While parents emphasized physical activity as part of the "childcare service" because it provided children with something "to do" and kept them from being "bored" and/or "restless," staff tended to emphasize physical education. Staff and volunteers believed that teaching about exercise and good exercise habits was especially important over the life course—and drew on their backgrounds in education to help provide this knowledge to children. They assumed these habits promote life-long fitness and well-being (Lubans et al. 2016, Penedo and Dahn 2005). As one staff member noted, "We have been doing quite a lot of physical activities, so trying to encourage the kids to become a bit fitter really." In short, while parents saw physical activity as a service, staff believed it was an educational experience. Children simply considered exercise and learning about different activities to be "fun" (e.g., "We do a lot of sports with [other children] which I like, and I am really enjoying it.")

Children often reported being engaged in formal educational activities while attending clubs. Staff tended to believe that children needed to remain "school ready." Staff who were also teachers brought their knowledge of schools to clubs by providing lesson plans and other educational opportunities to children during the summer. Staff noted that they were often anticipating what children would be learning that particular year in school so that they could prepare them in the club. One staff member pointed out the benefit of a summer head start: "In other years we focused on literacy. This year we did French because we are going to start doing French in [school in] September. They feel that they will already know a lot before they start."

In another case, a club with a volunteer teaching science reported, "Children will be learning about planets [in school], so I have had them doing quizzes this morning about Neptune and Saturn." Staff and volunteers universally believed that educational opportunities at clubs were important to children's well-being because they provided an "educational boost" to children residing in disadvantaged communities (Reardon and Portilla 2015; Schmitt et al. 2015).

Discussion and Conclusions

We set out to determine the range of resources that clubs provided. Consistent with Small's (2006) observations of childcare centers in the United States, we find that holiday clubs provide diverse resources that reflect the needs of children, staff, volunteers, and caregivers. While all holiday clubs relied on other organizations in the community to provide resources to participants, the extent and shape of each club's provision is clearly nuanced and dependent on club staff and volunteer networks. As a result, the delivery of resources at some clubs does appear to have relied more on staff and volunteer networks. Whether staff and volunteer ties produced more successful clubs and whether these ties become embedded in holiday clubs themselves should be the focus of future research.

We also set out to determine how staff and volunteers in clubs may acquire and broker resources by leveraging personal and professional networks. We discovered that many clubs were reliant on external networks and funding to acquire and broker resources. However, some clubs were highly dependent on volunteers and staff who worked within clubs to broker resources that improved the well-being of children, parents, and other caregivers. As we demonstrate, staff and volunteers helped several clubs to source and prepare food at little to no cost to the club, used their connections to arrange field trips, and provided equipment for children to use for activities while at a club.

Our results provide a starting point for a better understanding of holiday clubs in the UK. Such an understanding is critical as the UK government is currently considering how to support these clubs. We suggest that a universal and centralized funding scheme across the UK would benefit those clubs that have fewer networked staff and therefore appear to be more reliant on external funding sources. There are, however, reasons to be concerned about the way centralized funding is implemented. In particular, centralized funding schemes could disrupt important club functions that contribute to community well-being if clubs receiving funding are focused on singular and externally driven objectives.

UK policy-makers need only turn to the USDA Summer Program to better understand the likely consequences of a more singular focused and centralized funding scheme. In particular, evaluations of the USDA program suggest that it is often difficult to find program sponsors and reveal that attendance at the programs is low, even in the most deprived areas (Wauchoppe and Stracussi 2010). Providers often point out that reporting requirements for children and meals served are excessive and note that "a lack of activities at program sites are barriers to participation" (Wauchoppe and Stracussi 2010, 3). In the UK, many staff and volunteers working in the holiday clubs we studied also noted that their clubs were influenced by nonlocal networks and reporting requirements (see also Backman and Smith 2000, Guest 2000). These nonlocal networks present the potential for more formal coercive pressure via funding. For instance, the holiday clubs that we studied were all tasked with adhering to healthy eating guidelines as required by the provider who followed national food standards (Adamson et al. 2013). Thus, while clubs in North East England do more than feed children, they are simultaneously being pressured to pay more attention to and report on who they serve food to as well as the kinds and amounts of food served. This might be interpreted as a move toward a U.S. model that is distinctively focused on food provision.

In the end, our observations about club resources and staff networks provide us with optimism. First, we found that the resources that clubs provide matter to the parents, caregivers, and children who participated in our research. Second, while we believe that national directives aimed at clubs may be problematic, we also do not dismiss potential benefits of networks outside the community. That is, the central government and other national organizations have the capacity to mobilize significant levels of funding to support these holiday clubs and therefore can greatly expand well-being across the UK. More importantly, the national governmental and large nongovernmental organizations can help to direct needed funding and local mandates. Nevertheless, this must be done carefully and equitably by ensuring that all communities have access to these funds. Because our research suggests that clubs offer a diversity of resources that reflect community interests and because staff networks clearly matter for some clubs, we propose that any changes to club funding structures, especially at the national level, be carefully considered with significant input from a variety of clubs. By drawing attention to the various resources that clubs provide, along with the networks they leverage to acquire and broker resources, we hope that holiday clubs will continue to promote community well-being and health to their local communities.

References

Adamson, Ashley, Suzanne Spence, Lowri Reed, Ruth Conway, Alison Palmer, Eve Stewart, Jennifer McBratney, Lynne Carter, Shirley Beattie and Michael Nelson. 2013. School food standards in the UK: Implementation and evaluation. *Public Health Nutrition* 16 (6): 968–81.

Amato, Paul and Jiping Zuo. 1992. Rural poverty, urban poverty, and psychological well-being. *The Sociological Quarterly* 33 (2): 229–40.

Auerbach, Carl and Louise Silverstein. 2003. *Qualitative data: An introduction to coding and analysis.* New York, NY: NYU Press.

Babey, Susan, Richard Brown, and Theresa Hastert. 2005. Access to safe parks helps increase physical activity among teenagers. Los Angeles, CA: UCLA Center for Health Policy Research. Available from www.escholarship.org (accessed 19 August 2019).

Backman, Elaine, and Steven Rathgeb Smith. 2000. Healthy organizations, unhealthy communities? *Nonprofit Management and Leadership* 10 (4): 355–73.

Belle, Deborah. 1983. The impact of poverty on social networks and supports. *Marriage & Family Review* 5 (4): 89–103.

Bradshaw, Jonathan. 2016. *The well-being of children in the UK.* Bristol, UK: Policy Press.

Brass, Daniel, Joseph Galaskiewicz, Henrich Greve, and Wenpin Tsai. 2004. Taking stock of networks and organizations: A multilevel perspective. *Academy of Management Journal* 47 (6): 795–817.

Bratt, Rachel. 2002. Housing and family well-being. *Housing Studies* 17 (1): 13–26.

Bullman, May. 28 March 2019. The government can no longer claim that "absolute child poverty" is falling—it is time to acknowledge the crisis and act. *Independent.* Available from https://www.independent.co.uk/voices/child-poverty-crisis-relative-absolute-theresa-may-uk-government-austerity-conservative-a8844211.html (accessed 19 August 2019).

Caplan, Pat. 2016. Big society or broken society? Food banks in the UK. *Anthropology Today* 32 (1): 5–9.

Carroll, Glenn, and Michael Hannan. 2004. *The demography of corporations and industries.* Princeton, NJ: Princeton University Press.

Chatterjee, Helen, and Guy Noble. 2016. *Museums, health and well-being.* New York, NY: Routledge.

Colatruglio, Sarah, and Joyce Slater. 2014. Food literacy: Bridging the gap between food, nutrition and well-being. In *Sustainable Well-being*, eds. Frank Deer, Thomas Falkenberg, Barbara McMillan and Laura Sims, 37–55. Winnipeg: ESWB Press.

Craig, Gary, and Elizabeth Dowler. 1997. Let them eat cake! Poverty, hunger and the UK state. In *First World Hunger*, eds. Graham Riches, 108–33. London: Palgrave Macmillan.

Defeyter, Margaret, Pamela Graham, and Kate Prince. 2015. A qualitative evaluation of holiday breakfast clubs in the UK. *Frontiers in Public Health* 3, Article 199. Available from https://doi.org/10.3389/fpubh.2015.00199.

Defeyter, Margaret, Paul Stretesky, Zeb Sattar, and Elish Crilley. 2018. *Evaluation of a "day out, not a handout" holiday provision programme.* Newcastle, UK: Northumbria University. Available from www.children-ne.org.uk/ (accessed 19 August 2019).

DiMaggio, Paul, and Walter Powell. 1983. The iron cage revisited: Institutional isomorphism and collective rationality in organizational fields. *American Sociological Review* 48 (2): 147–60.

Fiese, Barbara, and Marlene Schwartz. 2008. Reclaiming the family table: Mealtimes and child health and well-being. *Social Policy Report* 22 (4): 3–17.

Galaskiewicz, Joseph, Wolfgang Bielefeld, and Myron Dowell. 2006. Networks and organizational growth: A study of community based nonprofits. *Administrative Science Quarterly* 51 (3): 337–80.

García, Robert, and Aubrey White. 2006. *Healthy parks, schools, and communities: Mapping green access and equity for the Los Angeles region.* Los Angeles, CA: The City Project Policy Report. Available from www.cityprojectca.org (accessed 19 August 2019).

Garthwaite, Kayleigh. 2016. *Hunger pains: Life inside foodbank Britain.* Bristol, UK: Policy Press.

González de la Rocha, Mercedes 1994. *The resources of poverty: Women and survival in a Mexican city.* Cambridge, MA: Blackwell Publishers.

Graham, Pamela, Paul Stretesky, Michael Long, and Emily Mann. 2018. Holiday hunger: Feeding children during the school holidays. In *Feeding children inside and outside the home*, eds. Vicki Harman, Benedetta Cappelline, and Charlotte Faircloth, 105–24. London: Routledge.

Graham, Pamela Louise, Eilish Crilley, Paul Stretesky, Michael Long, Katie Palmer, Eileen Steinbock, and Margaret Defeyter. 2016. School holiday food provision in the UK: A qualitative investigation of needs, benefits, and potential for development. *Frontiers in Public Health* 4, Article 172. Available from https://www.ncbi.nlm.nih.gov/pmc/articles/PMC4992941/ (accessed 19 August 2019).

Guest, Avery M. 2000. The mediate community: The nature of local and extra-local ties within the metropolis. *Urban Affairs Review* 35 (5): 603–27.

Guo, Chao, and Muhittin Acar. 2005. Understanding collaboration among nonprofit organizations: Combining resource dependency, institutional, and network perspectives. *Nonprofit and Voluntary Sector Quarterly* 34 (3): 340–61.

Jencks, Christopher, and Susan Mayer. 1990. The social consequences of growing up in a poor neighborhood. In *Inner-city poverty in the United States*, eds. Laurence Lynn and Michael McGeary, 111–86. Washington, DC: National Academy Press.

Kling, Jeffrey R., Jeffrey B. Liebman, and Lawrence F. Katz. 2005. Bullets don't got no name: Consequences of fear in the ghetto. In *Discovering successful pathways in children's development*, ed. T. S. Weisner, 243–81. Chicago, IL: University of Chicago Press.

Lambie-Mumford, Hannah, and Lily Sims. 2018. Feeding hungry children. *Children & Society* 32 (3): 244–54.

Long, Michael, Paul Stretesky, Pamela Graham, Katie Palmer, Eileen Steinbock and Margaret Defeyter. 2018. The impact of holiday clubs on household food insecurity. *Health & Social Care in the Community* 26 (2): e261–e269.

Lubans, David, Justin Richards, Charles Hillman, Guy Faulkner, Mark Beauchamp, Michael Nilsson, Paul Kelly, Jordan Smith, Lauren Raine, and Stuart Biddle. 2016. Physical activity for cognitive and mental health in youth. *Pediatrics* 138 (3): e20161642.

Machin, Richard. 2016. Understanding holiday hunger. *Journal of Poverty and Social Justice* 24 (3): 311–19.

Mann, Emily, Michael Long, Paul Stretesky, and Margaret Defeyter. 2018. A question of justice: Are holiday clubs serving the most deprived communities in England? *Local Environment* 23 (10): 1008–1022.

Mazelis, Joan. 2017. *Surviving poverty: Creating sustainable ties among the poor.* New York, NY: NYU Press.

Min, Pyong. 1992. The structure and social functions of Korean immigrant churches in the United States. *International Migration Review* 26 (4): 1370–1394.

Moore, Jeanne. 1998. Poverty and access to the arts: Inequalities in arts attendance. *Cultural Trends* 8 (31): 53–73.

Nord, Mark, and Kathleen Romig. 2006. Hunger in the summer: Seasonal food insecurity and the National School Lunch and Summer Food Service programs. *Journal of Children and Poverty* 12 (2): 141–58.

Nordenmark, Mikael, and Mattias Strandh. 1999. Towards a sociological understanding of mental well-being among the unemployed. *Sociology* 33 (3): 577–97.

Olson, Christine. 1999. Nutrition and health outcomes associated with food insecurity and hunger. *The Journal of Nutrition* 129 (2): 521S–524S.

Payne, Rupert, and Gary Abel. 2012. UK indices of multiple deprivation. *Health Statistics Quarterly* 53:1–22.

Penedo, Frank, and Jason Dahn. 2005. Exercise and well-being: A review of mental and physical health benefits associated with physical activity. *Current Opinion in Psychiatry* 18 (2): 189–93.

Purdam, Kingsley, Elisabeth Garratt, and Aneez Esmail. 2016. Hungry? Food insecurity, social stigma and embarrassment in the UK. *Sociology* 50 (6): 1072–1088.

Reardon, Sean, and Ximena Portilla. 2015. Recent trends in socioeconomic and racial school readiness gaps at kindergarten entry. *AERA Open* 2 (3): 1–18.

Rozin, Paul. 2005. The meaning of food in our lives: A cross-cultural perspective on eating and well-being. *Journal of Nutrition Education and Behavior* 37:S107–S112.

Sampson, Robert. 2003. The neighborhood context of well-being. *Perspectives in Biology and Medicine* 46 (3): S53–S64.

Schmitt, Sara, Megan McClelland, Shauna Tominey, and Alan Acock. 2015. Strengthening school readiness for Head Start children. *Early Childhood Research Quarterly* 30:20–31.

Simpson, Donald, Eunice Lumsden, and Rory Clark. 2015. Neoliberalism, global poverty policy and early childhood education and care: A critique of local uptake in England. *Early Years* 35 (1): 96–109.

Small, Mario. 2006. Neighborhood Institutions as resource brokers: Childcare centers, interorganizational ties, and resource access among the poor. *Social Problems* 53 (2): 274–92.

Small, Mario, and , |Monica McDermott. 2006. The presence of organizational resources in poor urban neighborhoods: An analysis of average and contextual effects. *Social Forces* 84 (3): 1697–1724.

Small, Mario, Erin Jacobs, and Rebekah Massengill. 2008. Why organizational ties matter for neighborhood effects: Resource access through childcare centers. *Social Forces* 87 (1): 387–414.

Small, Mario. 2009. *Unanticipated gains: Origins of network inequality in everyday life*: Oxford: Oxford University Press.

Social Metrics Commission. 2019. *Measuring poverty 2019*. Legatum Institute Foundation. Available from https://socialmetricscommission.org.uk/wp-content/uploads/2019/07/SMC_measuring-poverty-201908_full-report.pdf.

Stack, Carol. 1975. *All our kin: Strategies for survival in a black community*. New York, NY: Basic Books.

Stiehm, Walter. 2000. Poverty law: Access to healthcare and barriers to the poor. *Quinnipiac Health Law Journal* 24:279–85.

Utter, Jennifer, Simon Denny, Mathijs Lucassen, and Ben Dyson. 2016. Adolescent cooking abilities and behaviors: Associations with nutrition and emotional well-being. *Journal of Nutrition Education and Behavior* 48 (1): 35–41.

Valenzuela-García, Hugo, José Molina, Miranda Lubbers, Alejandro García-Macías, Judith Pampalona, and Juergen Lerner. 2014. On heterogeneous and homogeneous networks in a multilayered reality: Clashing interests in the ethnic enclave of Lloret De Mar. *Societies* 4 (1): 85–104.

Van Eijk, Gwen. 2010. Does living in a poor neighbourhood result in network poverty? A study on local networks, locality-based relationships and neighbourhood settings. *Journal of Housing and the Built Environment* 25 (4): 467–80.

Wauchoppe, Barbara, and Nena Stracussi. 2010. Challenges in serving rural American children through the Summer Food Service Program (Brief Number 13). Durham, NH: University of New Hampshire Carsey Institute. Available from https://scholars.unh.edu/cgi/viewcontent.cgi?article=1107&context=carsey (accessed 23 July 2019).

Wilson, William Julius. 2011. *When work disappears: The world of the new urban poor*. New York, NY: Vintage.

Wilson, William Julius. 2012. *The truly disadvantaged: The inner city, the underclass, and public policy*. Chicago, IL: University of Chicago Press.

A Divided Sisterhood: Support Networks of Trans Sex Workers in Urban Turkey

By
EZGI GÜLER

This article examines how transgender individuals operating in the underground sex economy in urban Turkey form supportive relationships and mobilize against various forms of violence, given structural conditions that encourage distrust and competition and undermine collective efforts among the sex workers. I found that, despite their conditions, workers heavily relied on each other for matters ranging from small-scale interpersonal exchanges of resources to community mobilization. However, the violent and unpredictable circumstances of their lives still generated repeated conflict, making their ties precarious. The article considers the importance of fictive kinship ties in this community, and discusses the coexistence of solidarity and conflict in sex workers' relationships.

Keywords: sex work; transgender; support networks; mobilization; ethnography

According to Amnesty International (Murphy 2015), sex workers face violence, stigma, discrimination, and other rights violations all over the world. In particular, transgender sex workers disproportionately become the targets of these violations (Lyons et al. 2017). In Turkey, this population encounters a deep intolerance for transgressing societal gender norms. The gentrification and urban renewal projects in the cities have resulted in the displacement and spatial discrimination of transgender communities, like other marginalized groups (Bayramoğlu 2013). Despite their particularly hostile circumstances, transgender (or trans) sex workers' experiences have been largely overlooked in the scholarly literature (Lyons et al. 2017).

Ezgi Güler is a PhD researcher in the Department of Political and Social Sciences at the European University Institute in Italy. Her research focuses on survival and resistance in sex worker communities.

NOTE: I am grateful to all those who welcomed me into their lives.

Correspondence: ezgi.guler@eui.eu

DOI: 10.1177/0002716220919745

Several studies document the lived experiences of violence of trans communities in various social contexts (e.g., Lyons et al. 2017; Perkins 1996; Zengin 2014). This line of research highlights that the intersecting vulnerabilities, which place this population in a particularly risky position, are created by a complex interplay of social structural factors (Lyons et al. 2017). Trans sex workers' vulnerability is an urgent issue in Turkey, where these individuals experience pervasive stigma about their gender identity, lack of employment due to discrimination, the criminalized and precarious nature of the street-based sex work they depend on for their livelihoods, and the policing practices sex work entails.

In this hostile context, where trans sex workers run high risks to their safety and economic survival, it is important to create support networks and a climate of solidarity; yet the violent and exclusionary structural forces that shape their environments also complicate their relationships and produce conflicts with each other. How do these networks operate? Using qualitative methods, this research focuses on a network of trans sex workers in urban Turkey, exploring how they form supportive relationships and mobilize against different forms of violence, given structural conditions that encourage distrust and competition and undermine collective efforts for safety, security, and sustenance.

Traditionally, debates on sex work have either privileged the structural constraints that lead people to engage in sex work and that have shaped sex workers' lives, or the agency of workers to choose such work (Choi and Holroyd 2007). Depending on the conditions under which they operate, sex workers' agency may be highly constrained. For example, marginalization results in street-based sex workers having diminishing control over the spaces in which they live and work and over their actions within these spaces (Scorgie et al. 2013).

While this may be true, research in various social contexts has also revealed that, within all the constraints, sex workers display considerable agency, thereby enhancing their personal protection and economic advantage (see Choi and Holroyd 2007; Morselli and Savoie-Gargiso 2014; Scorgie et al. 2013). Collective efforts, such as support exchanges or mobilization in the face of violent and exclusionary pressures, display their agency. Indeed, social structure not only shapes practice but is also reproduced or transformed by this practice (Giddens 1984). The relationship between social structure and agency should therefore be central to understanding sex workers' experiences. This research seeks to recognize the agency of transgender sex workers without dismissing the severe constraints undermining their ability to control their lives and their collective struggles.

The objectives of this case study are threefold. First, it aims to explore the structural conditions that foster support exchanges between trans sex workers, and the ways in which they mobilize against different forms of violence. Furthermore, it sheds light on the conditions that constrain workers' involvement in collective coping by critically engaging with their social practices and narratives, in both the presence and the absence of support. In doing so, the study relies on two bodies of literature, which focus on material and immaterial challenges undermining solidarity in sex worker communities. It attempts to show how these two sets of conditions simultaneously operate in limiting trans sex workers' support for one another. Finally, it describes how sex workers collectively respond to these pressures.

Sex workers' informal support networks used to cope with marginalized circumstances are facilitated by certain social elements embedded in their communities. For example, in China, bar hostesses' support networks were enabled by blood relationships, common background, native place, and mutual benefits (Zheng 2008). In Vietnam, "mommies" supported bar hostesses to fight back against violent clients, and the familial relationships among coworkers entailed sharing clothing, tips, advice, and responsibilities (Hoang 2015). In Australia, the sense of common suffering brought "male-to-female transsexual" sex workers together as a community (Perkins 1996). Other ethnographic studies have documented certain codes and practices ingrained in sex worker communities that have helped them to maintain a supportive environment (see Parreñas 2011). Thus, community characteristics, such as a shared identity; deeply rooted social relations, norms, and values; and the experiences of common difficulties motivated supportive practices among sex worker communities.

In addition to the interpersonal support exchanges, community members work together to achieve their common goals: for instance, they mobilize to counter the risks in their environments and pose challenges to the oppressive structures. According to social movement scholars (see della Porta and Diani 2009; Gamson 1992), mobilization is rooted in a collective identity in opposition to an oppressive out-group. In some contexts, sex workers' collective efforts indeed transformed their circumstances by establishing economic independence, combatting stigma, increasing physical safety (see Ghose et al. 2008), and motivating legal and policy changes (see Blankenship et al. 2006), such as decriminalizing sex work or introducing HIV prevention services.

However, structural forces may also pose challenges to collective efforts and create interpersonal conflicts. First are challenges that material pressures, including competition, inequalities, and financial concerns, create on sex workers' relationships and community dynamics. For example, the organization of sex work may result in competition for income, clients, and locations (see Busza and Schunter 2001; Campbell 2000; Hubbard and Sanders 2003), which in turn weakens companionship and solidarity among workers (Hofmann 2010) and render support networks unstable (Zheng 2008). In Turkey, the trans community acted in solidarity and cooperated in the face of state violence, exclusion, and discrimination (Cabadağ 2016; Zengin 2014), but financial disparities led to disagreement, tensions, and quarrels; divided them; and, on some occasions, undermined their political mobilization (Zengin 2014).

Second, social and political dimensions of marginalization, such as social exclusion, stigmatization, and hostility, limit support and generate conflict in sex worker communities. For instance, Perkins (1996) noted that oppression and negotiating survival in a hostile world undermined transsexual sex workers' support, cooperation, and sense of community. Similarly, the *travestis* in Brazil were in competition with one another; not only for financial reasons, but also for boyfriends, beauty, and femininity (Kulick 1998). Kulick further explained that distrust, betrayal, and violence may be rational responses to the violent world they live in or the consequences of internalizing the antagonism and discrimination they constantly experience.

In all these contexts, the precarious and competitive work or hostile circumstances complicated sex workers' relationships. In this article, I show how material and immaterial conditions simultaneously shape sex workers' collective struggles, such as support networks and mobilization, and explain how workers collectively try to counteract these elements, even with limited opportunities to do so. In the following, I briefly describe the legal, political, and economic context in which the study is situated.

Transgender Lives in Urban Turkey

The rights group Transgender Europe (2016) noted that "there is no safe country for transgender people," but the statistics from Turkey are particularly alarming. According to the data from this organization, between 2008 and 2018, 37 percent of the 139 murders of transgender people in Europe took place in Turkey (the highest rate in Europe), with nearly all being sex workers (Transgender Europe 2018). In large cities, trans communities have also become the targets of collective assaults, such as the attempts at lynching or forced eviction conducted by some residents or by the police (Human Rights Watch 2008). Moreover, revitalization and gentrification projects have taken place, which have led to the displacement of these populations (Bayramoğlu 2013). However, going beyond physical violence, transgender sex workers' experiences in Turkey take the form of "structural violence," a term coined by Galtung (1990). Structural violence describes the social arrangements that are embedded in political, economic, medical, and legal structures and that result in harm to certain populations (Farmer et al. 2006; Rhodes et al. 2012).

In 2011, around 8,000–10,000 transgender people were estimated do sex work in the large cities of Turkey, and approximately 15 percent of all sex workers in Istanbul were identified as transgender (quoted in Çokar and Kayar 2011). While the exact number is hard to establish, the involvement of trans people in sex work is widespread in Turkey. Whereas 15 percent of trans women in the United States reported having done sex work for income (Grant et al. 2011), an overwhelming majority of trans women in Turkey earn a living by participating in the sex economy, usually—not solely—due to the gender-based discrimination in the labor market (Çokar and Kayar 2011). In addition, most trans individuals are legally excluded from selling sex due to their gender identity, citizenship status, or age (UNFPA 2014)[1]. Even though Turkish law does not define prostitution as a crime, all necessary actions to conduct sex work outside of registered brothels are criminalized. These policies not only deprive them of economic and social security and safe working environments, but also compromise their access to legal protection channels (World Health Organization 2005).

The income made through sex work is highly variable. In a study conducted by the Red Umbrella rights organization with 233 trans women living in Turkey, the top one-fifth reported earning more than 3,000 liras ($1,350) per month from sex work, while the bottom one-fifth earned a minimum wage or less—around 1,102 liras ($500) per month (Ördek 2014). The majority of unregistered sex workers, despite not holding any social security or any resources other than the highly volatile income earned from sex work, often pay administrative fines imposed by law enforcers and high charges for healthcare expenses (UNFPA 2014). The most vulnerable sex workers—those who operate on the streets or struggle with poverty, homelessness, or health problems—are also the ones harmed by the institutional practices the most (Çokar and Kayar 2011). In these ways, legal, political, and economic structures render particularly the most disadvantaged groups of sex workers vulnerable to harm and poverty. Considering all of this, on one hand, trans sex workers in this context need to rely on each other to cope with and counter all these risks in their environments; on the other hand, the challenges they face might pose considerable barriers to their companionship and lead to conflicts. How do they tackle these contradictory dynamics?

Fieldwork

The current study took place in an urban neighborhood of a major city in Turkey, known as a community in which approximately 150–200 trans individuals live together and earn their livelihoods in the street-based sex market. I chose the particular area because there is an established trans community living and work-ing in this neighborhood with which I was familiar and to which I had relatively easy access. Nevertheless, it is not an exceptional case. Historically, trans indi-viduals in Turkey face similar pressures and try to stay safe by living and working as a community in large cities (Çokar and Kayar 2011; Zengin 2014). These characteristics differentiate them from nontrans sex worker populations.

A few of my interviewees reported that they have not defined their gender or that it varies over time. Besides, most sex workers in this study, whose assigned sex at birth was male, self-identify either as a woman or by using various local and transnational gender-variant terms: *travesti, lubunya, trans, transseksüel, gacı,* or cross-dresser.[2] A wide range of identities coexist under these broad categories, and they have the potential to challenge the reductionist and dichotomous con-ceptualization of gender identity.

The data collection was carried out during five rounds of fieldwork over two years from August 2017 to August 2019 through participant-observation and in-depth interviews. I spent an average of six hours a day for a total of six months with the workers in the streets while they were soliciting clients, and in their day-to-day activities, namely social gatherings, dinner times, beauty salon visits, and birthday parties.

I also conducted semi-structured in-depth interviews, using open-ended ques-tions in Turkish[3] with considerable probing. During the interviews, I adapted the order of the questions depending on the course of each interview so that it felt like a natural interaction. I collected comprehensive interview data on various forms of threats that workers recently experienced, as well as the corresponding coping strategies and support networks on which they relied. The particular research questions and some of the themes discussed during the interviews emerged in the course of my first round of fieldwork in August 2017. Following the fieldwork, recorded interviews were transcribed, and all interviews and field notes were read multiple times before being analyzed. In addition to some theoretically oriented priori themes, most themes arose from empirical data, resembling the grounded theory approach (Glaser and Strauss 1967), which allowed surprising connections to be integrated during data analysis (Charmaz 2008).

The interview sample includes thirty individuals, seventeen of whom were transgender sex workers, the principal interviewees of the study. The ages of the workers ranged from 18 to 45 with an average age of 25. Other actors were friends, shopkeepers, hairdressers, neighbors, managers, an ex-partner, an activist, a lawyer, and a local civil society representative, all of whom knew and commonly interacted with the community members. I started with convenience sampling, since the sampling frame was not predefined and access was difficult. As the research unfolded during the ethnographic investigation, and with a better understanding of the characteristics of the community, I identified the major subgroups of workers. Next, I continued with targeted sampling, an appropriate strategy to study "hidden" populations difficult to access "due to their attributed social stigma, legal status, and lack of visibility" (Watters and Biernacki 1989, 426). Accordingly, I interviewed trans individuals from various working flats and those who largely operated in other parts of the city, as these groups possessed slightly different characteristics. In sum, the construction of the interview sample was a multifaceted and dynamic process. Moreover, through participant observation, the voices of many more individuals were incorporated into the study.

I stopped conducting interviews when they provided little new information, yet most of the interviews took place in the first three rounds of data collection, over a period of three-and-a-half months. Having built trusting relationships, several months later I was able to hold casual chats and make more intimate observations, which offered new insights. Participation in the interviews was voluntary. If candidates agreed to participate, I introduced myself, broadly communicated the goals of the research, and reassured participants that they were free to skip any question or terminate the interview at any time. All interlocutors provided verbal informed consent. If they agreed, the interviews were recorded. The age of the interviewees, as well as interview characteristics, such as the place and date, were not revealed, for reasons of privacy and safety, and all names used here are pseudonyms.

Establishing rapport was the most challenging stage of data collection. During my initial visits, I met several shopkeepers who let me spend time in their establishments and introduced me to several members of the trans community. My regular visits to the neighborhood were an important step in helping the community to feel accustomed to my presence and helping me to establish a strong rapport with some of the workers. Over the course of the fieldwork, I spent time on the streets; at the tea garden, where I casually chatted with the people; and at the beauty salon, where I socialized and helped with cleaning and preparing dinner and shared meals. Ultimately, by combining interview data with ethnographic observation, and by interacting with various people concerning the same incidents, I succeeded in uncovering the process of an event and triangulating the validity of the information I received.

Description of the field site

Trans individuals have lived and worked in this inner-city neighborhood for many decades. Despite being directly adjacent to the business and the cultural center, it is located in a markedly less affluent part of the district, occupied by small traditional workplaces and emerging alternative restaurants and bars. More recently some community members have moved elsewhere or started working in other provinces, though they still frequent this area. The neighborhood hosts more than a dozen working flats, most of which are managed by the "mamas"— relatively more experienced trans women who are or used to be sex workers themselves. Clients come from a wide range of socioeconomic backgrounds and income and age groups.

On an ordinary day, I often saw trans women sharing their news, chatting, or gossiping while having a late breakfast or a glass of tea at one of the cafes. In the late afternoon, workers start standing on the street corners, which are their stable working spots. Various police groups, including the vice squad and uniformed officers, are in charge of preventing prostitution from taking place in the neighborhood every evening. With the police officers' arrival, workers try to remain vigilant and invisible, so they either stand at the entrances of the apartment buildings or make use of the time by going to the hair salon to get ready for the night's work. Their late-night chats at these places are generally intimate and entertaining. Early in the morning after officers leave, the neighborhood looks and sounds strikingly different; it feels noisy, dark, and unsafe. Despite the prevalent violent encounters with clients and passersby, this is the time when most of the trans women can finally begin to work.

Findings

Support networks

Nazlı has had an exceptionally supportive family with whom she has maintained regular contact throughout her transition and during her "new life." On the other hand, most of the other women I spoke with had experienced ostracism and estrangement when their families first became aware of their gender identity. For instance, Sevda, who had to leave her parental home and cut ties with her family members, has not been able to build accepting or trusting relationships with her family, even after returning to her home city and reconnecting with them. Derya, like many others, occasionally gets in touch with her family, but only over the phone. Several have undergone more traumatic family experiences: for example, when Aslı was a young teenager, she allowed an older male relative to take cross-dressed photos of her, which he then disseminated to all her extended family. After that, she fled her hometown and became part of the community in the neighborhood where the research was conducted. In addition, a few others abandoned their homes, even without coming out to their families. While some individuals were alienated from their biological families, several others were proud to share with me that they had reestablished relationships with them. Nevertheless, even those who had did not usually confide their problems to them, nor did they anticipate any assistance from them. Most importantly, they did not want to cause harm to or complicate their relationships with their families. Also, the families would usually be unwilling to support them or not know how to help them.

Violence was common in the everyday lives of these sex workers. Despite the devastating conditions, they had limited access to formal support structures; to the contrary, institutions were the places where they also felt vulnerable to harassment. All of the women I spoke with had unique life stories and different educational and socioeconomic backgrounds, political opinions, perceptions about sex work, and future aspirations. Regardless, they have all experienced similar forms of discrimination in schools, jobs, and public spaces and had become the targets of violent acts.

Given that trans sex workers' access to legal protection mechanisms and family support is limited, in many cases informal networks among workers served as physical, financial, and emotional assistance. Undoubtedly, there were differences in who was more disposed to help and which circumstances tended to evoke supportive patterns. While many of their peers were helpful in the event of serious violence, particularly those who operated in the same house or street were of greatest help. Notably, but not surprisingly, biological sisters in the community were extremely sensitive about each other's safety and security. A young worker, Aslı stated, "My sister and I protect each other like angels . . . I can't let any harm come to her." In the course of the research, I encountered three pairs of biological siblings, all of whom were trans sex workers affiliated with this neighborhood. These siblings lived and worked in the same houses, watched out for each other, and provided all kinds of support. Although many workers typically did not receive any assistance from their biological families, these sisters were deeply committed to one another, more than anyone else in the community.

At times, to get through a moment of crisis, the intimate friends also supported each other financially. This was the case when someone needed to repay a debt to a loan shark, was at risk of being imprisoned for fines, or when their property, such as a house, was seized by the authorities. For example, getting into trouble for her unpaid penalty for compulsory military service,[4] a well-known worker in the community, Handan, was taken into custody, where she called her friends to ask for help. She could be freed if she covered the fine, which was nearly twice her monthly rent, but she did not have the funds for it. Handan was a friend of four relatively affluent and popular women who worked together in the same house with a markedly protective and disciplined mama. Two days later, her closest peers, one of whom was advancing to becoming a mama, paid the fine so that Handan could be released. During my time there, Handan was paying small sums of money back to her friends. In the same way, if some people could not afford to rent a flat, their friends hosted them, or they slept in the working flats. Hence, in all these cases, the urgency of an adverse situation evoked a willingness to provide financial support among intimate friends.

Some of the workers have faced more grievous circumstances. Another time, Pınar, whom I see as one of the toughest workers of the community, told me that she once fell from the balcony of an apartment building. Even though she was lucky to escape without serious injuries, she hurt her feet and was unable to work. During her recovery, her friends, with whom she shared a house, provided for and nursed her. When she told me about this incident, she expressed her gratitude for her friends' care. In these examples, people struggling financially received help from those with whom they had intimate ties, namely biological siblings and close friends. Nevertheless, monetary assistance generally did not reach beyond these intimate ties.

Some narratives also referred to the reciprocal nature of these friendships. An experienced worker, Kamelya, said that she would undoubtedly lend money to her best friends in financial hardship, and then she immediately added, "They do likewise." Aslı mentioned that financial cooperation took place with her group of friends and her biological sister who lived in the same house, but not with the outsiders. Some women who had shared a house for many years cultivated familial relationships and trusted each other to pool resources at difficult times, getting involved in a "gift-giving economy" (Bourgois 1998), which reduced the risk of having severe crises.

Especially those who lived and worked together and thus had the same mama were closely bonded. These relationships indeed carried an intimate sense of sisterhood. At the time of the interview, Aslı said, referring to her best friends, "We are all the girls of the same house. We've shared a house; we've shared everything. We're like sisters. They know every little thing about me, and I know every little thing about them." These intimate relationships recall Kath Weston's work (1997), who noted that fictive kinship networks serve as emotional support and provide financial assistance and care to individuals of diverse gender and sexuality who have limited or no access to their families of origin.

Besides, all steady members of the community were acquainted and occasionally interacted with each other. For instance, while preparing for their evening of work in the beauty salons, many of them exchanged food, cigarettes, pantyhose, shoes, makeup products, and advice about appearance. In addition, both close friends and distant acquaintances gave each other psychological support, which included information (e.g., pieces of advice, suggestions, and experiences on various topics) as well as emotional support (e.g., close contact, intimate relationships, expressions of empathy, and care). In other words, the neighborhood has become home to these people, who cared for and protected one another, and their relationships provided some of the resources that were conventionally delivered by biological families, as Zengin (2014) also noted in her ethnographic research with the queer community in Istanbul.

In contrast to several flats that have had a stable composition for years, there has been labor mobility among the sex workers. Whereas some workers operated independently without a manager, others had a voluntary and informal agreement with a mama, which created a sense of interdependence. The local businesses, such as beauty salons, restaurants, and a tea garden, made encounters and connections more likely, which made it easier for such agreements to be struck. Indeed, workers were free to break the informal contract with the manager and join another house. In exchange for a room to conduct their work, they were required to pay daily rent to the mama, whether or not they worked. This roughly corresponds to the earnings from one sexual service. The interdependence between these parties sometimes materialized when the *girls* in a house needed financial support. One of the oldest members of the community, Esin *Anne*, is a respected mama who has lived in this city since the 1980s. She, for instance, clarified the role of a mama:

> Whom they call mama is a boss. Who is a boss? She isn't a bad person. She's rented a flat and opened her doors to trans women who escaped their villages to help them to acquire a livelihood. She guides them. That isn't a bad thing. . . [Imagine] a muscular guy arriving dressed as a woman. Among many other things, they remove the body hair and get breast implants. Who does all these? A boss gets them done. That's why they respect her. Because the boss transforms them.

Esin's narrative explains that managers helped workers to acquire the assets and skills to practice their profession, a financial exchange that emerged between people who had a direct work contract. Mamas were, in the first place, motivated to protect their business as the managers of the working houses; support and guidance were also part of the management of sex labor.

The community maintained a hierarchical social structure, in which all women regarded more senior mamas with respect. Regardless of whether they personally knew them, they called them *Anne*, which means mommy in Turkish. Not every experienced woman in sex work becomes a mama, however, and not every mama occupies an equally high position; those with considerable experience, a good reputation, and notable connections were respected and obeyed more than anyone else in the community. "Mother-daughter" relationships signify a common identity and express a sense of respect and responsibility between these parties, but they do not necessarily communicate intimacy. In all of these instances, the collectivity created around the neighborhood, working flats, and small businesses enabled supportive relationships. This collectivity took various forms, such as community, intimate friendships, and fictive families (both sisterhoods and mother-daughter relationships).

Community mobilization

Workers mobilized particularly against physical violence. They heavily relied on their community to stay safe; not only intimate friends, but also more distant associates had each other's backs. They stayed in close contact, stood in the streets in groups, warned others about dangerous clients, coached inexperienced peers, protested at the police station to save a friend, fought back during violent events, and collectively built a reputation to deter threats. A pressing concern shared by many of the workers, safety was treated as a collective responsibility, consistent with previous research with sex workers in various other contexts (see Hoang 2015; Sanders and Campbell 2007). For instance, an experienced worker, Mine, recalled a recent event when a client attempted to murder her neighbor while she was working, "Everyone went to help. I also ran [there] when I heard the noise." As I questioned how common this conduct was, she asserted, "When it comes to safety, we always help each other." Another time, refusing his request to lower the price of the date, Sevda was assaulted by a client in front of her apartment. She told me, "As soon as I started yelling, all the girls ran towards us with sticks and stones." These women were not only Sevda's close friends, but many of her peers who worked in the same or neighboring streets. Following these instances, large-scale mobilization almost immediately took place.

The primary subject, which brought many of them together, was violent encounters with clients and passersby while working. Those who aim to earn a comparatively higher income or do not manage to join a house operate in other neighborhoods of the city. However, working in remote or geographically dispersed locations is hazardous especially because workers go without the protection of their peers. A young worker, Tuna, explained:

> I work in [this neighborhood]. I went out to the [highway] for two weeks only. Compared to here, it's very dangerous there. It's also dangerous here, but there it's much worse. People go there to earn a higher income. At least, when something happens here, we can band together and become one. It's very difficult to gather there.

In fact, like Tuna, most of my respondents acknowledged that large-scale mobilization increased workers' safety, consistent with existing research (see Ghose et al. 2008). Workers further supported their associates in less-risky ways, such as informing them of the identity of unsafe men who they have encountered, and, more generally, warning each other of potential risks, discussed strategies, and shared tips and advice to stay safe.

Another serious concern for workers was policing practices, which they rigorously tried to counteract while doing their jobs. On a winter night in 2017, I was spending time at a beauty salon in the neighborhood with some customers who were waiting to have their hair and makeup done, when Feray *Anne* pushed the door open and rushed into the place together with two younger women. It was an attempt of the mama to conceal her *girls* from the police. This mama, who had her working flat two blocks away, announced to the others that the officers had arrived. Every night, a different group of police officers, some of whom normally operated in other districts, or even in neighboring cities, visited the neighborhood. They usually carried out ID checks and prevented sex workers from standing in the streets. At times, they completely blocked the streets, so that nobody could enter the area until the officers left. The restrictions imposed, however, varied depending on the officer in charge of the police team. Therefore, workers informed each other about which team was present each night, so that everyone could manage their work accordingly.

In fact, these policing practices created further vulnerabilities in the lives of trans sex workers. Their presence significantly reduced the number of clients and the income of the workers, while extending the working hours and forcing many women to solicit clients in the unsafe areas of the city, like industrial zones or certain highways. In those places, workers are also obliged to pay a daily "protection fee" to the organized crime groups. Hence, the punitive practices not only deteriorate their working and living conditions, but also result in the organized crime groups' profiting from the sex trade.

Certainly, community mobilization was not merely a strategic act; it was also a shared understanding, nurtured by the sense of community. The most common narratives about the collective protection included "bond of a common fate," "sharing a common gender," and "having formed a family together." Resting on collective identity and, most importantly, the shared experiences of suffering attached to this identity (see Perkins 1996), these narratives encompass trans individuals across different social classes and locations. We can conceive this in Nazlı's words, "Every day, some troubles break out. We protect each other because we share a common fate. Personally, I always back the others." In a like manner, according to Simge, "When something happens to somebody, we rush to help. After all, we all have a common fate."

Much like others, Esin *Anne* viewed the set of relationships in the community as a family attachment:

> When there is an external danger, we unite. It's always been like this. We've formed a family for ourselves, separately from our own mothers, fathers, and siblings. If I get harmed, they'll be saddened. If they get harmed, I'll be saddened. We go to help each other just as family members do.

In Esin's narrative, there is a clear separation between "we," characterized by a common identity, and the "other," posing a threat to them and therefore responsible for their conditions. The shared identity among trans women has been reinforced by the frequent encounters with the other subjects who intended to harm them. Past research has deemed these conditions as necessary for mobilization (Gamson 1992). Furthermore, dense social networks among workers helped them to more effectively mobilize support in their community (see della Porta and Diani 2009). Facilitating communication and coordination among individuals, these social networks also played a crucial role in the emergence of collective action.

Without question, large-scale collective protection was critical for their safety. Esin *Anne* also argued that solidarity in the community was indispensable:

> We might have arguments. Well, for one day. Next day, if something happens, again, she is the one who will lend a hand. . . . See, [the arguments] are forgotten immediately! Because she has no other [source of] solidarity, nowhere else to go. Only among ourselves. We can exercise solidarity here by ourselves. We may shout at each other. We may fight just like siblings in a family do, but the next day, nothing happens; it is forgotten. You see, we have the same.

Here, Esin drew an analogy between the nature of the relationships in this big trans family and the conventional understanding of sisterhood dynamics; there were fights and conflicts, but also a deep commitment to protect each other. She further emphasized that the community had no other reliable source of support, neither institutional nor familial. In fact, some workers had ties with the local political or nongovernmental organizations, which operated vigorously in the face of an oppressive political environment. However, these organizations usually had a limited reach and capacity to assist. In addition, workers spent considerable time with some of the shopkeepers, neighbors, and regular clients in the neighborhood, but these actors were also unable to help interfere with the violent events. Hence, Esin's insights tell us that despite conflicts in the community, solidarity among workers persisted, due to the common need for safety.

Mamas were chiefly responsible for the security of their own working flats, but even this was insufficient to keep everyone safe. Support networks formed only with intimate ties would be too small and spatially concentrated to be effective. As Derya put it, "In the end, if we don't unite, we'll all be wiped out." Therefore, the capacity of joint efforts was improved by enlarging support networks to individuals working in distinct houses and streets. In short, there was a desperate need for large-scale collective action to stay safe, and strong shared identity and dense networks, which enabled it.

It is important to note that large-scale collective action also deterred violence by collectively building a reputation for being fierce. The safety of the neighborhood was a commonly valued property because if it was weakened, all community members would risk getting harmed. Along with several others, Mine believed that these efforts were often successful: "The wicked people can't mess with us much because they know about us. [They know that] when an incident occurs, we help out each other." As Mine expressed, rigorous community efforts against violations not only helped community members to cope with their challenges, but also impeded perpetrators from committing an offense, thereby empowering the community and disturbing power dynamics. This was proudly repeated in the narratives of many others.

Another subject that brought the sex workers together was death and funerals. On November 2017, I heard that Sevda's mama, Yasemin *Anne*, had had a stroke and lost her ability to walk and talk so that she became dependent on other people to meet her essential needs. Sevda looked after her during that period, but not long after, Yasemin *Anne's* condition worsened. On several occasions, Sevda informed the social services that she had neither the knowledge nor the means to look after such a severely ill person, and sought help from them. Despite her calls, assistance never arrived. Three months later, Yasemin *Anne* passed away. As one of the oldest members of the community, she was known and respected by many. Therefore, most of the community members chipped in to organize a funeral. Some groups collected money and met certain expenses for the rituals, such as serving food to the public.[5] Although it was primarily Sevda who took care of the financial and administrative matters for the funeral, she would be unable to meet all the expenses herself. Beren, from whom Sevda would never seek help otherwise, paid for Sevda's household bills. To express their appreciation for her companionship, some shop owners who knew Yasemin *Anne* also did their part.

The functional and emotional support the trans community gave through these practices resembles what is usually provided by the biological family (see Zengin 2014). Here, it is critical to understand that, when biological family links are absent, many of the workers in the community hold similar concerns: "Who is going to hold a funeral when I die?" This common concern, in addition to a devoted care for one another, motivated large-scale material and immaterial mobilization in unity. Overall, what brought them together were these risky events or the moments of grief. Due to a pressing need for safety and protection from harm, the threatening events particularly mobilized social resources to a great degree (see Taylor 1991). These stories show that shared identity, a sense of common difficulties and suffering, dense interpersonal networks, and lack of other support structures enable or facilitate mobilization in this community.

Barriers and obstacles to support exchanges and mobilization

While informal support systems are a crucial resource to cope with and counter risks, these connections were not uniformly available. Even though, noticeably, many workers were in a deep financial struggle, money and other material resources were usually exchanged only among small and intimate social circles. My interviewees argued that this was due to social fragmentations, largely based on working flats, which differed slightly from one another in income, status, mobility rates, and management of the houses. For example, while Sevda was looking after her ill mama, her financial situation significantly worsened; she was struggling to make ends meet for several months. On one of these days, she voiced her disappointment about her wealthier peers, who worked next door, "They know my situation. Why don't they offer any support?" Likewise, she did not receive any assistance from other peers, like Beren, who worked on the same street as Sevda. Erol, the waiter at a tea garden in the neighborhood, explained the nature of their relationships:

> If Sevda turns to Beren [to ask for money], Beren would not recognize her. They occupy separate corners and earn separate bread [earnings]. They've never sat, eaten, or drunk together. Sevda has no possibility of asking her for money. Everyone has a best friend [whom they can count on]. . . There is nothing like everyone supports everyone.

Being acquainted with both Sevda and Beren, Erol stated that particularly among peers who had never shared resources or engaged in a material exchange, it was not expected to seek or offer financial support.

On the contrary, workers commonly expressed distrust, especially toward their distant peers. Working in the same house did not always generate a habit of sharing either. Mine, who did not feel attached to anyone in the community, was cautious about being taken advantage of financially. Similarly, Melike appeared doubtful that her peers would pay back if she lent them money. Several others said that, even if they were asked to, they would refuse to help their associates financially. In fact, they often kept their earnings hidden from their peers. Even intimate friends would at times treat each other with a certain wariness. For example, recall Handan, who avoided going to prison because her friends intervened and paid her fine. Despite being good friends with Handan for several years, her friends did not trust her to pay back her debt. To monitor her spending, they had her move into their own working flat. These mechanisms, however, seemed to function only in close-knit groups.

Moreover, some women who were struggling financially were held responsible for their circumstances. Hilal criticized some of her peers, "No one defends those who are young and capable of working. If a sex worker can't afford rent, she either misuses all her money on her lover or consumes drugs. These are the practices not approved of by wise trans people." In a similar way, Melike blamed others for their financial difficulties, "They must be something like drug-addicts. They don't need money in the same way a [non trans] family does." Hence, when it comes to financial struggles, they often adhered to the narratives of divisions, distrust, and personal failings, which hindered mobilizing support.

Tensions and conflicts are anticipated in every relationship, but the circumstances of their lives exacerbated these conflicts. I witnessed workers expressing resentment toward their peers, quarreling with each other, and spreading rumors. Some of them maligned their peers to the clients and belittled them in the presence of others and in private conversations. Sometimes half-jokingly, sometimes seriously, they criticized their friends' appearances, clothing, makeup, and plastic surgery. Over time, I came to realize that a great deal of these quarrels were seen as natural and as codes of interaction in the community. The contentious nature of these social interactions helped them to bond, release tensions, and form alliances. Yet in some cases, hostile comments and practices turned self-destructive, harmed relationships, and undermined solidarity. Given the violent world these women live in, a safe and supportive environment is vital to surviving and transforming their circumstances.

There could be several underlying reasons for distrust and conflicts. The vulnerability to economic hardship varied from person to person. Earnings depended on many factors, such as age, working capacity, and social skills. Whereas some workers were well-to-do—they could even save money and purchase hard assets such as property—others struggled to earn a living. Several workers I spent time with told me that, due to the unpaid administrative fines, they could neither put money into their bank account, nor buy any property, which limited their capacity to create financial security. Much like Zengin (2014) described, there were large economic disparities among these women. Therefore, financial struggles were not viewed as a common difficulty and did not always mobilize workers' support networks. These women also shared physical work space in the informal sex market. As in other contexts (see Hofmann 2010), the work structure created a competitive environment, which at times gave rise to heated arguments over "stealing" others' clients or working spots. When their regular client picked another worker, they sometimes expressed resentment to the client as well as to their peer. Although they needed each other to define the market and attract clients to the neighborhood, everyone found work for themselves in this concentrated urban space. Consequently, economic interdependence was in part constrained by the inequalities and competition between workers.

Furthermore, material pressures also impeded community mobilization. For instance, a sense of insecurity created by the precarious living and working environments gave rise to a reluctance to mobilize against violence and social and economic exclusion. Some workers had restricted their participation in physical and political mobilization in their neighborhood, because they were afraid that such protests would reduce the number of clients and intensify policing practices, thereby negatively impacting their livelihood. This was repeated in the narratives of many community members. Some workers even disapproved of their colleagues who engaged in assertive collective resistance such as organizing political action, fighting back, and revolting against police misconduct.

However, the negative relational dynamics were not only a result of material divisions or material pressures. Similar to transgender sex workers in other contexts (see Kulick 1998; Perkins 1996), the relationships of those in my study were affected by social and political dimensions of marginalization, such as discrimination, social exclusion, and violence; these circumstances created distrust, conflicts, and rivalries among workers (see Bourgois 2001). This may be interpreted as a practical necessity for self-protection in a hostile world (see Kulick 1998). Or a psychological process may be at work, according to which they may have internalized the stigma they constantly faced during daily struggles and projected it onto their peers (see Tajfel and Turner 1979). In any case, the structural conditions of violence, which affect their lives in various significant ways, were reflected in their relationships.

Friends and acquaintances in the context of my study were very supportive of fighting against serious violent events and other external threats to the community. In other words, the code of acting collectively to ensure safety was respected to a large extent. On the other hand, these social ties could also be demoralizing and troublesome, as I have explained (see Rook 1984). In sum, the material pressures, such as precarious labor, economic disparities, and competition; and the immaterial conditions of marginality, such as stigma and hostility, simultaneously shaped transgender sex workers' environments. These conditions further undermined their support network and capacities to mobilize.

Conclusion

This article explored the structures that foster or constrain collective efforts in a transgender sex worker community in Turkey. It further shed light on how a community with limited opportunity responds to violent and exclusionary pressures and copes with tension between solidarity and conflict in their day-to-day lives. In an attempt to transcend discourses of victimization, this research recognizes these workers' agency amid the complexities and contradictions of their daily lives.

In particular, it documents the ways in which sex workers are often able to mobilize emotional and material support. First, in the absence of a biological family and other support networks outside the community, fictive kinships are used to convey rights and duties to people living in the same house, such as the expectations to support one another and to respect mamas. Furthermore, events such as violence, death, and funerals brought the wider community together and bred unity and cooperation despite competition and conflicts in other areas.

However, their marginalized circumstances, in addition to shaping sex workers' environments, also complicated their relationships. In this hostile context, where workers typically relied on one another for various resources, their relationships and collective efforts were also fraught with distrust, conflicts, and competition. Material and immaterial conditions (such as financial pressures, precarious work, and stigma) operated together to limit trans sex workers' support for one another and create conflicts.

My ethnography was useful to explore the structural foundations of the community dynamics and grasp the complexity of collective efforts in this community of sex workers. The friendships among my study population were ridden with contradictions, as Mine described, "We, trans women, always hold onto each other, but, at the same time, fight each other tooth and nail." That is, the relationships may provide support and protection, but they are also prone to conflict and rivalry. Despite being exhausted by their marginalized conditions, these workers were able to offer assistance, support, and care, which helped them to subsist in a hostile environment. In this way, the dynamics of their relationships allowed solidarity and conflict to intimately coexist. Indeed, these contradictory dynamics are not specific to sex worker communities; other marginalized populations, particularly those whose livelihoods rely on the informal economy, have similar experiences (see Snow and Anderson 1993).

Finally, this research has several policy implications. The criminal and administrative sanctions and the threat and reality of police harassment disrupted the lives of my study participants, and displaced them into unsafe and isolated locations where they had to work illegally without peer support networks. Understanding how various pressures shape the living conditions of trans individuals can inform legal and political practices designed to transform the circumstances for this population. Particularly, replacing punitive practices with public policies that address the safety and economic needs of transgender people may help them to report violence, work in safer areas, access social services, and find employment outside the sex trade.

Notes

1. To register themselves in a legal brothel, trans women need to have completed their transition and hold a female identity card. See Çokar and Kayar (2011) for the legislation.
2. See Zengin (2014) for the local meanings attached to these gender identity terms.

3. Some excerpts of the transcribed interviews and field notes were translated into English for this article.

4. Trans women can get exempted from compulsory military service if they obtain a medical report, as they are considered to have "sexual identity and behavior disorder."

5. As a tradition, people distribute a large amount of food or dessert to the public to receive a blessing for the person who had died.

References

Bayramoğlu, Yener. 2013. Media discourse on transgender people as subjects of gentrification in Istanbul. In *Queer sexualities: Diversifying queer, queering diversity*, eds. Vikki Fraser, 41–48. Leiden: Brill.

Blankenship, Kim M., Samuel R. Friedman, Shari L. Dworkin, and Joanne Mantell. 2006. Structural interventions: concepts, challenges and opportunities for research. *Journal of Urban Health* 83 (1): 59–72.

Bourgois, Philippe. 1998. The moral economies of homeless heroin addicts: Confronting ethnography, HIV risk, and everyday violence in San Francisco shooting encampments. *Substance Use & Misuse* 33 (11): 2323–2351.

Bourgois, Philippe. 2001. The power of violence in war and peace: Post-Cold War lessons from El Salvador. *Ethnography* 2 (1): 5–34.

Busza, Joanna, and Bettina T. Schunter. 2001. From competition to community: Participatory learning and action among young, debt-bonded Vietnamese sex workers in Cambodia. *Reproductive Health Matters* 9 (17): 72–81.

Cabadağ, Nazlı. 2016. Negotiating queer public visibility: Experiences of LGBTI residents in Kurtuluş, Istanbul. PhD diss. Sabanci University, Turkey.

Campbell, Catherine. 2000. Selling sex in the time of AIDS: the psycho-social context of condom use by sex workers on a Southern African mine. *Social Science & Medicine* 50 (4): 479–94.

Charmaz, Kathy. 2008. Grounded theory as an emergent method. In *Handbook of emergent methods*, eds. Sharlene Hesse-Biber and Patricia Leavy, 155–72. New York, NY: Guilford Press.

Choi, Susanne Y.P., and Eleanor Holroyd. 2007. The influence of power, poverty and agency in the negotiation of condom use for female sex workers in mainland China. *Culture, Health & Sexuality* 9 (5): 489–503.

Çokar, Muhtar, and Habibe Yılmaz Kayar. 2011. *Seks işçileri ve yasalar: Türkiye'de yasaların seks işçilerine etkileri ve öneriler*. İstanbul: İnsan Kaynağını Geliştirme Vakfı.

della Porta, Donatella, and Mario Diani. 2009. *Social movements: An introduction*. Oxford: Blackwell.

Farmer, Paul, Bruce Nizeye, Sara Stulac, and Salmaan Keshavjee. 2006. Structural violence and clinical medicine. *PLoS Medicine* 3 (10): 1686–91.

Galtung, Johan. 1990. Cultural violence. *Journal of Peace Research* 27:291–305.

Gamson, William. 1992. *Talking politics*. Cambridge: Cambridge University Press.

Ghose, Toorjo, Dallas Swendeman, Sheba George, and Debasish Chowdhury. 2008. Mobilizing collective identity to reduce HIV risk among sex workers in Sonagachi, India: The boundaries, consciousness, negotiation framework. *Social Science & Medicine* 67 (2): 311–20.

Giddens, Anthony. 1984. *The constitution of society*. Cambridge: Polity Press.

Glaser, Barney, and Anselm Strauss. 1967. *Grounded theory: The discovery of grounded theory*. Chicago, IL: Aldine.

Grant, Jaime M., Lisa A. Motter, Justin Tanis, Jack Harrison, Jody L. Herman, and Mara Kiesling. 2011. *Injustice at every turn: A report of the national transgender discrimination survey*. Washington, DC: National Center for Transgender Equality and National Gay and Lesbian Task Force.

Hoang, Kimberly Kay. 2015. *Dealing in desire: Asian ascendancy, Western decline, and the hidden currencies of global sex work*. Berkeley, CA: University of California Press.

Hofmann, Susanne. 2010. Corporeal entrepreneurialism and neoliberal agency in the sex trade at the US-Mexican border. *Women's Studies Quarterly* 38 (3/4): 233–56.

Hubbard, Phil, and Teela Sanders. 2003. Making space for sex work: Female street prostitution and the production of urban space. *International Journal of Urban and Regional Research* 27 (1): 75–89.

Human Rights Watch. 2008. *We need a law for liberation: Gender, sexuality and human rights in a changing Turkey*. Available from www.hrw.org/report/2008/05/21/we-need-law-liberation/gender-sexuality-and-human-rights-changing-turkey.

Kulick, Don. 1998. *Travesti: Sex, gender, and culture among Brazilian transgendered prostitutes*. Chicago, IL: University of Chicago Press.

Lyons, Tara, Andrea Krüsi, Leslie Pierre, Thomas Kerr, Will Small, and Kate Shannon. 2017. Negotiating violence in the context of transphobia and criminalization: The experiences of trans sex workers in Vancouver, Canada. *Qualitative Health Research* 27 (2): 182–90.

Morselli, Carlo, and Isa Savoie-Gargiso. 2014. Coercion, control, and cooperation in a prostitution ring. *The ANNALS of the American Academy of Political and Social Science* 653 (1): 247–65.

Murphy, Catherine. 14 August 2015. Sex workers' rights are human rights. Amnesty International.

Ördek, Kemal. 2014. *Violence directed towards sex worker trans women in Turkey: A struggle for existence caught between crossfire of invisibility and impunity*. Ankara: Red Umbrella Sexual Health and Human Rights Association.

Parreñas, Rhacel S. 2011. *Illicit flirtations: Labor, migration, and sex trafficking in Tokyo*. Stanford, CA: Stanford University Press.

Perkins, Roberta. 1996. The 'drag queen scene': Transsexuals in Kings Cross. In *Blending genders: Social aspects of cross-dressing and sex-changing*, eds. Richard Ekins and Dave King, 53–62. London: Routledge.

Rook, Karen S. 1984. The negative side of social interaction: Impact on psychological well-being. *Journal of Personality and Social Psychology* 46 (5): 1097–1108.

Rhodes, Tim, Karla Wagner, Steffanie Strathdee, Kate Shannon, Peter Davidson, and Philippe Bourgois. 2012. Structural violence and structural vulnerability within the risk environment: Theoretical and methodological perspectives for a social epidemiology of HIV risk among injection drug users and sex workers. In *Rethinking social epidemiology: towards a science of change*, eds. Patricia O'Campo and James Dunn, 205–30. New York, NY: Springer.

Sanders, Teela, and Rosie Campbell. 2007. Designing out vulnerability, building in respect: violence, safety and sex work policy. *The British Journal of Sociology* 58 (1): 1–19.

Scorgie, Fiona, Katie Vasey, Eric Harper, Marlise Richter, Prince Nare, Sian Maseko, and Matthew F. Chersich. 2013. Human rights abuses and collective resilience among sex workers in four African countries: A qualitative study. *Globalization and Health* 9:1–13.

Snow, David A., and Leon Anderson. 1993. *Down on their luck: A study of homeless street people*. Berkeley, CA: University of California Press

Tajfel, Henri, and John Turner. 1979. An integrative theory of intergroup conflict. In *The social psychology of intergroup relations*, eds. William G. Austin and Stephen Worchel, 33–47. Monterey: Brooks Cole.

Taylor, Shelley E. 1991. Asymmetrical effects of positive and negative events: the mobilization-minimization hypothesis. *Psychological Bulletin* 110:67–85.

Transgender Europe. 2016. Minority groups should not be played out against each other. Available from tgeu.org/minority-groups-should-not-be-played-out-against-each-other (Accessed 8 March 2019)

Transgender Europe. 2018. Trans murder monitoring report. Available from https://transrespect.org/wp-content/uploads/2018/11/TvT_TMM_TDoR2018_Tables_EN.pdf

UNFPA. 2014. *Türkiye'de seks işçileri cinsel sağlık ve üreme sağlığı durumu: İhtiyaçları ve öneriler*. Available from http://www.kirmizisemsiye.org/SourceFiles/pdf-201852514943.pdf

Watters, John K., and Patrick Biernacki. 1989. Targeted sampling: Options for the study of hidden populations. *Social Problems* 36 (4): 416–30.

Weston, Kath. 1997. *Families we choose: Lesbians, gays, kinship*. New York, NY: Columbia University Press.

World Health Organization. 2005. *Violence against women and HIV/AIDS: Critical intersections—violence against sex workers and HIV prevention*. Available from www.who.int/gender/documents/sexworkers.pdf

Zengin, Asli. 2014. Sex under intimate siege: Transgender lives, law and state violence in contemporary Turkey. PhD diss. University of Toronto.

Zheng, Tiantian. 2008. Complexity of life and resistance: Informal networks of rural migrant karaoke bar hostesses in urban Chinese sex industry. *China: An International Journal* 6 (01): 69–95.

Asymmetries in Transnational Social Protection: Perspectives of Migrants and Nonmigrants

By
BAŞAK BILECEN

This study investigates the extent to which migrants' embeddedness in two formal social protection systems (country of origin and host country) influences the resources they exchange in their informal supportive relationships. I analyze the support networks of a matched sample of Turkish migrants in Germany and their significant others in Turkey to illuminate the conditions and meaning of reciprocal resource exchanges, finding that both migrants and nonmigrants perceive formal social protection offered by Germany as superior to that of Turkey. I show that those perceptions have implications for how financial support is exchanged with the family but have less impact on friendships. These implications for family included unequal power relationships, changes in equity among siblings and family, different valuation processes of resources, and thus, (reciprocal) exchanges.

Keywords: transnational social protection; international migration; reciprocity; personal networks; multisited research; matched sample; low-income families

Millions of people around the world use migration as a strategy to overcome poverty, not only for themselves but also for their close family members who stay behind in their country of origin. Migrants send financial remittances home to support their partners, children, and other relatives in their country of origin (Garip 2014; Massey and Basem 1992;

Başak Bilecen is an assistant professor of sociology and the Rosalind Franklin Fellow at the University of Groningen, the Netherlands and affiliated researcher at the Center on Migration, Citizenship and Development at Bielefeld University, Germany. Her research focuses on international migration, international student mobility, transnational studies, social inequalities, social support/protection, and social networks. She is the author of International Student Mobility and Transnational Friendships *(Palgrave 2014) and has co-edited special issues in the* Journal of Ethnic and Migration Studies *(2017),* Social Networks *(2018), and* Comparative Migration Studies *(2019), among others.*

Correspondence: b.bilecen@rug.nl

DOI: 10.1177/0002716220922521

Menjívar et al. 1998), and the people whom migrants leave behind provide the migrants with emotional support, a sense of belonging (Ryan 2011; Zontini and Reynolds 2007), and an array of services (e.g., childcare, help with housing and business investments) (Mazzucato 2011). Yet migration can also disrupt social networks (Putnam 2000) that protect individuals against risks like poverty and social exclusion, as ties are lost or watered down over time (Lubbers et al. 2010), creating a need for migrants to strengthen such networks locally (Ryan 2007).

While transnational care arrangements have received considerable scholarly attention in recent years (Baldassar 2007; Boccagni 2015; Bryceson and Vuorela 2002; Parreñas 2001), there is still little understanding of migrants' personal support networks given that their lives simultaneously span two nation-states' formal protection structures. In general, research into social support (Berkman and Glass 2000; Taylor 2011) often ignores the fact that social support exchanged between persons is embedded in the formal protective schemes of nation-states, such as welfare regimes. For instance, international migrants with a steady income may send financial remittances back home to their siblings so that they can hire nurses to care for elderly parents or relatives, because there may not be sufficient state infrastructures to do so without financial help from the migrant relative. The opposite could also be true: grandparents may go to the country of destination to care for grandchildren so that parents can work, perhaps because childcare is costly or there are few childcare facilities in the country of destination. When a person migrates, their relationships to people who stay behind are embedded in the protective schemes of two nation-states (the origin country and the destination country). I argue that these regimes affect the ways in which informal social protection exchanged in these relationships is understood and negotiated. The double embeddedness can give migrants and nonmigrants certain benefits, but it can also alter support mechanisms. In particular, I argue in this article that this double embeddedness affects the reciprocity of support exchanges and the power balance between the giver and the receiver of support. A better understanding of transnational social protection is important to design more effective social policies for families of migrants in a globalized world. Families of migrants are geographically separated and are subject to different welfare regimes, which might widen existing inequalities within and between societies. More generally, an accumulation of knowledge in studies like this one can shed light on how societal contexts affect mechanisms of informal social protection.

In this research, I investigate patterns of social protection for Turkish migrants in Germany and their significant others in Turkey by adopting a matched sample in a multisited research design (Barglowski, Bilecen, and Amelina 2015; Bilecen

NOTE: This research was funded by a grant from the German Research Foundation (DFG) within the framework of Collaborative Research Centre 882 "From Heterogeneities to Inequalities" at Bielefeld University, which I am grateful for. I thank all my interviewees who shared with me their perspectives, lives, and experiences. I am thankful for Gül Çatır, and Aslı Orhon, who conducted the matched-sample interviews in Turkey. I also thank the guest editors Hugo Valenzuela García, Miranda J. Lubbers, and Mario L. Small for their feedback on the earlier versions.

2016; Mazzucato 2009). Instead of the term *social support*, I adopt the concept *informal social protection* (Faist 2013; Faist et al. 2015) to highlight the complementarity of such protection with nation-state protection frameworks, as I outline in the next sections. The examination of givers' and receivers' perspectives of social protection across borders contributes to an in-depth understanding of the meanings attached to resources and norms of reciprocity, as migration is never only an individual experience.

Apart from the focus on the embeddedness of personal protective relationships within national welfare schemes, the study extends previous research in two other ways. First, the majority of studies on transnational social protection are conducted with only one of the two people in a relationship. In so doing, exchanges of protective resources are evaluated from only the migrants' perspective or from only the perspective of those who were left behind (exceptions include Dankyi, Mazzucato, and Manuh 2017; Marchetti-Mercer 2012; Poeze, Dankyi, and Mazzucato 2017). Because social protection is relational, de facto, it involves at least two people. By analyzing both people's evaluations of resource exchange, we can understand the relationships between the givers and receivers better, as well as the instability and inequality in resource exchanges.

Second, migration research emphasizes family ties over other nonkin relationships that might be equally important. However, when individuals migrate, their "left-behind" ties include not only their immediate family members but also, for example, childhood friends and former neighbors. Although family ties are important, the literature highlights other types of relationships that have different supportive functions (Small and Sukhu 2016; Wellman and Wortley 1990). In the seminal study of East Yorkers, Wellman and Wortley (1990) found that while ties between parents and children are the most supportive mainly in terms of emotions, friends tend to be companions. This study therefore focuses on both family members and friends.

The empirical material comes from an international collaborative research project[1] that involves interviews with Turkish migrants who live in Germany ($n = 20$) and their significant others in Turkey ($n = 10$) through a matched sample (see also Barglowski, Bilecen, and Amelina 2015). Turkish migrants in Germany represent a crucial case to investigate because they are the largest ethnic minority in the country and are marginalized. The long migration history of Turkish migrants started in 1961 with a guest-worker agreement between Turkey and Germany. Most migrant workers had a lower educational background than did Germans and worked in manufacturing and construction, and, in the late-1960s, in the lower levels of the service sector (Abadan-Unat and Bilecen 2020). There is ample evidence of their limited access to education and self-exclusion due to discrimination from the majority society (Çelik 2015; Song 2011). The second generation still tends to have disadvantages in the labor market, even if they have the necessary training and educational credentials (Song 2011; Sürig and Wilmes 2015). Thus, Turkish migrants represent a stigmatized minority group in Germany, grounded mainly in their different ethnicity, cultural, and religious practices and usually a lower educational background (Barwick 2016).

Conceptual Framework

Transnational social protection

Social protection refers to the complex assemblages of "strategies to cope with social risks arising in capitalist economies in fields such as employment, health care, and education" (Faist 2013, 3; cf. Faist 2019; Faist et al. 2015; Levitt et al. 2017; Sabates-Wheeler and Feldman 2011). Such social risks comprise unemployment, lack of care, poverty, and social exclusion. Social protection comprises formal elements, i.e., opportunity structures codified in nation-state rules and regulations; and informal elements, i.e., resources embedded in personal networks (Bilecen and Barglowski 2015). Although there is considerable overlap between the concept of informal social protection and that of social support due to their relational constitution, the term informal social protection acknowledges that resources embedded in interpersonal networks complement and are closely interlinked with welfare state provisions.

International migration can lead to a reevaluation of both formal and informal social protection practices. Notably, migrants may have multiple connections to at least two welfare regimes that are regulated through social policies and regulations or bilateral agreements, even though sometimes they are excluded from one or even both.

For transnational informal social protection, most of the literature focuses on family- and ethnically based community networks or religious communities that help migrants to minimize social risks (see Glick Schiller 2005a; Ryan 2011). These networks and communities play an especially crucial role in the lives of migrants. They are embedded within and across borders that are spatially bound to certain laws, rules, and regulations of welfare schemes, including health, employment, education, and family benefits. Thus, the dynamics of different social policies frame informal social protection relationships with the family members and friends who remain in their country of origin.

First, migration policies might pose legal constraints on families. In this sense, transnational migration research finds that state infrastructures and policies affect migrants' ability to move in the first place. For example, Bilecen and colleagues (2015) found that it was difficult for families from Turkey to visit and support their grandchildren in Germany due to visa regulations and the hardships of obtaining one; while Polish grandmothers did not encounter such difficulties, because Poland is an EU Member State, which enabled Polish people to move freely across national borders (Barglowski, Krzyżowski, and Świątek 2015).

Second, the state's territorial control (Faist 2000; Glick Schiller 2005a) and social protection frameworks (Faist 2019; Faist et al. 2015; Levitt et al. 2017) also affect the formation of transnational networks and communities. It is important to investigate how migrants and nonmigrants in different countries interact with a range of state institutions and policies as well as their perceptions of both contexts and their participation in discourses about society, nation, and migration phenomena (Glick Schiller 2005b). Once we understand migrants' and nonmigrants' perspectives and interactions with a nation-state, we can then articulate the influence of nation-state frameworks, such as welfare regimes, on personal relationships, social locations, social worth of welfare, and perceived social inequalities.

Geographic distance and state regulations affect informal social protection; but informal social protection also depends on personal relations that change due to migration. Some personal relationships are preserved, while others are disrupted or dissolved over time and through geographic separation, or they change in their content. For example, when women migrate and become the main breadwinner of the family, while leaving their children in their home countries, there are implications for gender dynamics, child care, and current and future intergenerational protective relations (Parreñas 2001).

Reciprocity in transnational social protection

Continuous reciprocal exchanges (e.g., gift exchanges between friends, neighborly exchanges of small items like a cup of sugar for coffee) are a main mechanism of maintaining personal ties. Simmel (1950) theorized that reciprocal exchanges tend to maintain relations by fostering feelings of gratitude. For Simmel, gratitude is "the moral memory of mankind" (1950, 388). Following Simmel, Gouldner (1960) posited that reciprocity works as a social mechanism, mainly by creating new social relationships, and he applied the concept to the contexts of power imbalances. He distinguished between *reciprocity as a pattern of mutually contingent exchange* and *the generalized norm of reciprocity*. Gouldner noted that some people might want to get more than they give, which results in imbalances and, eventually, exploitation. Even when there is a propensity for exploitation, however, reciprocity as a *norm* would function as a safeguard. According to Gouldner, when one end of the social tie feels obligated to give much more than the other end, asymmetries in relationships will surface. Building on Gouldner's work, Hansen (2004) argued that the rules of reciprocity and the ways in which they are invoked are largely determined by social class. For example, in studying childcare networks, Hansen (2004) examined class contingencies of reciprocity and found that reciprocation differs between upper and working classes because of material and time costs associated with reciprocation. Because upper-class mothers have wealth and status, they tend not to ask for support from their personal ties, whereas lower-class respondents mainly have support from their family ties and tend not to ask for support from other personal ties when they perceive reciprocation would be a burden for them.

Social mechanisms of such resource exchanges are important not only because of who gives what, where, and in exchange for what, but because of their unequal implications for both migrants and nonmigrants (Bilecen, Çatır, and Orhon 2015; Faist et al. 2015). Ideally, givers and receivers of supportive resources have shared beliefs about the type and value of the resource. If not, problems in reciprocity might emerge. Research has argued that one type of resource can be "returned" as another type, signaling "generalized reciprocity" (Sahlins 1965). The value of certain types of support might change over time. In addition, perspectives about the value of resources might be different in the eyes of the receivers and givers. Individuals evaluate resources based on cultural norms and values. International migration may affect individuals' evaluation processes, which could result in a change in the value ascribed to a resource by the receiver. Givers might attach value to such resources that, in the eyes of the receiver, were not as important or as highly regarded before migration. Those mismatches are important to study as a means to understand the wider consequences of international migration. To counterbalance the overly optimistic studies that indicate that international migrants' sending financial remittances home to support their significant others leads to development (see De Haas 2007 for a critical review) and that such transactions have only pure economic implications (e.g. Taylor 1999; World Bank 2006), the current study evaluates the nuances of such protective exchanges and shows the discrepancies between what is actually being exchanged and how these exchanges are (re-)evaluated depending on the social and national context.

Transnational research: Those who stayed

In contrast to earlier research that highlighted migrants' financial remittances to those in their country of origin and their implications for the country's development (Durand, Parrado, and Massey 1996; Massey and Basem 1992; Portes 2007), contemporary research has been interested in resource exchanges across borders. In addition to financial resources, migrants also remit ideas and knowledge to their country of origin, known as "social remittances ":

> What migrants bring and continue to receive from their homelands affects their experiences in the countries where they settle. This, in turn, affects what they send back to non migrants who either disregard or adopt these ideas and behaviours, transforming them in the process, and eventually re-remitting them back to migrants who adopt and transform them once again. (Levitt and Lamba-Nieves 2011, 3)

Along similar lines, Mazzucato (2011), who studied Ghanaian migrants in Amsterdam, found reciprocal support exchanges between family members who resided in both places and emphasized the importance of support that comes from the stayers, which she called "reverse remittances."

The literature suggests that there is a great power asymmetry between migrants and left-behind extended family members (Menjívar and Agadjanian 2007; Schmalzbauer 2008). For example, Menjívar and Agadjanian studied wives who were left behind in Armenia and Guatemala and found that gender inequality increased over time because wives became much more dependent on their husbands' financial remittances. In a similar vein, McKenzie and Menjívar (2011), who studied the meanings given to remittances and exchange relationships by Honduran women whose husbands migrated for work, found that the separation of couples put a lot of stress and anxiety on the shoulders of the left-behind wives. Similarly, wives in Turkey, whose husbands migrated to work in Europe, also talked about their difficulties, mainly in terms of being economically dependent on their husbands and their living situation with their in-laws in

Turkey, who had excessive demands (e.g., that they do all the household chores and/or take care of their husbands' elderly parents alone) and control (Çelik, Beşpınar, and Kalaycıoğlu 2013). Focusing on relationships beyond the nuclear family, Fuller-Iglesias (2015), who studied extended families from Mexico whose lives spanned Mexico and the United States, noted that, although some families strongly felt the geographic separation, others (usually return migrants) felt much closer to one another (mainly in their spousal relationships). Those who felt family fragmentation were usually parents whose multiple children had migrated to the United States, and some spouses who were living across borders for long periods reported strains on their relationships.

Recent research has looked at the perspectives of the left-behind family members in different contexts but has not addressed left-behind friendships. This is mainly because research has recruited only family members residing in the countries of origin. Although such a research design is a useful strategy, when asking migrants with whom they have protective relations, I found that migrants mentioned both important friendship relationships and family ties (Bilecen 2016, 2019).

Research Design and Sample

Empirical data for this study were collected between 2011 and 2013 and comprised participant observations, in-depth interviews, and personal network maps collected both in Germany ($n = 20$) and in Turkey ($n = 10$) as part of a collaborative research project. A multisited research design was implemented, whereby some of the initial respondents' personal connections were contacted and interviewed by the research team (Barglowski, Bilecen, and Amelina 2015; Bilecen 2016; Marcus 2011; Mazzucato and Wagner 2018). In so doing, the team was able to follow the movement of protective resources that connected different sites across borders and the meanings that different actors gave to those resources.

I interviewed and collected personal network data from all respondents. Data in Germany were collected through multiple access points to increase the heterogeneity of respondents, starting with randomly selected religious (e.g., Alevi organizations, mosques) and nonreligious organizations (e.g., integration courses, schools) in two urban areas, and continued with snowball sampling (with maximum two referrals). Five respondents were recruited through religious organizations and eight through nonreligious organizations, and snowballing yielded seven additional interviews, mainly with spouses, siblings, friends, and acquaintances of migrants. Although there are two couples and one pair of siblings, there is also one pair of acquaintances and a mother-son pair in the sample. Table 1 displays the characteristics of the respondents in Germany. The respondents are of Turkish and Kurdish ethnicities, and twelve respondents had at least one child. Three were retired, nine were unemployed (of whom two were students, and four were homemakers), and eight worked in sectors such as catering, construction, security, real estate, and sales. The sample in this study comprises low-income individuals in Germany. The interviews were conducted in Turkish.

TABLE 1
Respondent Characteristics in Germany

Name	Gender	Age	Marital Status	Migrant Status	Labor Market Status	Years spent in Germany
Ali	Male	21–30	Married	2nd generation	Student/Part-time worker	11–20
Ahmet	Male	21–30	Relationship	2nd generation	Student	21–30
Ömer	Male	31–40	Married	2nd generation	Part-time worker	21–30
Lale	Female	41–50	Married	Labor migrant	Part-time worker	31–40
Faruk	Male	31–40	Married	Labor migrant	Self-employed	11–20
Süleyman	Male	61–70	Married	Labor migrant	Self-employed	41–50
Adnan	Male	71–80	Married	Labor migrant	Pensioner	41–50
Murat	Male	31–40	Married	2nd generation	Employed	31–40
Nilgün	Female	61–70	Married	Family reunification	Homemaker	31–40
Berrin	Female	21–30	Married	2nd generation	Unemployed	21–30
Münevver	Female	51–60	Widowed	Family reunification	Pensioner	31–40
Hülya	Female	41–50	Single	2nd generation	Unemployed	31–40
Mustafa	Male	31–40	Single	Asylum seeker	Unemployed	11–20
Aylin	Female	61–70	Married	Family reunification	Homemaker	41–50
Bora	Male	31–40	Married	2nd generation	Part-time worker	31–40
Berna	Female	41–50	Married	2nd generation	Part-time worker	21–30
Elif	Female	61–70	Single	Labor migrant	Pensioner	41–50
Sema	Female	41–50	Single	Asylum seeker	Unemployed	11–20
Selda	Female	41–50	Married	Asylum seeker	Homemaker	11–20
Cemil	Male	31–40	Relationship	2nd generation	Student	21–30

The interviewees were asked to name as many relationships as they wished in response to the name-generator question: "From time to time, most people need assistance, be it in the form of smaller or bigger tasks or favors. Who are the people with whom you usually exchange such assistance?" At the same time, they were given a network map with four concentric circles of importance of people in their lives (very important, important, less important and unimportant; Kahn and Antonucci [1980]), into which they placed their contacts ("alters") and later reflected on the importance of each. Once the network maps were completed, I asked several questions about their relationships, including gender, location, type of relationship, and other aspects as a means to further understand the relationships that they maintained. Respondents were also asked about the relationships *among* alters. In 20 personal networks, a total of 301 alters were named as protective ties. Networks of migrants comprised between 8 and 27 contacts, with an average network size of 15. The average density score was 0.66, indicating that networks were closely knit. They comprised family (61 percent) and friendship ties (39 percent), and 50 percent of the ties were considered very important; 39 percent, important; 11 percent, less important; and 0.01 percent, unimportant. Of the ties, 65 percent were living in Germany; 29 percent in Turkey; and 6 percent in other countries.

Participants were asked to indicate who could be interviewed by the research team in Turkey. Unlike previous research that has sought respondents in the countries of immigration with personal ties in a predetermined city in the country of origin (Mazzucato 2009; Poeze, Dankyi, and Mazzucato 2017), or recruited respondents in their country of origin with migrant family members (Çelik, Beşpınar, and Kalaycıoğlu 2013; McKenzie and Menjívar 2011; Menjívar and Agadjanian 2007), the respondents in this study decided whom to name as their personal relationships, and only after that did the research team ask for their location. Eight participants in Germany gave their ten significant others in Turkey. Table 2 contains information on the respondents in Turkey. Out of the ten in Turkey, four were siblings of the interviewees in Germany, and six were friends. The research team was surprised by this, as they were expecting participants to name mainly family members, given the prominence of ties between family members in the literature and because 61 percent of the ties identified through network analysis with participants were family. Nine of the siblings and friends were interviewed by the research team in Turkey in three different urban areas, while one was visiting Germany and was interviewed by the author there. All participants from Turkey were middle-income.

The author also conducted participant observations through attending family gatherings, such as breakfasts and birthdays, as well as through lending circles[2] over two years, organized by women (Bilecen 2019). Although the fieldwork conducted in this study is not representative of all Turkish migrant families in Germany, the long relationships developed in the field over the years led the author to talk to many others who were not in the sample of the study but appear in the field notes. Informal conversations with neighbors, artists, medical personnel, and friends of friends as well as field observations in both contexts complemented the information obtained through the fieldwork. The next section presents the findings in two parts: the embeddedness of informal social protection in formal protection, and the evaluation of asymmetries in resource exchanges across borders. Family and friendship ties in countries of both emigration and immigration are analyzed as well and are discussed as part of the findings for social protection and asymmetries. To protect the identities of respondents and those in their networks, all names are pseudonyms.

Findings: Transnational Social Protection from Both Ends

Informal social protection embedded in formal protection systems

Migrants and stayers agreed that the German welfare state was superior to the Turkish one. This perception justified migration, but it also served as a source of

TABLE 2
Respondents Characteristics in Turkey

Name	Relationship to the migrant respondents	Importance for migrants	Importance for stayers	Gender	Age	Marital Status	Labor Market Status
Hale	Berna's friend	Important	Very important	Female	41–50	Single	Employed
Nazlı	Berna's friend	Important	No mention	Female	41–50	Single	Employed
Necati	Faruk's friend	Less important	Very important	Male	31–40	Single	Employed
Hüseyin	Faruk's friend	Less important	Important	Male	31–40	Single	Employed
Selim	Sema's friend	Important	No mention	Male	41–50	Divorced	Employed
Buğra	Bora's friend	Important	No mention	Male	31–40	Single	Employed
Şükrü	Berrin's brother	Very important	Important	Male	15–20	Single	Student
Ayşe	Ali's sister	Very important	Important	Female	21–30	Single	Student
Süheyla	Münevver's sister	Very important	Very important	Female	41–50	Married	Employed
Çetin	Süleyman's brother	Very important	Important	Male	51–60	Married	Pensioner

stigma for migrants. Contrary to the findings of McKenzie and Menjívar (2011), who interviewed staying wives with husbands who had migrated, in this study no stayers wished that their network contacts had not migrated, even if close family. I should note, however, that there were no couples who were geographically separated. The participants in Turkey had always supported or at least understood the need for migration because everyone in this study perceived Germany as a "super-state" (see also Bilecen, Çatır, and Orhon 2015).

Berna. Berna was born in Germany and then "returned" to Turkey with her parents, later migrating to Germany in the 1990s through marrying a second-generation migrant. Although Berna had a Turkish high school diploma and a good command of German, she did not find employment right away, as her educational credentials were not recognized in Germany. At the time of the interview, she was working part time at a department store while her husband, who is a second-generation migrant with vocational training, had a full-time, stable job. Berna spoke extensively about the German state as an advanced welfare state that offered employment, unemployment benefits, and educational assistance for individuals in every segment of society. She believed that, unlike in Turkey, individuals in Germany could achieve a better socioeconomic status because of the formal social protection in the country that contributes to the livelihood and life chances of individuals and their families. Although Berna is considered working class, she felt secure in terms of her life chances and access to healthcare in Germany.

Berna emphasized the importance of a well-developed state assistance mechanism funded by a well-functioning tax system to prevent economic and social deprivation, even if a person is unemployed or has a low salary, as she did. She noted that she managed to send some financial remittance to her parents, who could barely make ends meet. Berna's parents had retired in Turkey, and their only income was one pension tied to her father's employment. Because of a one-time contribution from the German state when they returned to Turkey in the early 1970s after the oil crisis, they could buy a house and live there with Berna's unemployed, adult brother. Berna's perception of the superiority of the German state was shared by Hale and Nazlı, Berna's friends in Turkey. Berna's family was familiar with the welfare state regime in both countries given their first-hand experience in Germany and their move back to Turkey; they knew what benefits she had access to, which made them aware of her social position in German society. Thus, her family had a more realistic view and expectation than did her friends. Berna wished that her parents could visit her in Germany regularly, but that required considerable financial capital for visa fees and flights. So, Berna visited them once a year.

Süleyman. Süleyman, who came to Germany in the 1960s for work, agreed with Berna's view that the welfare state in Germany is well-functioning. "Germany is a super-state," he said. "It helps everybody and everybody around me. . . . One can get unemployment benefits, what they call Hartz IV. They get it and they can live perfectly." Although his migration history is somewhat different from Berna's, they share the same perspective on how state policies, such as unemployment benefits, work to protect the poor. Süleyman is a first-generation migrant who came to Germany from Istanbul via the guest-worker agreement between the two countries. He immediately started work in a factory and, later, married Aylin, a woman from his neighborhood back home. She later joined him in Germany. Figures 1 and 2 represent their respective networks. While Süleyman was surrounded by many friends and family members, he only received care (e.g., household tasks, illness related matters, etc.) from his wife and provided financial protection to two of his siblings in Turkey. He also gave care to his son and his daughter-in-law through occasionally spending time with his grandson.

Aylin. Aylin tried to learn German but was unsuccessful. She, thus, perceived herself as distant from the majority society and socially excluded but "proud to [have] raised two children who are successfully employed in Germany." Although Aylin wanted to find a paid job, she had been held back by family obligations, such as taking care of the children and the household. She indicated that she had also been held back by her father as a child. Her parents were divorced and her sister, Hümeyra, had been living with her father while Aylin had been living with her mother. Aylin's father forced her to quit her studies after middle school, and later when she started to work he forced her to quit her job to stay at home. She has long been the caregiver to family members. She is now the primary caregiver to her elderly mother, who lives with them for six months of the year (the maximum amount of time on a visa that her mother could get). As a result, Aylin is not entitled to receive a pension from either Turkey or Germany. Although she could always choose a private scheme for the pension system in both contexts,

FIGURE 1
Süleyman's Personal Network

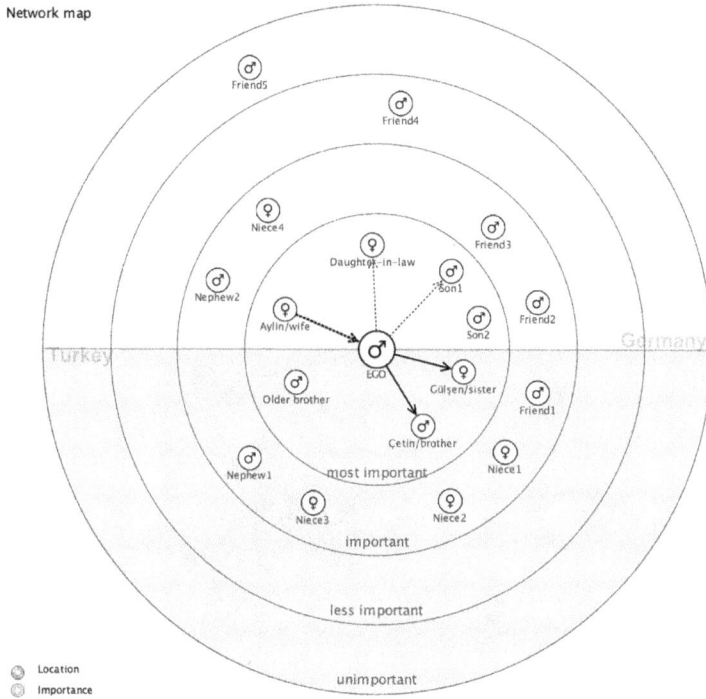

NOTE: On the network maps, drawn with the software VennMaker (Figures 1–3), information exchange is indicated with a dashed-dotted line, care relations with a dotted line, and financial protection with a straight line. The more types of provision or receipt of protection an actor is involved in, the thicker the arrows. Arrows indicate directionality of the exchange, the absence of arrows in the relation indicate their bidirectionality.

she never had the means. Due to Süleyman and his sons' hard work, they were able to buy a house in Germany and two in Turkey, even though each of their monthly incomes is average by German standards. As Figure 2 shows, Aylin had quite a few friends in Germany, all of whom were Turkish migrant women. With them, she had been organizing a lending circle called the "day of gold," which made financial capital and emotional support available to its members during the monthly meetings (Bilecen 2019). Süleyman's older sister, Gülşen, lived in Süleyman and Aylin's flat in Istanbul, which is in the same building as the flat in which his brother Çetin lived, which Süleyman helped to buy. When Aylin and Süleyman go to Istanbul, they stay with Gülşen. Because of long lasting resentments after her parents' divorce, Aylin has a somewhat complicated relationship with her sister, yet Hümeyra is still in her network map and from time to time Aylin sends her some money. During my interview with Aylin, it became clear that because Hümeyra was left behind in Turkey with an oppressive father, Aylin

FIGURE 2
Aylin's Personal Network

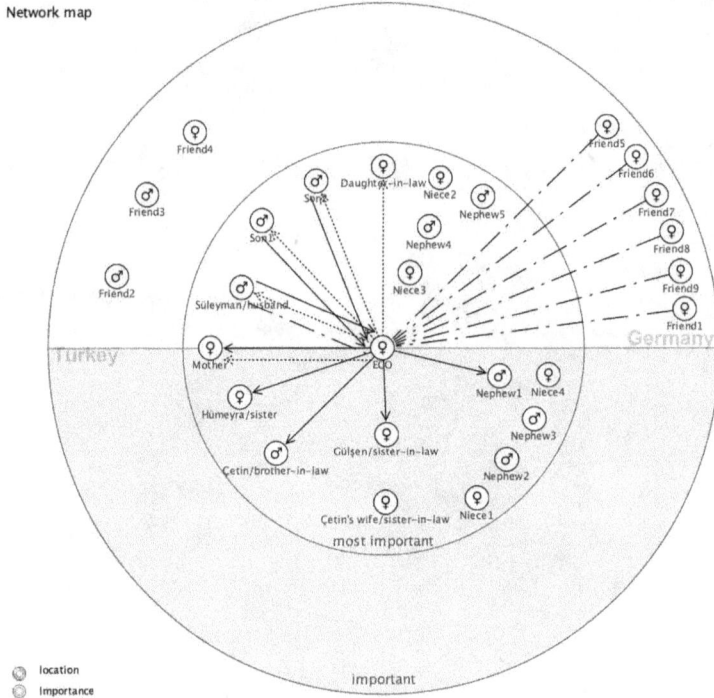

Network map

felt that she was in a position to contribute to Hümeyra's well-being and that of her three children through financial protection when needed. When I asked about their relationship, Aylin told me that even though Hümeyra had the means to visit her in Germany, she had only done so once, but that they tended to see each other during Aylin's yearly summer visits to Turkey. Because of the hardships Hümeyra and her children face, Aylin does not expect Hümeyra to reciprocate and rather sees her as disadvantaged, and thus entitled to receiving support.

Çetin. Süleyman's and Aylin's family members in Turkey had similar perceptions of the German state infrastructures as being superior to Turkey's. They perceived Süleyman and his sons as doing very well financially. (The Euro was over twice the value of the Turkish Lira at the time of the interviews.) Aylin often hinted that Süleyman's family in Turkey had unrealistic financial expectations for them. Süleyman's brother in Turkey, Çetin, also felt that the nation-state infrastructure functioned well in Germany and that migrants were "backed up" by the state, unlike in Turkey. Çetin also briefly implied that, because they live in a strong welfare state, migrants to Germany do not need any resources from their personal relationships. Çetin also wanted to migrate, but he was not able to obtain a work permit. He lived on his pension from Turkey and is married to a

FIGURE 3
Çetin's Personal Network

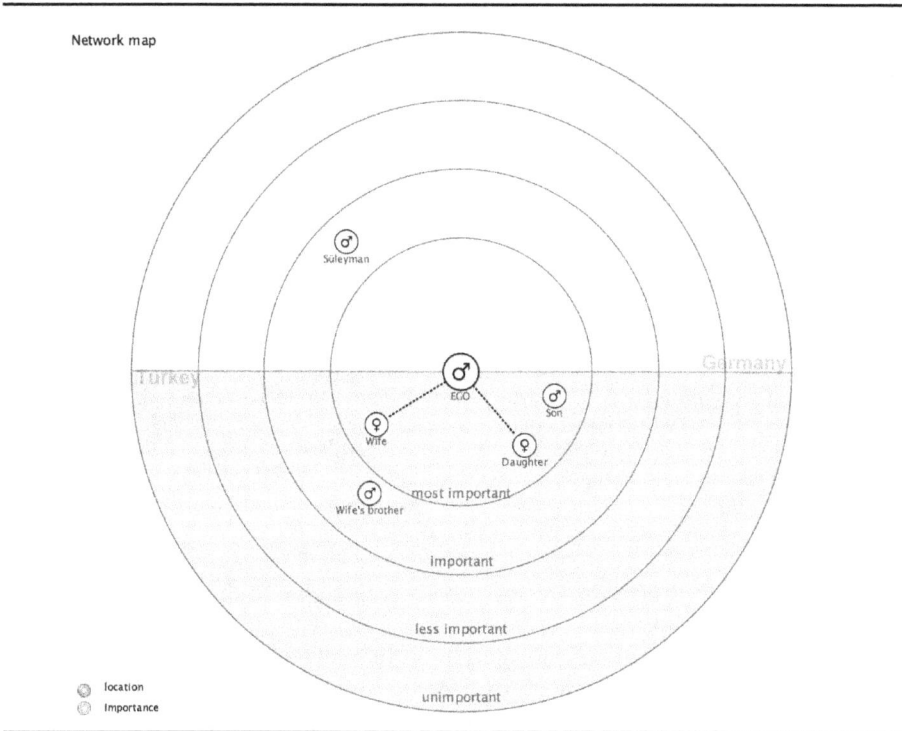

Network map

Süleyman

EGO

Son

Wife

Daughter

most important

Wife's brother

important

less important

location

Importance

unimportant

Turkey   Germany

homemaker and has three children; he is not in a condition to contribute financially to his brother, Süleyman, in times of need. Figure 3 represents Çetin's network map, which only contains his family members in Turkey and Süleyman in Germany. He mentioned care exchanges with his wife and daughter and did not even mention that Süleyman sends them money every month. Unlike his brother and sister-in-law, he has a rather small network. When asked about his friends, he said that none is qualified to be on the network map.

While Gouldner (1960) argues that indebtedness exists until a favor is returned, Çetin's accounts do not hint at any feelings of indebtedness to his brother or to Aylin. This could perhaps be because Çetin and Süleyman do not see the transaction as a one-time favor but, rather, as a normalized, continuous family obligation because Süleyman sends him remittances every month. This perspective is in line with Gouldner's notion of *normative reciprocity*, which results from status duties; that is, although migrants are in a low-income group in the countries of emigration, migrants are expected to contribute to transnational family welfare even if the stayers are not low-income. From a network perspective, Çetin is at a disadvantage because of his small network size, dependence on family members only, and a low resource exchange capacity in comparison to Süleyman and Aylin. Boccagni and Decimo (2013) argue that nonmigrants try to impose social control over migrants through reaffirming the power of original bonds by, for example, bringing up their status in the family. Çetin—the younger brother who could not migrate although he wanted to and who had a small social network—seemed to exert this control, according to Aylin, as he often implied that he was entitled to receive financial support from Süleyman. As Hansen's (2004) work indicates, there are status obligations. Çetin is the younger brother and Süleyman is the migrant brother; both statuses have meanings in the wider family and are socially recognized by both brothers, as well as by others in the network, such as Aylin.

Similarly, migrants' friends in Turkey perceive migrants in Germany as being well protected by the German state, such that migrants do not need personal protection from their friends back home. For instance, Necati, a friend of another participant, Faruk, has seven siblings and extended family members who live in Germany and France. He stated:

> In terms of social protection, those who live abroad are a bit luckier than us [in Turkey]. We [Turkey] are not a developed country in that respect. For example, when a German gets sick here, the German government sends an airplane over here. I think that is something you cannot compare to anything else. [. . .] Of course, they [family and friends in Europe] are better off than us, unfortunately, as a more developed country than us.

This widely held perception of superiority is reflected in the general discourse in Turkey, led migrants to be stigmatized, and normalized the expectation that migrants should contribute to their family welfare. The Turkish term *almancı* or *gurbetçi* emerged in the language to describe migrants who had left for better opportunities or selfish reasons. The two terms imply that migrants are not well-educated, and thus belong to the working class, and that they do not comply with Turkish social norms. In addition, migrants are portrayed by the society in Turkey as persons who put value on material things. My findings are in line with those in Fuller-Iglesias's (2015) research, who found that mainly former neighbors or in-laws criticized or gossiped about migrants. For those in Turkey without migrant family members, migrants are seen as having a higher socioeconomic position but are also perceived as traitors who left the country to seek a better income. These perceptions can be somewhat explained by feelings of envy or resentment that result because of the social inequalities among stayers with and without migrants in their families. Although my findings point to corroboration between movers and stayers who are entangled in formal and informal social protection systems, accounts from participants also brought out concerns about financial exchanges and the value of various resources.

Perceived asymmetries in informal social protection: Family and friendships

The initial years of migration from Turkey to Germany in the 1960s proved to be important because the financial flows back to stayers helped the Turkish economy. First-generation migrants were perceived as earning a great deal of money in the eyes of the stayers. Not only did immediate family members gain economic resources but communities and villages also prospered; thus, those in small villages wanted to keep sending family members to Europe (Çelik, Beşpınar, and Kalaycıoğlu 2013). Although having a migrant in the wider family meant a general prosperity, not all family members benefited to the same degree. As Boccagni and Decimo (2013, 4–5) state:

> Every interaction between money senders and recipients involves much more than a merely economic transaction. No less significant are the symbolic value, the expected destination, the roles and the power relationships that are attached to, and negotiated through, migrant monies.

The symbolic value of resources also depends on the perspective of the beholder, and the values attached to certain resources might change over time depending on the relationship between the giver and receiver. Some of my migrant respondents described being dissatisfied with and resenting certain family members or friends who had become too demanding and who made contact only when they were in trouble or needed financial assistance. For example, Aylin thought that she and her family in Germany gave too much financial protection to relatives who remained in Turkey. Aylin felt that family members in Turkey expected her to financially contribute because they perceived her as having a better socioeconomic position in Germany than those who remained in Turkey. Although migrants are obliged to give when they are asked, Aylin nevertheless felt that they had not received much in return. Although her brother-in-law, Çetin, thought that because they are a family, they all need to take care of each other, and, thus, that all resources should be granted to other family members by default; Aylin thought otherwise. She stated, "Well, we can't get what we give, actually. I can't say that it is equal because we always give, we do not really get— perhaps 'once in forty years'" [Turkish expression of rarity]. Participant observations yielded many accounts when migrants discussed that they had severed ties with family members because they were demanding. Aylin, too, had conflicting relationships with her nieces and nephews, who had sometimes demanded financial help. Although many of these family members were listed in Aylin's sociogram, they were listed as ambivalent ties.

Although Aylin resented being the provider in almost all cases, during our informal meetings after the interviews, it became clear that she enjoyed having "the upper hand" because it translated into power in the family—she had more say in what to buy, where and how much to save, and had a dominant place in daily decisions in the household. And she perceived an upward social mobility among her extended family that was made possible through her migration. According to her husband, Süleyman, the stayers are family members in need; thus, he sent a regular financial remittance to Çetin, and to his sister, Gülşen. He conceded bluntly that he was on the giving side in his family that remained in Turkey. For Süleyman, the help he gives is unequal, however, not because he does not receive anything back or receives something of a lower value, but because he cannot help his older brother and extended family such as nieces, nephews, and cousins to the same degree. He felt guilty or ashamed because he did not have the means to help these other family members. Süleyman's accounts also hinted at the norm of equity, that every sibling had the right to be equally supported by him.

Münevver. Two sisters who I interviewed, Münevver and Süheyla, commented on financial exchanges. Münevver first came to Germany in 1975 at the age of 21 and has never had a paid job. Right after she got married in Turkey, her husband left to work in Germany. Two years later, she joined him. She maintained close ties to her family, but after a while, she lost track of her friends in Turkey. Although her sister Süheyla and her brother from Turkey took care of their mother in Turkey on a daily basis, Münevver sent them money from Germany via her husband's income and, after he passed away, from her pension. Because she could not be in Turkey physically to take care of her mother (her low income restricted her from traveling frequently), Münevver sometimes felt guilty . She expressed appreciation to her siblings for their time and effort. As a daughter, Süheyla recounted that she did what she had to do and interpreted her care for her mother as a family obligation rather than a resource to be exchanged with her sister. In Süheyla's eyes, she could not reciprocate Münevver properly for the financial support that Münevver provided. Although Süheyla was a full-time employed civil servant in Turkey who was entitled to all state benefits, she and her family needed Münevver's regular financial contributions to sustain their livelihood while caring for Süheyla and Münevver's mother.

Although elderly care or emotional support are very important sources of protection, they are not considered a tangible resource in the eyes of both the sender and the receiver among my participants. Süheyla and Münevver desired a direct reciprocity of resources, but the reciprocity took different meanings. Süheyla noted, "Those who live abroad, well, my sister, I mean, it is just, you know, spiritually [I can provide support], in the phone calls, how much, through sharing their problems, barely that much. We don't have so much opportunity." Süheyla seemed to be unsatisfied with the exchanges she had with her sister, because she did not perceive the reciprocity to be equal in value and felt as if she was not providing enough. In contrast to Çetin, Süheyla felt that she had to reciprocate, most likely because she had a good job in Turkey and because she was aware of her sister's low socioeconomic status in Germany.

Münevver felt that, by taking care of their mother, her siblings gave her protection which could not be reciprocated financially. Münevver felt guilty about not being able to help and perceived the care for her mother as a favor and not as a resource. She could not care for her mother for an extended time, because if she were in Turkey for more than six months she would lose her residence permit in Germany, and thus, formal social protection entitlements such as access to health care would be jeopardized. The two sisters should care for their mother equally, but because one had migrated and thus was subjected to two nation-state schemes, the other took on the care of their mother. So, the care for their mother was perceived as a favor that needed to be returned, but it could not be matched by financial means because of its nonreciprocal emotional dimension.

All first-generation migrants in the sample spoke about their financial obligations and the mismatch with resource exchanges. Second-generation migrants in the sample, Berna and Murat, whose parents were labor migrants, were the only ones who sent financial remittances to their returned elderly parents in Turkey. As the only person with a stable income (even though it was a low income) in her parental family and as the only female child, culturally Berna was expected to contribute to her parents financially and emotionally. I had the chance to observe Berna in many different settings and during many occasions (see also Bilecen 2019). I learned through these observations that she saw her financial contributions to her parents as necessary to maintain her parents' daily activities. With her contribution, her parents could buy better groceries and undertake a small construction project in their home to enhance their living conditions.

Moreover, as I have discussed elsewhere (Bilecen 2016), Berna relied on her two very close female friends in Turkey (Hale and Nazlı) to help with her parents. For example, she asked them to visit her parents from time to time to keep them company and to check on them. Berna was very much aware that there was a limit to the help from her friends, but sometimes she would consult with her female friends about her parents, even more so than with her brother. For Berna, their help with her parents was very important, while both Hale and Nazlı spoke mainly about the emotional support they exchanged with Berna on a weekly basis. Similarly, Murat sends his mother money when necessary. His mother and other family members in the household use the money for their daily necessities and to make ends meet most months. Although there are six siblings, Murat is expected to send money regularly because he has better and more stable employment and, more importantly, because he is a man.

Financial protection was usually given by family members, whereas friends did not exchange money but, rather, exchanged emotional support or the social status achieved from having a friend living abroad. For example, Nazlı, who works at her family's company in international trade and belongs to the middle-class in Turkey, and, therefore, had access to formal social protections in Turkey, visited Berna once in Germany, and they were in touch regularly. During Nazlı's visit with her family, Berna introduced Nazlı to her friends in Germany. Although she did not mention Berna in the network map, Nazlı described their relationship as very close: "Berna is very important for me; she is beyond a friend for me." Moreover, through her visit to Germany and with Berna's friends, Nazlı accumulated information about the German welfare state, which can be understood as "social remittances."

Faruk. Another participant, Faruk, migrated to Germany from Turkey in 1999 in his twenties to continue his studies in Germany. When his previous academic work in Turkey was not recognized, however, Faruk opened a small business. But the business failed, and at the time of the interview he was working in catering. Faruk was in his thirties when I interviewed him, and he was in frequent contact with his friends and relatives in Turkey through daily calls and yearly visits. In addition to these cross-border activities, he occasionally sent small amounts of money to his two brothers in Turkey. For our research, he indicated his friends, Necati and Hüseyin, could be interviewed, and both were. Neither of them ever mentioned any financial exchanges with Faruk but implied that having a friend abroad was a great way to be connected with the world.

Although asking for money among friends is not easy, Faruk made it clear to me on several occasions that he would always be there for his friends because he would like to share his success with the "stayers."

Different from family members' "taking protection for granted" or having normative attitudes about obligations, friends tended to be cautious when it came to money and, even more so, had a fear of receiving money as they might not be able to pay it back or would have to reciprocate some other way that would not be perceived as equivalent by their friend. As Hansen (2004) has argued, individuals do not tend to ask for favors when the price of reciprocity seems too high. Thus, friends in Turkey in my sample may have thought that the price to repay financial help from their friends in Germany would simply be too high or might not be valued as equal or matching the initial favor. Another factor was the economic and social positions of migrants and stayers in their respective countries. In the case of Necati and Hüseyin, the staying friends had their own businesses and were middle-class in Turkey even though they had not been educated to the same degree as Faruk, who was in the low-income group in Germany. In the sample, friends in Turkey seemed to be doing well, so perhaps they did not need financial protection from their friends in Germany, and such friendships across borders served to fulfill emotional needs instead.

Clearly, not all friendships are the same, and friends can perceive the same things differently. For example, Sema arrived in Germany during the end of the 1990s as an asylum seeker, escaping political violence in Turkey. She put all of her contacts in the important circle in the network map and differentiated her family members from friends, not through their importance in her life, but through what kind of protection she actually exchanged and theoretically would exchange with them. Sema felt close only to her family members and would accept financial means from them, but mentioned her reluctance to exchange such resources with friends. To her, friends were there to socialize with and to exchange useful information. She talked at length about how important her friend Selim was in her life. When the research team interviewed Selim, he never mentioned Sema during the interview or in his network map.

For migrants, despite the physical distance, relationships continue to exist with those in their origin country. However, the "staying" friends may feel that the migrants' lives went on and that they made new friendships in their new country. Perhaps the staying friends also have opportunities to meet new people and to create new friendships, while the ones with those who migrated dissolve over time. This may have been the case with Sema and Selim. Sema had never visited Turkey after she left, and Selim might value face-to-face relationships and spending time together, and that is, perhaps, why he did not mention Sema in his interview. Having migrant status (Sema) might have disrupted the friendship in the eyes of the stayer (Selim).

This analysis shows that power dynamics were changed in family relationships as a result of migrants' double embeddedness in nation-state social protection systems. Through migration, some individuals had power over resources, but stayers' continued non-reciprocation was seen as a loss of resources by migrants. While friendships were more easily dissolved than family ties, due to geographical and emotional distance, they were the least affected by migrants' embeddedness in two nation-states. Being in a stronger welfare state, migrants are perceived to be doing better, and, thus, become burdened by family expectations.

Discussion

Like other articles in this special issue, this article focuses on financial protection, the norm of reciprocity, and the differentiated role of family and friendship. This study considers these central issues of the volume from a transnational perspective, in which two formal social protection systems rule. This has implications for the movers and stayers depending on the type of relationship (family and friendships). Moreover, this article shows how asymmetries in power and unequal flows of social and financial protection are perceived by both sides in dyadic (migrant/ nonmigrant) relationships.

This article makes three novel contributions to research on social protection: it provides a discussion of personal networks' embeddedness in formal systems; it goes beyond a unilateral view of resource exchanges (e.g., financial remittances); and it extends beyond the primary focus on kin in the social network literature.

First, the analysis shows how migrants' double embeddedness within nation-state frameworks impacts which resources flow and in what direction, and how relationships are shaped. The social welfare scheme in Germany helped the migrants in my study to be financially secure, even if considered lower class in Germany, which allowed them to be able to send remittances home to Turkey. Residency-based social policies limited their ability to provide physical care to family members in their country of origin. It is important to note that the "superior" welfare scheme of Germany changed the power balance in personal relationships for my participants, giving migrants the upper hand in family decisions, even though their social position in Germany was lower than the social positions of those who stayed in Turkey. Both migrants and stayers perceived the country of emigration as superior and, thus, normalized the financial flows from migrants to staying family members. In the eyes of the stayers, migrants lived in a superior welfare state. This view overlooks migrants' vulnerabilities, such as social exclusion or not having all of the perceived entitlements, such as pensions. Family members felt entitled to migrants' remittances without any reciprocation because migrants lived in a "superior" state, even though their social position was not high in Germany. Friends of migrants who stayed in Turkey did not ask for anything from their migrant friends; the fear of reciprocity held them back. Friends were concerned that they might not be able to reciprocate the favor at all, or even if they did, they worried the value might not be perceived as matching that of their friends' favor. In my sample, although staying friends belonged to the middle-class in Turkey while migrants were low-income in Germany, friends still perceived migrants as doing better. Friendships among the migrants and stayers in this study were mostly about companionship, as previous work has also demonstrated (Wellman and Wortley 1990).

Second, this study looks at the dynamics of reciprocity within personal networks. Both movers and stayers shared certain meanings they attributed to migration (Germany has superior state infrastructures, which justified migration and stigmatized migrants and the idea that migrants do "better" economically, so that they need to send financial remittances), and the negotiation of resource flows were influenced by these attributions. Building on Gouldner's (1960) and Hansen's (2004) work, this study investigates the dynamics of reciprocity between migrants' family members and friendships. The multisited matched sample design led to a fine-grained understanding of the implications of migration on the stayers. In such a design, not only who gives what and to whom, but also the value of what is given from different perspectives, is analyzed. For instance, my findings suggest that friends were more aware and cautious about expectations bound by normative reciprocity that might have been evoked through asking for support. In line with one of the Hansen's (2004) rules of reciprocity, friends in my study did not ask for resources when it necessitated a return that was too costly or might not have been of equivalent value.

Third, this study provides an extension beyond the primary focus in the literature on kin and the heterogeneity of relations. Although earlier research has made it clear that family ties have a critical place in the lives of migrants (e.g., Boccagni 2015; Mazzucato 2009, 2011; Parreñas 2001), this study shows how friendships are also important for migrants, mainly for emotional support and companionship on both ends. For some in the sample, sending money to family members was perceived to be a necessity, but friendships had different dynamics and not all friendships were considered equal or as having resources that could be tapped into. Although some of the friendships involved resource exchanges, others dissolved over time in the view of the stayers but not necessarily in the eyes of the movers. Although the evidence in this study indicates that there are more resource exchanges between family members, friendships were still very important for some of the migrants and their transnational friends. Further studies could investigate what makes certain friendships dissolve while others continue across borders.

Understanding how protective resources are exchanged and evaluated by movers and stayers is fundamental to designing effective social policies for contemporary migrant families that do not necessarily match the "ideal" family living in only one nation-state. My findings suggest that, whether with family members or friends, transnational ties are a crucial part of migrants' lives and should be considered when devising social protection programs and policies for international migrants. For example, my interviews with migrants showed that elderly care from a distance came up against some obstacles because formal social protection policies are designed mainly to meet the needs of citizens within the boundaries of a given nation-state. Family and formal welfare systems in other parts of the world may be unable to provide elderly care, and migrant family members might be called upon to provide such care. Thus, social policies in the countries of emigration should assist migrants who need to give care in the countries of origin through securing or at least not jeopardizing their entitlements in the countries of destination. Moreover, social and economic policies need to be designed with modern family formations (i.e., transnational families) and shifting gender dynamics in families in mind.

Notes

1. The project, "Transnationality, the Distribution of Informal Social Security and Inequalities," was funded by the German Research Foundation (DFG) within the framework of the Collaborative Research Centre (SFB) 882 at Bielefeld University (2011–2015). For more information about the project, see https://sfb882.uni-bielefeld.de/en/projects/c3.html. The project also collected data from migrants with Polish and Kazakh origins as well as data from various sources, such as document analysis, expert interviews, and matched interviews with interviewees' significant others in the respective emigration countries.

2. Lending circles are rotated savings and credit associations (ROSCAs) based on trust, solidarity, and reciprocity pooling together a preset amount of money periodically. Every member gets the accumulated sum in turns over time (Bilecen 2019).

References

Abadan-Unat, Nermin and Başak Bilecen. 2020. The Turkey-Germany migration corridor. In *Routledge handbook of migration and development*, eds. Tanja Bastia and Ronald Skeldon, 458–63. London: Routledge.

Baldassar, Loretta. 2007. Transnational families and the provision of moral and emotional support: the relationship between truth and distance. *Identities: Global Studies in Culture and Power* 14 (4): 385–409.

Barglowski, Karolina, Başak Bilecen, and Anna Amelina. 2015. Approaching Transnational Social Protection: Methodological Challenges and Empirical Applications. *Population Space and Place* 21 (3): 215–26.

Barglowski, Karolina, Łukasz Krzyżowski, and Paulina Świątek. 2015. Caregiving in Polish–German transnational social space: circulating narratives and intersecting heterogeneities. *Population Space and Place* 21 (3): 257–69.

Barwick, Christine. 2016. *Social mobility and neighbourhood choice: Turkish-Germans in Berlin*. London: Routledge.

Berkman, Lisa F., and Thomas Glass. 2000. Social integration, social networks, social support, and health. In *Social epidemiology*, eds. Lisa F. Berkman and Ishiro Kawachi, 137–73. New York, NY: Oxford University Press.

Bilecen, Başak. 2016. A personal network approach in mixed-methods design to investigate transnational social protection. *International Review of Social Research* 6 (4): 233–44.

Bilecen, Başak. 2019. *"Altın Günü"*: Migrant women's social protection networks. *Comparative Migration Studies* 7 (11). DOI: https://doi.org/10.1186/s40878-019-0114-x.

Bilecen, Başak, and Karolina Barglowski. 2015. On the assemblages of informal and formal transnational social protection. *Population Space and Place* 21 (3): 203–14.

Bilecen, Başak, Gül Çatır, and Aslı Orhon. 2015. Turkish-German transnational social space: Stitching across borders. *Population Space and Place* 21 (3): 244–56.

Boccagni, Paolo. 2015. Burden, blessing or both? On the mixed role of transnational ties in migrant informal social support. *International Sociology* 30 (3): 250–268.

Boccagni, Paolo, and Francesca Decimo. 2013. Mapping social remittances. *Migration Letters* 10 (1): 1–10.

Bryceson, Deborah F., and Ulla Vuorela. 2002. *The transnational family: New European frontiers and global networks*. Oxford: Berg.

Çelik, Çetin. 2015. "Having a German passport will not make me German": Reactive ethnicity and oppositional identity among disadvantaged male Turkish second-generation youth in Germany. *Ethnic and Racial Studies* 38 (9): 1646–62.

Çelik, Kezban, Umut Be pınar, and Sibel Kalaycıoğlu. 2013. Experiences of stay-behind women in international migration. In *Migration, familie und soziale lage*, eds. Thomas Geisen, Tobias Studer, and Erol Yıldız, pp. 235–50. Wiesbaden, Germany: Springer.

Dankyi, Ernestina, Valentina Mazzucato, and Takyiwaa Manuh. 2017. Reciprocity in global social protection: providing care for migrants' children. *Oxford Development Studies* 45 (1): 80–95.

De Haas, Hein. 2007. International migration, remittances and development: myths and facts. *Third World Quarterly* 26 (8): 1269–1284.

Durand, Jorge, Emilio A. Parrado, and Douglas S. Massey. 1996. Migradollars and development: A reconsideration of the Mexican case. *International Migration Review* 30 (2): 423–44.

Faist, Thomas. 2013. Transnational Social Protection: An Emerging Field of Study. *COMCAD* Working Papers No. 113. Center On Migration, Citizenship and Development: Bielefeld.

Faist, Thomas. 2019. *The transnationalized social question: migration and the politics of social inequalities in the twenty-first century*. Oxford: Oxford University Press.

Faist, Thomas. 2000. *The volume and dynamics of international migration and transnational social spaces*. Oxford: Oxford University Press.

Faist, Thomas, Başak Bilecen, Karolina Barglowski, and Joanna J. Sienkiewicz. 2015. Transnational social protection: Migrants' strategies and patterns of inequalities. *Population Space and Place* 21 (3): 193–202.

Fuller-Iglesias, Heather R. 2015. The view from back home: Interpersonal dynamics of transnational Mexican families. *Journal of Ethnic and Migration Studies* 41 (11): 1703–24.

Garip, Filiz. 2014. The impact of migration and remittances on wealth accumulation and distribution in rural Thailand. *Demography* 51 (2): 673–98.

Glick Schiller, Nina. 2005a. Transnational social fields and imperialism: Bringing a theory of power to transnational studies. *Anthropological Theory* 5 (4): 439–61.

Glick Schiller, Nina. 2005b. Transborder citizenship: An outcome of legal pluralism within transnational social fields. In *Mobile people, mobile law: expanding legal relations in a contracting world*, eds. Franz von Bender-Beckman and Keebet von Bender-Beckman, 27–50. London: Routledge.

Gouldner, Alvin. 1960. The norm of reciprocity: a preliminary statement. *American Sociological Review* 25:161–78.

Hansen, Karen V. 2004. The asking rules of reciprocity in networks of care for children. *Qualitative Sociology* 27 (4): 421–37.

Kahn, Robert L., and Toni C. Antonucci. 1980. Convoys over the life course: Attachment, roles, and social support. In *Life-span development and behavior*, eds. Paul B. Baltes and Orville Brim, 254–83. New York, NY: Academic Press.

Levitt, Peggy, and Deepak Lamba-Nieves. 2011. Social remittances revisited. *Journal of Ethnic and Migration Studies* 37 (1): 1–22.

Levitt, Peggy, Jocelyn Viterna, Armin Mueller, and Charlotte Lloyd. 2017. Transnational social protection: setting the agenda. *Oxford Development Studies* 45 (1): 2–19.

Lubbers, Miranda J., José Luis Molina, Jürgen Lerner, Ulrik Brandes, Javier Ávila, and Christopher McCarty. 2010. Longitudinal analysis of personal networks. The case of Argentinean migrants in Spain. *Social Networks* 32(1): 91–104.

Marchetti-Mercer, Maria. 2012. Those easily forgotten: The impact of emigration on those left behind. *Family Process* 51 (3): 376–390.

Marcus, George E. 2011. Multi-sited ethnography: Five or six things I know about it now. In *Multi-sited ethnography: Problems and possibilities in the translocation of research methods*, eds. Simon Coleman and Pauline von Hellermann, 16–32. New York, NY: Routledge.

Massey, Douglas S., and Lawrence C. Basem. 1992. Determinants of savings, remittances, and spending patterns among united-states migrants in four Mexican communities. *Sociological Inquiry* 62 (2): 185–207.

Mazzucato, Valentina. 2009. Bridging boundaries with a transnational research approach: A simultaneous matched sample methodology. In *Multi-sited ethnography: theory, praxis and locality in contemporary research*, eds. Mark-Anthony Falzon, 215–32. Farnham, England: Ashgate.

Mazzucato, Valentina. 2011. Reverse remittances in the migration development-nexus: Two-way flows between Ghana and The Netherlands. *Population, Space and Place* 17: 454–68.

Mazzucato, Valentina, and Lauren Wagner. 2018. Multi-sited fieldwork in a connected world. In *Handbook on the geographies of globalization*, eds. Robert C. Kloosterman, Virginie Mamadouh, and Pieter Terhorst, 412–21. Cheltenham, England: Edward Elgar Publishing.

McKenzie, Sean, and Cecilia Menjívar. 2011. The meanings of migration, remittances and gifts: Views of Honduran women who stay. *Global Networks* 11 (1): 63–81.

Menjívar, Cecilia, and Victor Agadjanian. 2007. Men's migration and women's lives: Views from rural Armenia and Guatemala. *Social Science Quarterly* 88 (5): 1243–62.

Menjívar, Cecilia, Julie DaVanzo, Lisa Greenwell, and R. Burciaga Valdez. 1998. Remittance behavior among Salvadoran and Filipino immigrants in Los Angeles. *International Migration Review* 32 (1): 97–126.

Parreñas, Rachel S. 2001. Mothering from a distance. Emotions, gender, and inter-generational relations in Filipino transnational families. *Feminist Studies* 27 (2): 361–91.

Poeze, Miranda, Ernestina K. Dankyi, and Valentina Mazzucato. 2017. Navigating transnational childcare relationships: Migrant parents and their children's caregivers in the origin country. *Global Networks* 17 (1): 111–29.

Portes, Alejandro. 2007. Migration, development, and segmented assimilation: A conceptual review of the evidence. *The ANNALS of the American Academy of Political and Social Science* 610 (1): 73–97.

Putnam, Robert. 2000. *Bowling alone. The collapse and revival of American community*. New York, NY: Simon and Schuster.

Ryan, Louise. 2011. Migrants' social networks and weak ties: Accessing resources and constructing relationships post-migration. *Sociological Review* 59:707–24.

Ryan, Louise. 2007. Migrant women, social networks and motherhood: The experiences of Irish nurses in Britain. *Sociology* 41 (2): 295–312.

Sabates-Wheeler, Rachel, and Rachel Feldman, eds. 2011. *Migration and social protection: Claiming social rights beyond borders*. New York, NY: Palgrave.

Sahlins, Marshall D. 1965. On the sociology of primitive exchange in the relevance of models for social anthropology. In *The relevance of models for social anthropology*, eds. Michael Banton, 139–236. New York, NY: Praeger.

Schmalzbauer, Leah. 2008. Family divided: the class formation of Honduran transnational families. *Global Networks* 8 (3): 329–46.

Simmel, Georg. 1950. Faithfulness and gratitude. In *The sociology of Georg Simmel*, eds. Kurt H. Wolff, 379–95. New York, NY: Free Press.

Small, Mario L., and Christopher Sukhu. 2016. Because they were there: access, deliberation, and the mobilization of networks for support. *Social Networks* 47:73–84.

Song, Steve. 2011. Second-generation Turkish youth in Europe: Explaining the academic disadvantage in Austria, Germany, and Switzerland. *Economics of Education Review* 30 (5): 938–49.

Sürig, Inken, and Maren Wilmes. 2015. *The integration of the second generation in Germany*. Amsterdam: Amsterdam University Press.

Taylor, Edward J. 1999. The new economics of labour migration and the role of remittances in the migration process. *International Migration* 37 (1): 63–88.

Taylor, Shelley E. 2011. Social support: A review. In *The handbook of health psychology*, eds. M. S. Friedman, 189–214. New York, NY: Oxford University Press.

The World Bank. 2006. *Global economic prospects: Economic implications of remittances and migration 2006*. Washington, DC: The World Bank.

Wellman, Barry, and Scot Wortley. 1990. Different strokes from different folks: community ties and social support. *American Journal of Sociology* 96 (3): 558–88.

Zontini, Elisabetta, and Tracey Reynolds. 2007. Ethnicity, families and social capital: Caring relationships across Italian and Caribbean transnational families. *International Review of Sociology* 17 (2): 257–77.

This commentary provides a synthetic overview and analytic framework for understanding the papers in this volume of The ANNALS, which focuses on sharing networks in a comparative context. Economic crises endemic to capitalist societies generate the need for support networks, while welfare state configurations influence their importance as an additional survival tool. Social norms set the stage for the degrees of reciprocity and durable obligation that networks engender and the boundary conditions that enable or disable the most vulnerable members of the social hierarchy to tap the resources of more privileged contacts.

Keywords: social networks; economic crises; poverty; reciprocity

Ties that Bind/ Unwind: The Social, Economic, and Organizational Contexts of Sharing Networks

By
KATHERINE S. NEWMAN

Sendhil Mullainathan and Eldar Shafir, two of the leading lights in behavioral economics, lead readers into the cognitive jungle that is poverty in their 2014 book, *Scarcity*. Their mission is to reveal the underlying logic beneath what appears to be the most self-defeating aspects of life at the bottom of the class ladder. In particular, they highlight the toll that unpredictability takes on people who are fully capable of "delayed gratification," but for whom practicing long-term thinking makes no sense. This group of people cannot count on the steady flow of resources that is the bedrock of middle-class economic logic and instead must focus on getting through today and tomorrow. While next week or next month is not too far off to imagine, it is too far away to plan for. Their underlying message: poverty takes an exhausting toll on

Katherine S. Newman is Torrey Little Professor of Sociology and interim chancellor of the University of Massachusetts, Boston. She is the author of fifteen books on topics such as urban poverty, downward mobility, poverty and policy, and lethal violence in American schools. Her most recent book is Downhill from Here: Retirement Insecurity in the Age of Inequality *(Metropolitan Books 2019).*

Correspondence: Katherine.Newman@umb.edu

DOI: 10.1177/0002716220923335

decision-making, where no solution is truly a good one, and the psychological cost of arriving at the best deficient solution is debilitating.

For social scientists steeped in the field work tradition, the cognitive load that bedevils people who must live under conditions of insecurity and—above all—scarce resources does not defeat the poor. It spurs them toward solutions that enlarge the universe of people and institutions that can insert assets when the ship appears to be going down, who can come to the rescue when childcare fails, a key person in the ecosystem gets sick, a parent gets left behind in the wake of emigration needs support, food will not stretch far enough, or the police crack down.

The ties poor people cultivate spell the difference between survival and defeat. And because they know this, even the most marginal cultivate social relationships ranging from intergenerational bonds to sibling ties to friendships to fictive-kin ties between similarly situated minorities.

The articles in this volume of *The ANNALS* add important insights to our understanding of these human connections. They touch on at least the following important topics, arrayed roughly from the most macro to the most micro elements:

—Economic conditions: The role of the economy and its fluctuations in creating crises that place a premium on the possession of a support network;
—Welfare state context: How the provisions for social support within and between countries enters into the redistributive possibilities and cultural expectations of sharing networks;
—How ties are born: The role of formal and informal organizations in creating opportunities for interaction and hence the development of interpersonal bonds;
—The relationship between material deprivation and social isolation, social solidarity, and the limbo states in between;
—The output of sharing networks: What do they actually produce in the way of social support, financial support, and information transfer;
—How/whether ties are activated since the mere possession of a network is not enough; and
—How durable are social relations in the face of stress that creates the conditions for failed reciprocity?

Drawing upon survey, interview, and participant observation research across many continents, the volume presents material that can be drawn into a conceptual framework that is important for resolving puzzles in the literature on sharing networks, while leaving other issues for future research.

Economic Pressures, Economic Crises

Those at the very bottom of the class ladder experience degrees of chronic poverty in capitalist societies. Persistent scarcity punctuated by extreme deprivation is particularly problematic for adults with dependent children. It threatens their hold on shelter, food, warmth in winter, adequate clothing, basic hygiene, and access to medical care. Poverty destabilizes parents by forcing them to choose between holding a job and caring for a sick child. These are conditions character-istic of "normal poverty," meaning the kind that is omnipresent even when the overall economy is robust. Because these conditions routinely plague the poor, structural responses emerge in the form of formal organizations and informal networks that redistribute money, goods, and services that help those in dire need get over the hurdles of daily life.

Economic crises inject even more disruption into this already precarious situ-ation. If normal poverty finds individuals and families arrayed along a continuum from stressed but managing to overwhelmed by life-threatening deprivation, an economic crisis shifts the proportions sharply toward the more extreme end of the spectrum. It triggers forced migration, violence, and the collapse of social networks. Social networks that can bridge the gaps under conditions of normal poverty are stressed to the breaking point and often disintegrate entirely under conditions of economic crisis precisely because few possess the extra resources needed for any form of redistribution. Under these circumstances, even family bonds—usually the most durable—shatter.

Most of the articles in this volume focus on social networks that form under conditions of normal poverty. They illustrate how these relationships enable the poor to manage scarcity by redistributing resources including childcare and elder care, food, money, shelter, clothing, and social solidarity or psychological com-fort. While extended family is often the bedrock of these networks, friends and similarly situated minorities (sexual, ethnic, migrant) can form an even more durable set of ties because they are less burdened by normative definitions of fealty and reciprocity and are therefore freer to adapt to conditions that make conformity to those norms problematic.

Normal poverty may or may not lead to durable and dependable relations within these networks, and here in the volume the articles present some contra-dictory conclusions. Mazelis's (this volume) study of the Kensington Welfare Rights Union of Philadelphia argues that it is precisely the vulnerability of its members that causes networks to enlarge and renders them resilient even in the face of material deprivation, while González de la Rocha (this volume) observes that prolonged dependence on social networks under conditions of economic disaster lead relations among the poor to become tense and networks to shrink. Carol Stack's (1983) classic work, *All Our Kin*, presents the best example of the former perspective, in which neighbors and acquaintances develop fictive kin relations through the exchange of child care, cementing social ties through recip-rocal exchange, even if it is often delayed. Networks enable volatility in resources to be smoothed by redistribution of money and services, while a careful calculus sees to it that these favors are returned if not by the original "debtor" than by someone else understood to be responding to that obligation.

Matt Desmond's (2017) much celebrated work, *Evicted*, looks at the networks of the poor in almost the opposite terms: shrunken, instrumental, brittle in the face of challenge, spurred mainly by the extraordinary vulnerability of those who have been evicted and hence face homelessness or extremely tenuous living arrangements. To pose the matter as Mario Small does in several of his works, including his piece in this volume, (Small and Gose, this volume), the question is not whether the networks among the poor conform to the Stack model (as Mazelis might hold) or the Desmond model (as González de la Rocha or Lubbers et al. might argue), but under what conditions they exhibit features of expansion/ durability or retraction/brittleness. Where earnings and welfare benefits provide for a relatively dependable, though clearly meager, flow of resources, networks are born to smooth momentary crises and can withstand the strain of borrowing and lending under assumptions of reciprocity. Where resources are pushed past the breaking point, or are entirely unreliable, breakdowns are likely and instrumental or "market" logics will overtake the social solidarity that derives from more fortunate circumstances.

Both sets of circumstances exist under conditions of normal poverty. Under the specter of economic collapse, however, breakdown due to overuse and persistent strain is much more widespread. The long overhang of the worldwide Great Recession engulfed southern European countries, including Greece, Portugal, and Spain, and created massive unemployment that has taken more than a decade to subside. An insolvent banking system and EU-imposed austerity policies created pressures on social networks and kinship bonds in Barcelona that were vulnerable to breakdowns due to overuse and insufficient bandwidth to respond to demands within the networks (Lubbers et al., this volume). Similar conditions embroiled the urban poor of Guadalajara and led them to pull away from normative relations of exchange and inter dependence into "market logics" of instrumentality and monetization, a total breakdown of normative expectations (González de la Rocha, this volume).

The point here is that the larger economic context is crucial in understanding the conditions under which the networks described in these articles form and add to the coping mechanisms necessary to survival among the poor. The evidence in these articles suggests that as long as there is a minimal surplus and a minimal capacity for redistribution, networks will persist and form an important informal support structure for daily life and for the care of children and the elderly. But economic crises—which we normally think of as large, national and international events—undermine these networks because they withdraw resources below that minimal level and lead to a more individualistic, every man for himself, mentality.

Welfare States as a Conditional Element in Sharing Networks

The inadequacies and contradictions of official welfare state provisions are often the institutional context for the study of sharing networks. Notably, the old "man in the house" rules of AFDC in the United States penalized women and children by withdrawing benefits designed for single parent households if there was evidence of men living among them. These welfare regulations were indicted by researchers for their role in breaking families up, isolating poor men from their kin, and setting up the desperate conditions that often lead to crime as a last resort. The "workarounds" that mothers and wives concocted to maintain relations with the men in their lives, binding them into sharing networks despite the official rules, was a staple topic in fieldwork among the poor for many years. In the articles in this volume, the welfare state is less the pernicious actor and more a framework within which reliable benefits are conveyed, especially in the social democracies, as a contrast to the less reliable sources of income: especially wages.

The relative generosity and predictability of benefits in Western Europe, compared to what is available in non-Western nations, emerges as an important contextual factor in the operation of international sharing networks that unite kin and friends across the distance of divergent welfare states. Bilecen (this volume) shows that all parties, on either side of an immigration divide, believe that German benefits provide a steady stream of resources to Turkish migrants. Turkish retirement benefits are far less generous than those in Germany and unemployment support is negligible. Accordingly, relatives who stay behind in Turkey expect that migrants to Germany will send remittances based on welfare benefits and in exchange take care of social obligations for the care of dependent relatives back home. Kin in sending countries are unaware of the pressures that high expenses impose on their migrant members and even regard them as "spoiled" by their residence in "superior" states. They are critiqued for avoiding the social responsibilities of kin and expected to provide financially to make up for defaulting on social contracts. A litany of moral inequalities, social accusations, and awkward ruminations accompany these transactions and upend familial bonds.

Bilecen's work complements the literature on transnational migration that has long emphasized wages as a source of family sustenance and local development (see especially Rob Smith [2005] on financial linkages between Mexico and New York). The focus on a hierarchy of generosity in welfare state structures adds an important element to our understanding of linkages across international boundaries. Researchers in federal states should take note: State benefits in Mississippi are significantly less generous than New York and internal migrants may undergo a similar calculus. I am not aware of studies that examine this question.

The Birth of Ties

There is an old and rich literature on how sharing networks form (e.g., Stack 1983). The articles in this volume are, not surprisingly, influenced by the novel approach to this question, introduced by one of its editors, Mario Small. In his award winning book, *Unanticipated Gains: Origins of Network Inequality in Everyday Life*, Small (2010) focuses on the role of organizations, especially nonprofit childcare centers, that create opportunities for people to meet, bond, and then share services, support, and information that is vital to security and stability. A safety net can be forged out of these ties and often comprises more varied, "bridging" linkages than those that form in neighborhoods where people are of similar economic means. The variety provides for more heterogeneous sources of information and enables redistribution in ways that homogeneous networks may not.

Small and Gose (this volume) extend this framework through a critical literature review that points toward the structural features of organizations that can increase or decrease the likelihood of network formation. They note that what may appear to be an organizational logic—requiring parents to participate in the activities of a day care center—has implications for the frequency of contact and the likelihood that ancillary social relations will develop. Hence the presence and the internal structure of organizations creates the context within which vitally important safety nets form. Neighborhoods blessed with many such opportunities, organized to promote contact, will spout a richer array of cross-cutting ties than those that lack them.

Stretesky et al. (this volume) examine "holiday clubs," organized to provide food for children in high poverty regions of northern England for whom the summer months without school meals creates deprivation. Although the formal purpose of these clubs is to feed children who might otherwise go without, to avoid stigma, children from families of different incomes are allowed to participate and activities that provide stimulation and enjoyment are often organized by staff. Here we find a formal organization, established for one narrow (but critical) purpose, branching out to become a broader and more inclusive institution that promotes cultural capital (visits to unfamiliar places) and social relations across income boundaries. Whether these ties outlast the summer months would require additional research to discover.

Material Deprivation and Social Isolation, or its Opposite

Are the poor socially isolated from the rest of society, from each other, and from the organizations that serve them or, by contrast, integrated (whether on favorable or unfavorable terms) with all of these levels of social organization? This is a long-standing dispute in the sociological literature. William Julius Wilson's (2012) classic work, *The Truly Disadvantaged*, argues that as unemployment deepens, the poor are cut off from critical mainstream institutions. Their social isolation is amplified by economic segregation in housing and schools, and underlined in cities where transit systems fail to reach into poor neighborhoods, creating geographic barriers that are hard to overcome.

The opposite conclusion is derived from classic works by Liebow (2003) and Hannerz (2004) from the 1960s, and more contemporary accounts by Eli Anderson (2000), Sandra Susan Smith (2010), Mary Patillo (2013), and Katherine Newman (2000), who argue that the poor are socially integrated, in the sense that they have ties to working class relatives and homeowners, know many people who are gainfully employed, and often live in neighborhoods adjacent to the middle class. Yet they often fail to benefit from these ties because the poorer members are considered morally suspect or socially contaminating. It is not the lack of contact, but often the opposite—continuous but tension-filled interactions—that underlie the fragility of the poor and render the networks less than optimally useful.

In both instances, material deprivation is omnipresent and creates the impetus for social support, lending and borrowing, and specific and generalized exchange. But on the former account, the helpful are beyond reach because they are unknown and both socially and physically distant—almost willfully beyond reach.

Many of the papers in this volume underline the wisdom of the latter perspective. Güler's (this volume) article on transgender sex workers makes clear that they have myriad ties to family members, friends, and officials, but that most of these relations are fraught. The ties that truly bind are, instead, to like-situated sex workers who look out for one another and support each other, even as they are locked in competition for clients. González de la Rocha's observations of the strains endured by Guadalajara's poor under conditions of extreme and widespread poverty make it clear that these networks contain people who are better off, but over time wither under the pressure of repeated demands.

It may well be that in time the conclusions drawn by Desmond regarding "disposable" ties come to dominate, and the difference lies in the time frame of observation. What starts out as a heterogeneous network may fracture as the pressures spawned by need become too much to bear. Biosca's (this volume) research, drawn from financial diaries of low-income families in Glasgow, makes clear the extraordinary frequency of borrowing to meet daily needs. Reliance on informal sources limits the ability to create credit histories that will enable the poor to access formal lending institutions. But more importantly, the repeated reliance on friends and family to get by, especially if compounded by an inability to reciprocate, will erode those ties. Researchers observing the early use of these ties will come to different conclusions about their durability than those who can draw upon data compiled over time, when the consequences of repeated reliance become clearer.

What Sharing Networks Share

Stack's (1983) classic account of sharing networks defines the household as a unit that may stretch across a number of domiciles to provision children. Children move between them as a symbol of trust and a definition of family. Family are the people who care for kids, whether they are actually related or not. The resources that move across these households are monetary and in-kind, a point Edin and Lein (1997) reinforce in their book, *Making Ends Meet*. Indeed, survival is dependent on being able to access support from legal and illegal sources, because the welfare system does not provide enough to get by.

In these articles, the emphasis seems to have shifted, or perhaps is taking for granted, the material exchanges that are crucial to survival. Instead, the emphasis seems to be more on the social solidarity that builds up among the most marginal members of the social order. This may reflect the contemporary concern with social exclusion over material deprivation that originally developed in the literature based on fieldwork in the more generous social welfare regimes of the Nordic countries and France. In Güler's (this volume) contribution, we see that while transgender sex workers need each other and the "mamas" who oversee their business, they are even more desirous of the comfort that comes from social acceptance and shared identity.

"Us against the world " might be an appropriate summation of what these papers are telling us about support networks.

Failed Reciprocity

It is axiomatic among students of sharing networks that reciprocity is key. Freeloading is an anathema in these circles; the omnipresent mental monitoring that undergirds the process of redistribution and repayment is evidence of the fear and suspicion that lurks just under the surface. The least trustworthy members of a savings circle, especially newcomers who are not well known and lack credit histories, will be positioned at the end of the distribution cycle to guard against providing a windfall that could lead to an early exit from obligations to the "moneyround" (or menage) (Biosca, this volume).

Among the most interesting observations is Mazelis's that relatives are particularly difficult partners with whom to exchange because one is constrained to continue relationships with them even if they default on promised repayments. Blood is thicker than water, but it can coagulate into resentment. Friends may be more reliable or at least less difficult because the relationship truly depends on reciprocity, and hence the cost of defaulting is the loss of the bond altogether.

The original anthropological studies of delayed exchange—especially Malinowski's (1984) work based on the Kula Ring in the Trobriand Islands— posed a romantic image of social relations sustained by reciprocity. Accounts of the spectacular give-aways chronicled by Franz Boas (1975) and Marcel Mauss (2018) in ethnographies of the "potlatch" cultures of the Pacific Northwest underlined an anthropological corrective to rival accounts of utilitarian economics. Exchange, so the theory went, is not about profit and loss; it is about social solidarity and the preservation of culturally defined relations of respect and obligation. People do not need the cowry shells or the decorated shields; indeed, in some versions of the potlatch, the goods are ultimately destroyed. What they "need" are the social ties that exchange underlines.

The articles in this volume return to that classic understanding of exchange as the stuff of social life and belonging, rather than simply the goods and services needed to survive. It is in this context that the failure to reciprocate takes on the most damaging aura. To default on the social obligation is to walk out of the circle of friends or like situated survivors and face the hardship of going it alone. That it happens under conditions of economic crises is evidence for the powerful impact of an overwhelming collapse of social relations.

Questions Left Unanswered

This volume provides a rich array of studies of social ties and sharing networks, organizations that foster them, conditions that shape them or undermine them, and the limits of their utility when the members of exchange groups are under continuous or extreme economic pressure. The articles take us across continents, into the divergent conditions of different welfare regimes, and trace the calculus of migrants who participate in the legal structures of sending and receiving countries at the same time. Some of these articles dwell on families locked in what I have labeled "normal poverty," the condition of scarcity that plagues individuals and families at the bottom of class structures in capitalist countries. Others focus on the impact of economic crises in countries already characterized by weak to virtually nonexistent welfare states. Individuals can, of course, find themselves in extreme conditions of vulnerability even when the economy around them is robust. But the likelihood that millions will plunge below the level of sustainability is greatly increased when the general economy is in a state of collapse, as so many are at the time of this writing, in the context of a pandemic-inspired recession.

All of these articles note the resilience and ingenuity of the poor, for whom the cognitive calculus described by Mullainathan and Shafir is an exhausting, but necessary, aspect of survival. And all note the limits of resilience, the erosion of ties when they are in constant use and reciprocity becomes impossible. As González de la Rocha notes, under these circumstances, a market logic erupts and disrupts normative obligations.

What, then, are the questions that remain? There are many, including:

—The studies in this volume all focus on relatively wealthy societies at least when compared, for example, to sub-Saharan Africa or the flood plains of Bangladesh. What do we have to learn about networks and survival when communities are pushed to the limit and ejected from their homelands? The swelling of refugee populations around the globe is a terrifying social fact. Can this kind of research help us to understand the social organization of survival under these conditions?

—We have a tendency to think in national units. This volume helpfully posits the study of welfare states in the middle of social networks comprising migrants. Should the same model be used to understand internal migration in federalist countries where social benefits are highly variable?

—Organizations create interaction patterns that create opportunities for network formation, especially when they enable repeated and sustained encounters. Is that feature random or organized? Are organizations "classed" such that those located in the interstices of different socioeconomic groups are more likely to call for that kind of repeated interaction while those that draw from a more uniform population, or even a more affluent one, avoid it?

—Economic crises clearly place sharing networks under extreme pressure. What happens to them when the crises abate and the stress declines? Elapsed time could be a decade or more and some never recover at all. Still, the Spanish economy has seen unemployment decline from 27 percent in 2013 to 14 percent in 2018 (Plecher 2020). That is still 4 percentage points higher than it was in 2005, before the crisis. But the improvement is unmistakable.

What happens to those frayed bonds when better days unfold? Are they restored or is the damage too deep and hence they remain disconnected?

The comparative material presented in this volume provides us with a great deal of food for thought. Case studies drawn from South America, Europe, the Middle East, and the United States teach us to widen the lens and consider a variety of contexts and pressures, through the common lens of sharing networks and adaptations to poverty. That it leads us to think about more questions is a compliment to the authors and editors.

References

Anderson, Elijah. 2000. *Code of the street: Decency, violence and the moral life of the inner city*. New York, NY: W. W. Norton and Company.

Boas, Franz. 1975. *Kwakiutl ethnography* (Classics of Anthropology). Chicago, IL: University of Chicago Press.

Desmond, Matthew. 2017. *Evicted: Poverty and profit in the American city*. New York, NY: Broadway Books.

Edin, Kathryn, and Laura Lein. 1997. *Making ends meet: How single mothers survive welfare and low wage work*. New York, NY: Russell Sage Foundation.

Hannerz, Ulf. 2004. *Soulside: Inquiries into ghetto culture and community*. 2nd ed. Chicago, IL: University of Chicago Press.

Liebow, Elliot. 2003. *Tally's corner: A study of negro streetcorner men*. 2nd ed. London: Rowman and Littlefield Publishers.

Malinowski, Bronislaw. 1984. *Argonauts of the Western Pacific*. Reprint ed. New York, NY: Waveland Press.

Mauss, Marcel. 2018. *The gift: Form and reason for exchange in archaic societies*. Glendale, CA: Bibliotech Press.

Mullainathan, Sendhil, and Eldar Shafir. 2014. Scarcity: *The new science of having less and how it defines our lives*. New York, NY: Picador Press.

Newman, Katherine S. 2000. *No shame in my game: The working poor in the inner city*. New York, NY: Vintage.

Patillo, Mary. 2013. *Black picket fences: Privilege and peril among the black middle class*. 2nd ed. Chicago, IL: University of Chicago Press.

Plecher, H. 2020. Unemployment rate in Spain. Available from https://www.statista.com/statistics/263706/unemployment-rate-in-spain/.

Small, Mario. 2010. *Unanticipated gains: Origins of network inequality in everyday life*. London: Oxford University Press.

Smith, Robert. 2005. *Mexican New York: Transnational lives of new immigrants*. Berkeley, CA: University of California Press.

Smith, Sandra. 2010. *Lone pursuit: Distrust and defensive individualism among the black poor*. New York, NY: Russell Sage Foundation.

Stack, Carol. 1983. *All our kin: Strategies for survival in a black community*. New York, NY: Basic Books.

Wilson, William Julius. 2012. *The truly disadvantaged: The inner city, the underclass, and public policy*. 2nd ed. Chicago, IL: University of Chicago Press.

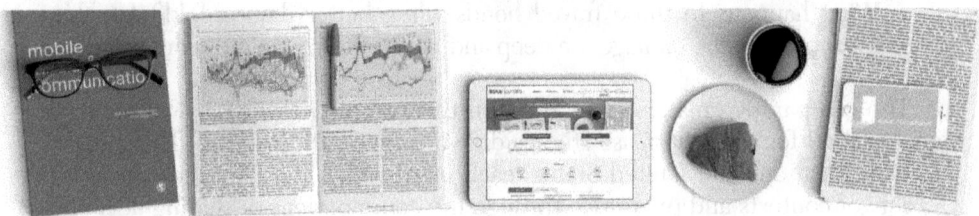

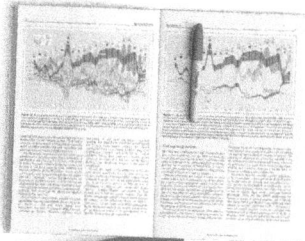

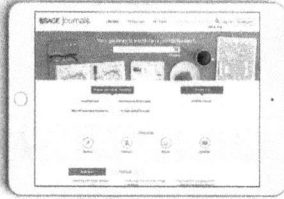

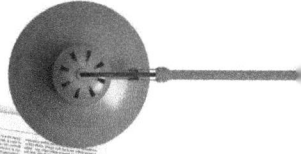

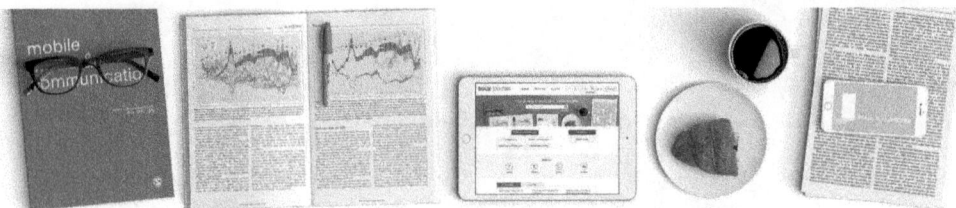

www.ingramcontent.com/pod-product-compliance
Lightning Source LLC
Chambersburg PA
CBHW060321030426
42336CB00011B/1147

9 7 8 1 0 7 1 8 2 3 7 5 0